TABLE OF CONTENTS

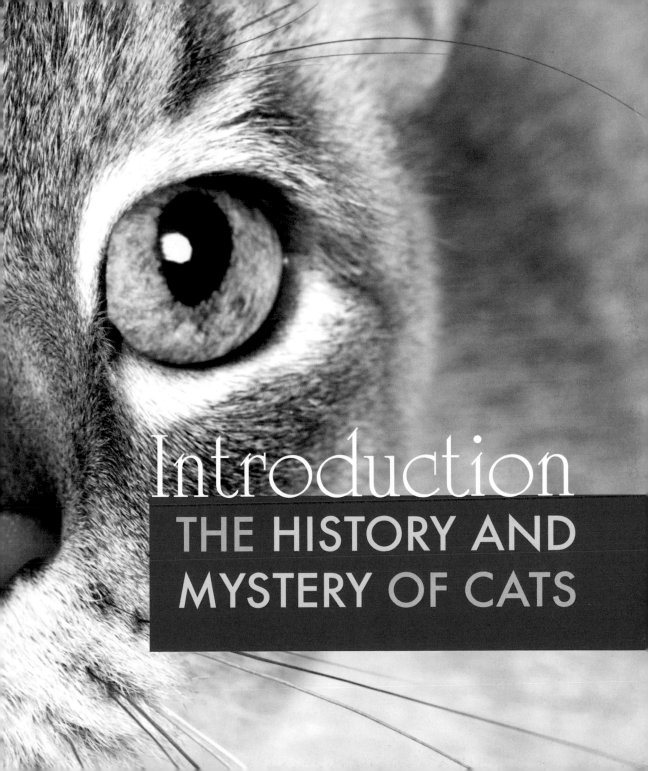

Introduction
THE HISTORY AND MYSTERY OF CATS

"In the beginning, God created man, but seeing him so feeble, He gave him the cat."

— Warren Eckstein

In case you didn't know, cats are magical. They are so magical that no one knows exactly how, when, or where they decided to make friends with us. However, science is beginning to give us more substantial clues, and it turns out that cats may not have materialized out of thin air after all. Instead, the modern magic of DNA fingerprinting, combined with an amazing archaeological discovery, has revealed some intriguing new information. An 8000-year-old grave, complete with commingled cat, mouse, and human bones, has been found in Cyprus, an area that was settled by Neolithic farmers from Turkey who brought their domesticated animals with them.

This discovery of a cat buried

with her human owner was somewhat shocking to the experts, who until very recently believed that feline domestication took place in Egypt at a much later date. It was thought that the ancestors of our domestic cat were one or more species of African wildcat, who may have scavenged scrap heaps and hunted vermin that inhabited the developing towns of early man. The assumption was that ready sources of food made adapting to man and sticking around his encampments on a permanent basis a rather attractive proposition.

What's in a Name? The Egyptians named the cat Ma after the sound she makes. This obvious example of mimicry seems to be a common phenomenon. The Chinese have a similar word for cat, which is Mao. It is probable, however, that the most common derivation for many of the modern names for the cat (cat, chat, katt, cattus, gatous, etc.) came from the Egyptian word "utchat," which was the magical and sacred "eye" possessed by Bast, the goddess of cats.

Although the domestication theory still holds, the location that it took place has been reconsidered. After examining DNA from the cat remains found at the Cyprus burial site, it is now believed that all 600 million of today's house cats are descended from one of five "matriarch cats" who lived about 9500 years ago in regions of the Near East. The results of genetic testing suggest that the origin of the domestic cat is more likely to have been in the Near East instead, and the remains at the Cyprus dig would back this up because the date of burial far precedes Egyptian civilization.

Still, the Egyptians caught cat fever early on, although so-called full domestication took another 4000 years. Presumably, the cat's prowess in ridding the grain fields of mice and rats endeared them to the ancient Egyptians. However, the Egyptians had a penchant for the graceful, elongated style of beauty that the cat just happens to possess, so I think that must have been part of her charm as well.

Not only did the cat eventually take up residence in Egyptian households, but she came to be exalted and worshipped as being godlike. It was illegal to kill a cat (unless you were sacrificing one, I guess), and you were supposed to get the cat out of a burning house before any humans got out. A formal cat cult was even instituted, and it lasted for two millennia. The most famous cat goddess in the world, Bastet, was revered by the ancient Egyptians. She was often depicted as having the body of a woman and the head of a domestic cat. (All Egyptian deities had animal heads and human bodies, for some reason.) The Egyptians loved Bastet so much that she became a household goddess and

Many experts believe that the cat's relationship with humans began around the end of the Stone Age, with the earliest records of cats dating back 8,000 years.

protector of women, children, and domestic cats. She was also the goddess of beauty, grace, and fertility, just as the cat herself is.

Cats were so admired by the Egyptians that they shaved their eyebrows off as a sign of grief when the family cat passed on to the Field of Bulrushes. You were supposed to deliver the body, wrapped in linen, to a priest who made sure she died a natural death. If foul play was suspected, the owner was in serious trouble. Once examined, the cat was mummified. Over 300,000 cat mummies were found in one excavation alone at Beni-Hassan in middle Egypt in the 1800s. Unfortunately, most of them got ground up and shipped to England to be used for fertilizer. Modern Egyptians are more pragmatic than their ancient ancestors. On a much darker note, they apparently sacrificed young cats—a rather large number of cats with broken necks have been found in excavation sites. It can't always have been an accident.

This seems to be a pattern because cats have been both revered

Family of Cats

All cats are members of the family Felidae. Scientists believe that the cat family split from other mammals at least 40 million years ago, making them one of the oldest mammalian families. Today, it is estimated that there are more than 500 million domestic cats.

and reviled throughout history. Honored and hated, protected and persecuted, they have been associated with wise women as well as with witches. The Greeks equated their own goddess Artemis (Diana) with Bastet. Unfortunately, during the Middle Ages, Diana was presumed to be the goddess of witches, and cats at that time were inextricably linked with witchcraft and sorcery. Even today, while the tensile grace and toughness of the cat is universally noted, many people fear or even loathe these beautiful creatures, an attitude possibly tracing back to medieval times.

As everyone knows, a black cat is said to be unlucky. Pseudo-Albertus, a writer during the early Renaissance, proclaimed that if you took the ear of a black cat, boiled it in the milk of a black cow, and then wore it on your thumb, you would become invisible. Even today, some people still swear that a cat will "suck away a baby's breath" if given the chance to do so, despite the fact that such a thing has never happened. Any cat lover can tell you that cats bring good fortune and joy to anyone lucky enough to own one.

It's been a complicated relationship, but one thing is certain: This is a provisional friendship. Unlike dogs who accept even cruel or bad owners with simple-minded good grace, cats have standards. You will need to prove yourself worthy of your feline friend every day. Also, unlike dogs, cats are not loyal unto death. They're much too smart for that. They will not risk their lives to save yours, although one may condescend to alert you if there's a fire because she wants to get out of the inferno herself. Nor can it even be said that cats are truly domesticated. Conservative in nature, cats have maintained their size, body type, and character despite frantic efforts to distort and twist them into unnatural shapes to satisfy some human whim. Cats have kept their present form for thousands of years now and show no signs of changing their minds about it. They have managed to remain true to themselves—willing to share your home and hearth, but not to surrender their pride or principles.

Treat a cat well, and she will reward you with sensible, wise companionship. Treat her ill and she's out the door. It has been said that every alley cat is potentially a house cat, and vice versa. Cats like to keep their options open, and they are flexible enough to change their living style. They will not, however, change their character. It is the human being who must learn to be accommodating to this most elegant, finicky, and sophisticated being: the family cat. If you invite one (politely) into your life, you will be blessed indeed.

Part 1

A GOOD
START

Chapter One

Getting a Cat

"A home without a cat—and a
well-fed, well-petted, and properly
revered cat—may be a perfect
home, perhaps, but how can
it prove title?"
from *Pudd'nhead Wilson*
by Mark Twain

I probably don't even have to tell you. Cats are clean, quiet, intelligent, self-reliant creatures who are well-suited to many lifestyles. Sophisticated enough for the city, sensible enough for suburbia, and robust enough for a life in the country, the cat has won America's heart. So if you want a cat, join the crowd. According to a recent survey by the American Pet Product Manufacturer's Association (APPMA), 37.7 million U.S. households own at least one cat; that's over a quarter of the households in America. The total is over 90.5 million pet cats.

Read No Further If...

I hate to be negative. To me, cats are the perfect pet. But the fact is that cats aren't for everyone. The millions of cats that end up in shelters around the country every year attest to the fact that there are more cats than people who need or want them. It's really important to deeply consider undertaking the responsibility of caring for and sharing a home with this unique animal.

Here is my short list of people who should remain catless, at least for now:

People who don't really want one: Please don't get a cat just because you think it would be good for the kids to have one. Cats were not put on earth to teach your children to be responsible; that's your job. You are the adult and

Cats are clean, quiet, intelligent, self-reliant creatures who are well-suited to many lifestyles.

the one whose responsibility it is to care for the family pet. In the same way, if you really want one, but your spouse does not, reconsider. Don't assume he will magically fall in love with her afterwards, although this happens more frequently than you might suspect. This advice is in spades if you ever, for any reason, suspect that your spouse or children may be abusive to an animal. And don't get a cat just because you have a mouse problem. Not all cats kill mice.

People who are seriously allergic: There is no truly hypoallergenic cat breed. And while some breeds such as the Devon or Cornish Rex, the Sphynx, and the Siberian seem to produce less of the culprit allergen than other breeds, there is more of a difference between individuals than between breeds. Neutered cats are less allergenic than their intact counterparts, and females less so than males. If you love cats beyond all measure and are determined to have one despite your allergy, there are several steps you can take to reduce your exposure, but nothing is guaranteed. (See the resource section at the end of the book for sources of more detailed information.)

People who have a cat-aggressive dog: If you have a dog that menaces cats or chases them, please don't add a cat to your household. You cannot train a prey-driven dog not to chase a cat any more than you can train a cat not to kill a mouse. Some dogs are cat-chasers, and some aren't. And that's about it. Dog breeds with high prey drive around cats include Greyhounds, Weimaraners, and Siberian Huskies, and while some members of these breeds are wonderful around cats, I have seen too many cases where the dog killed a cat after months of apparently ignoring the animal.

People who really (truly) don't have time for a pet: While cats famously do not require as much upkeep and attention as a dog, they are domestic animals who do not relish being alone for endless hours every day. Some individuals are more independent than others, but all cats enjoy a few minutes (at least) of petting and kind attention. Exercise and mental stimulation are very important to your cat's well-being, and your pet will rely on you to provide these outlets as well.

People whose lease agreement won't let them have a cat: Don't try to sneak a cat in past your landlord. You will be found out, and then you'll have to move

Cat Resources

It is a fact that a lot of people sort of "end up" with cats rather than going out in search of them. They pick up strays, acquire a kitten from a neighbor whose cat just had a litter, or just keep the one that the roommate left behind.

The largest and best known nationwide network for information about adopting a cat (or any other pet) is Petfinder. You can visit them online at www.petfinder.com. You can also visit your local shelter or humane society, or check with your vet. My vet runs a cat adoption service in conjunction with the local humane society.

If you have a specific breed in mind, visit the Cat Fancier's Association of America at www.cfainc.org. Their website will guide your search, as well as give you lots of other helpful information about cats and their proper care.

Out in the Cold

I do have to say that quite often cats insist upon joining a family whether they are invited to or not. For instance, one just shows up at the door and won't leave. This situation works out most of the time, but in some instances it can be a disaster. You must consult your deepest feelings and make a humane choice: either keep and love the animal (which you've probably already done or else you wouldn't be reading this book) or try to find a good home for her elsewhere. Please do not turn her back out into the cold.

or give up your pet. Move to a cat-friendly environment first. Then get a cat.

People on the move: College students, military personnel, and others in a fluid life situation should probably avoid getting a cat until they settle down. Shelters and rescues are full of animals whose owners have given them up because they are "moving."

People who are unable or unwilling to spend the money it takes to keep a cat: Even if you acquired your cat for nothing, it won't stay that way. Your cat will need to be altered, vaccinated, and fed. Inevitably, she will require veterinary attention at some time in her life. You will have to pay for litter, toys, a traveling crate, and bedding. The fact is that it will cost a few hundred dollars a year to keep a cat in good shape. Only you know if this is what you want to spend your money on.

But let's say you are the opposite sort of person: You love cats, have a stable environment, and are willing to spend the time and money that your cat (and all cats really) so richly deserves. If this sounds like you, you are eligible to join the elite and proud club of "cat people."

Finding the Perfect Cat

While most people seem to come by a cat naturally, there are situations in which you may find yourself in a cat-seeking mode. This can occur either because you are looking for a special breed or because none of your neighbors or friends are currently giving any away. But do not despair. Your perfect cat is close by.

WHERE TO START

You can get a cat from your neighbors, a free-to-a-good-home newspaper ad, a shelter, cat rescue, or a breeder of purebred show stock. Millions of homeless cats are left in shelters and rescues every year. Certainly one of them is right for your home. Another reason I love humane animal welfare groups is that there is an incredible variety of cats to choose from—all ages, colors, hair types, and backgrounds.

Shelter and rescue organizations are motivated not by money or "prestige," but in finding good homes for homeless pets. No-kill shelters tend to keep cats longer and have more time to work with each one to diagnose and even solve behavior problems. On the other hand, shelters that euthanize after a period of time often have a better selection because they have a higher turnover. Sad, but true. Rescues have the added advantage of placing their cats in foster homes first so they can be evaluated and can adjust to a homelike atmosphere. There are also a number of "purebred" rescues that work with only one breed of cat, such as Siamese or Persian.

Some shelters and rescues offer the added advantage of testing their cats for contagious diseases and will vaccinate and even alter them prior to re-homing them. Many have websites on which they post photos of cats and kittens available for adoption, making it easy to do your research prior to visiting the facilities or locating a pet that may be out of your immediate locale.

If your heart is set on getting a purebred kitten, you will probably have to visit a breeder. To find one, you may want to check the breeder listings in cat fancier magazines like *Cat Fancy* or *Kittens USA*. Also, breeder lists are available at the Fanciers Breeder Referral List at www.breedlist.com. Many national and local cat associations also may provide breeder lists (see the Resources section).

If you get a chance, go to a cat show and see the various breeds and their breeders in action—although to be truthful, most cats do little at a show but sit and sleep. However, many reputable breeders will be there, and you will

Despite their famously independent nature, most cats bond closely to their human families.

Consider a Mixed Breed Cat

About 25 percent of the pets turned in to animal shelters and pounds are purebred, but the other 75 percent, are lovable, wonderful mixed-breed pets just waiting to be given a chance to be adopted into a new home. Don't be fooled into thinking that these cats were relinquished because they were "bad." Shelter pets for adoption are most often loving companions who became the victims of a family's changing circumstances (moves, new jobs, etc.), a beloved owner's death, or an irresponsible individual who did not understand the care needed by a dependent animal.

Mixed breed pets also have less inbreeding, have generally less inherited disease, and are therefore healthier and happier pets overall! And the best place to find one is at a humane society or an animal shelter in your area or through a referral from your vet.

have an excellent opportunity to talk to them about the breed you're enamored of and to find out more about them from the experts. You can also ask about any upcoming litters in the event that you are ready to acquire your new pet.

TYPE: PET OR SHOW CAT?

Do you go for the slender, airy, elegant feline, the fluffy longhair, or the solid and no-nonsense domestic shorthair? In the cat world, many people have a decided color preference. Some like a Siamese-pointed cat, some a solid or smoke. The tabby and black have their aficionados, as does the ever popular tuxedo cat. However, you cannot judge a cat by the color of her coat, but rather by the content of her character. Purebred or mixed breed, all cats make loving, charming, and entertaining companions.

While different breeds do have subtle personality differences, these differences are more individual than associated with a particular breed. Nowhere in the cat world will you find the physical divergence that exists between dog breeds such as the Mastiff and the Shih Tzu. Cats are pretty stubborn that way. And as for body type and size, all cats are basically the same, although some cats, such as the Maine Coon, tend to be comparatively large. There is also a noticeable difference between sleek, elongated cats like the Siamese and the rounded features of the Persian.

However, cats probably differ most in color and coat types: cats come in an array of glorious colors and have eyes of green, gold, blue, amber, or anything in between. It's a rainbow world in cat land. The main consideration for many people is the length of the coat. What is your fancy—the elegance and dramatic lines of the sleek shorthair or the luxuriance of the longhair?

If you have a taste for the bizarre, there are other options. One breed, the Sphynx, has no hair at all; the Devon or Cornish have "rexed" or tightly waved hair, and others run the gamut from the domestic shorthair to the Persian. Hair length is of concern if your worry is grooming. In most cases, longhaired cats have hair that mats; if less shedding is a priority, you should know that shorthaired cats tend to shed more. That's because the hair growth and replacement cycle is shorter. For instance, we humans have long hair if it's left to grow out, and we don't shed much. But ask someone with a Dalmatian what their shedding is like. In addition, short hair seems to stick to furniture more stubbornly than long hair.

There are more than 40 cat breeds recognized by various registries, and if you want a purebred kitten with "papers," then a responsible breeder is your best choice. On the other hand, purebred cats end up in shelters and rescues just like "alley cats" and if you are patient, sooner or later you may find the breed of your choice while still doing a kind deed.

KITTEN OR ADULT?

There is nothing cuter than a kitten, and plenty of them are available from your local shelter. But so are adult cats who are also looking for a good home—and with the odds stacked against them. An adult cat is usually litter-

Kittens should not be taken from their mothers until they are at least eight weeks of age.

box trained. She is also a known commodity as far as size, hair length, and behavior. Of course, the animal may have behavior problems that caused her first owners to give her up, but chances are that there's nothing at all wrong with the cat and that she was simply "superfluous" to their lifestyle.

Kittens are adorable and terribly entertaining, but they can be destructive and overly energetic for some families. A lot of them play really rough. If you have toddlers, it's probably better to get a more self-sufficient adult cat. Besides, all kittens turn into cats eventually, so you might as well focus on other considerations as more important prerequisites for making your choice.

If you think you may prefer a kitten, bear in mind that she should been weaned from her mother and able to eat solid food on her own, usually after eight weeks of age. Removing a kitten from her mother and siblings too early can result in emotional and practical problems because the animal may not have been taught essential behaviors. Kittens will also have special needs that an adult cat would not require.

Once a kitten has been taken away from her mother and littermates she may feel a little insecure and abandoned and will need lots of extra attention from her new family. Kittens also need to eat a special "kitten formula" diet. Depending on what age you adopt your pet, she may also need to be taught how to use a litter box. You'll have to be patient with her because it may take a bit of time and she will have a few accidents along the way. Remember that she is still a baby learning to function in the world around her.

Many people want to adopt a kitten so they can watch her grow up into a beautiful, adult cat with which they can share many experiences over the years. But a mature cat is equally capable of giving you the love and companionship you are looking for in a feline friend…and so many adult cats are just hoping for a second chance.

SEPARATING THE GALS FROM THE GUYS

Telling the sex of a kitten is harder than telling a male from a female puppy, but it's not impossible if you know what to look for. Lift the tail. Below the anus you will see the genital opening. It's round in males and vertical in females. Some people say that when you look under the tail, males have a colon and females an exclamation point. But you do have to know your punctuation for that method to work.

You might also get a hint from the fur color. Almost all tricolor (calico and tortoise shell) kittens are female. Most orange and white kittens are male. Beyond that, it's anyone's guess.

MALE OR FEMALE?

There is no objective standard that says females make better pets than males or vice versa. Some people will swear the male is more affectionate; others are equally positive the female is more loving.

Females are more expensive to alter, and males are more subject to cystitis, but other than that it is pretty much a wash. If you are not planning to alter your cat (and you need to have a very good reason for that choice), you do have to worry that a male will spray strong-smelling urine all over the house. Unspayed females are extremely noisy when they are in season. These are two extremely good reasons to get your cat altered. Spaying or neutering is beneficial to your pet: he or she will live longer, won't stray from home, and will become more affectionate. More importantly, altering your male or female helps to control the overpopulation problem that accounts for the euthanization of almost half a million cats each year!

HOW MANY CATS?

 "One cat just leads to another," claimed Ernest Hemingway. He was an expert on this topic because he had 60 of them himself. Today we would call such a person a "hoarder." Today, animal hoarding is a recognized psychological condition that needs to be treated. But if you are considering two or more cats, your best bet is to acquire littermates who already know each other. With littermates I don't think it matters what the genders are. I have successfully owned sisters, brothers, and mixed pairs without any trouble at all. Don't get any more cats than you can adequately care for, however, and remember that every cat you add to the household adds additional stress and responsibility to the mix. You also need to remember that eventually you will own two or more very old cats.

TIMING

Not every time is the best time to acquire a new cat, especially if you have any choice in the matter. Holidays can be stressful for anyone, and dealing with Christmas decorations and a new kitten who is anxious to tear them apart may not make for the best introductions. If you're planning on leaving for a grand tour of Europe, postpone getting a new cat—and if you already did, don't take her along. Unlike dogs, cats are conservative by nature and don't really enjoy being shoved in a cat carrier and hauled all around the country, or even around the block for that matter. They prefer their own familiar surroundings in which they can lord it over the rest of the family.

For your pet's benefit as well as your own, make adopting a cat a family decision.

If you are under major life changing stress like having a baby, moving, going away to school, or getting a new job, it's better to wait until the excitement dies down before you take on this added responsibility.

Selecting a Healthy Cat or Kitten

Of course, choosing a kitten is not really possible. As every cat lover knows, it's the kitten who chooses you and makes you love every minute of it. It may seem obvious, but choosing a cat should be a family decision. It is unwise and perhaps even in the long run cruel to "surprise" the household with a kitten. This is a decision you should all agree on. Some people pressure the rest of the family into adopting the "cute" kitten, only to end up returning her when she is considerably older and less adoptable. If anyone in your household is so unenlightened as to be cold to the idea of a feline family member, reconsider. Perhaps a gerbil, or no pet at all, would be a better choice. But if you have the wholehearted approval of the gang, it's definitely time to adopt.

For the widest possible choice, head not to your nearest breeder (who is an expert on one kind of cat alone) but to your nearest shelter or cat rescue where you'll meet a wide variety of kittens. There you will find the cat who will touch your heartstrings, and the true cat lover is more about heartstrings than bloodlines. (While it's possible to find a purebred cat in a shelter, it's not likely. Only about 25 percent of shelter cats are purebred, although that's a higher number than you can find in the general cat population!)

When you go, take along your entire mature family. Very young children may find some shelters too upsetting to visit, although most up-to-date ones have family visiting rooms where you can see a whole litter of kittens in a pleasant, home-like setting. But beware—the biggest danger is that you'll be tempted to take them all!

There are all kinds of ways to decide if a particular cat is for you, and the standards you use depend on your own needs. Most people want a cat that is healthy, handsome, and affectionate.

SELECTING A KITTEN

For your best shot at getting a friendly and well-adjusted kitten, look for one that has been with her mom for *at least* eight weeks. As a general rule, the longer kittens stay with their mother and siblings, the more sociable they will be. Take a good look at mom, pick her up, and pet her. Most kittens inherit their temperaments from their mothers. Still, although meeting the mom will take out some of the guesswork, don't count on it to give a complete picture of her offspring's temperament or looks. Not only did the mom (probably long gone by now) have an influence, but cats are well known for forming their own characters despite the best efforts of their parents (or owners) to mold them.

Look for a kitten that is playful and fearless. Kittens that seem fearful, lethargic, or very anxious may have serious physical or psychological issues. And if you are looking for a healthy cat, avoid the runt of the litter no matter how appealing she may be in other ways. Runts often failed to get proper nourishment during the critical first few days of life and may suffer health problems ever after.

SELECTING AN ADULT

Most adult cats won't be charmed by your first overture. Don't expect the cat to leap into your arms. However, if she struggles

The Tragedy of Hoarding

Animal hoarding is a recognized mental illness. It often begins when someone takes in a homeless animal, and then over many years acquires more and more. Animal hoarders often believe they are saving their charges from death at a shelter. But unfortunately, as the disease progresses, the animals are kept in conditions worse than death: with no sanitation, adequate shelter, or veterinary care. Most hoarded animals are malnourished, sick, or dying. In their misguided attempts to help, animal hoarders often neglect their own health and sanitation, and their homes become so infested with disease that they have to be torn down.

This behavior has been observed in people of all ages, sexes, and income brackets. It has even been seen in veterinarians, veterinary technicians, and animal rescuers. Cats are one of the most common animals hoarded because they are easy to acquire and to hide in a house. Researchers believe that there are currently over a quarter million animals being hoarded in the United States alone. These people are not animal lovers, but instead have unwittingly become criminal abusers who subject their charges to a lifetime of neglect and misery.

If you suspect someone of animal hoarding, please report it.

fiercely to get away from you when you pick her up, there is a chance you will never be able to make a friend of her. If the cat seems content to be picked up (and especially if she begins to purr), you are in luck. Take her home. Some people like the idea of adopting an older, calmer animal, but worry that the cat won't bond to the family. It is true that cats are not Labrador Retrievers, but adult cats are remarkably adaptable. They will soon figure out what is in their best interest.

Both cats and kittens should be well groomed, have clean eyes and ears, good muscle tone, and a dry nose. However, you cannot tell if an animal is healthy just by looks alone. Always take your new kitten to the vet as soon as possible for a thorough checkup.

The Most Popular Cat Breeds

If you have a specific look, hair type, and character in mind, you might wish to consider selecting a purebred cat. (Remember, you can find them at a shelter or Petfinder.com as well as from a breeder.) I am providing a profile of some of the most popular cat breeds, but if none of them quite suits the bill, keep looking. A magical mix may turn up at your shelter tomorrow. You can also find out more about your favorite breed online; many of the national registries include breed profiles on their websites.

ABYSSINIAN

Friendly and beautiful, the primitive-looking, shorthaired Abyssinian is one of the world's most playful, courageous, and charming cats. The breed first arrived in America in the 1900s. Despite the name, however, these cats probably come from Southeast Asia, not Abyssinia, although some Abyssinian experts insist that this breed is a direct descendant of the sacred cats of Egypt. Perhaps DNA studies of cat mummies will clear all this up one day. Abyssinian cats were first shown in the United States in 1909.

These are tough, muscular cats with big ears, a rounded wedgy head, and almond eyes. They come in warm brown, red, and blue; however, all colors are agouti (with banded hairs). This is the same natural coloring as that of the jungle cat and indeed the breed seems genetically close to the African wildcat, *Felis silvestris lybica*! The hair is short, fine, and close-lying. The tail is thick at the base, fairly long, and tapering. The eyes may be gold or green and are accentuated by a dark line. The feet are small and oval.

Abyssinians require little grooming, although some lines seem prone to dental disease and amyloidosis, a kidney problem. These cats are emotional bandits, too. They demand and deserve all your attention; however, many do

Before you acquire your feline, be sure to do your homework. It is beneficial for both you and your breeder to learn more about each other before you make decisions or sign an agreement on a cat of your choice.

A good breeder will let you visit and spend some time at his facility. He will guarantee that your kitten is in good health and free from illnesses such as feline leukemia virus (FeLV) and feline immunodeficiency virus (FIV). He will also require that you have your kitten neutered or spayed at the appropriate age, unless you have a show contract. Always demand a written sales agreement that describes all terms of the sale, including the breeder's health guarantee and the neuter/spay agreement.

Here are some basics to consider when evaluating a breeder or rescue:

- You may consider it an invasion of privacy, but a good breeder or rescue coordinator will not just dump a cat in your arms and take a check. He'll ask you many questions about your home situation and may even want to speak with your veterinarian. Although these procedures can seem intrusive, a good breeder or rescue coordinator is looking out for the welfare of his cats.

- A good breeder has a spotless kennel. The animals should appear clean, healthy, and well cared for and should be housed in clean, roomy cages with fresh food and water.

- A good breeder will offer you a contract that clearly outlines both of your responsibilities in regard to the cat you are purchasing. Be sure to read it carefully and question anything you don't understand before signing it.

- A good breeder has a warm and chummy relationship with his cats. It's very important that young cats be introduced to the kind of life and circumstances they will be expected to live under by the time they are separated from their mom and littermates.

- A good breeder will happily provide references from former buyers.

- A good breeder is knowledgeable about the positives and negatives of his breed (no breed is perfect). He may show his cats.

- A responsible breeder will have had his cats tested for certain genetic problems and inherited diseases. He will show you proof that your cat has passed these tests.

not enjoy lap-snuggling and would rather be worshipped at a distance. They may have the highest activity level of all cats, so get out your roller blades.

AMERICAN SHORTHAIR

This sturdy, handsome cat came to America on the Mayflower in 1620 and has the honor of being America's first domesticated shorthaired breed. The breed was officially "recognized" at the turn of the 20th century. There are plenty of mixed breed cats who look just like the American Shorthair, but only those with a pedigree get the official title.

The American Shorthair is well-known for its mousing ability and comes in almost any color. The coat is thick and dense and tends to shed. The shorthair is neither aloof nor clingy, but manifests a sensible balance of love and independence. The first American shorthair to be registered in the United States (in the early 1900s) was a tabby named Belle. Ironically, Belle was transported from England.

BALINESE

The Balinese is basically a longhaired Siamese who began showing up in otherwise standard Siamese litters in the early 1900s. Some people suspect that these lines were somehow "tainted" with genes from other breeds; others believe it was a naturally occurring mutation. At any rate, these cats are not from Bali, but were given the name Balinese because their namer, Helen Smith, thought their movements resembled the graceful movements of Balinese dancers.

Like the Siamese, the Balinese is a very vocal cat, as well as playful and intelligent. Under the long hair, they are built along tapering, elegant Siamese lines, with wedge heads, very large ears, long legs, and a delicate bones structure. The long coat has no undercoat.

BIRMAN

Some say this "sacred cat of Burma" is a cross between a Siamese and Persian, and it certainly has some of the best features of each and is less demanding than either. It was once considered a "sacred temple cat" of that country.

This cat comes in 20 color variations, with the original seal being perhaps the most popular. Other colors include blue, chocolate, lilac, red, cream, as well as tortie and tabby patterns. No matter what the color, it should be evenly and symmetrically marked.

Birmans always have white paws. Legend tells us that they turned white when the founder of the breed placed his paws on the body of a favorite Buddhist monk as he lay dying, and so they have stayed to this very day. No matter what color the coat is, the eyes should be sapphire blue. The Birman cat was first recognized in France in 1925, when the breed standard was written, and the breed arrived in the United States in 1967.

BURMESE

This breed is indeed from Burma. The first Burmese to arrive in the United States, a brown female named Wong Mau, came in 1930. Wong Mau herself was a hybrid Siamese, and today's Burmese does have many Siamese traits; however, it lacks the exaggerated Siamese body type. The CFA has not permitted cross-breeding with Siamese since 1947.

The Burmese comes in many colors, but different fancies recognize different colors. Most popular are sable, champagne, blue, and platinum. This is a hard, well-muscled type of cat. Golden yellow eyes are preferred. These cats are affectionate, amusing, and loyal. There are two basic types of Burmese recognized today: the regular Burmese and the European Burmese, which has a longer, narrower muzzle and head. The European Burmese comes in brown, blue, chocolate, lilac, red, cream, seal tortie, blue tortie, chocolate, tortie, and lilac tortie.

CORNISH REX

As the name indicates, the Cornish Rex comes from Cornwall, England. The first known example was discovered in 1950, and the first recognized individual was named Kallibunker. The breed arrived in the United States in 1957 and was at first outcrossed with Siamese, Havana Browns, American Shorthairs, and domestic shorthairs to increase the gene pool and to provide a selection of colors.

The breed appears in any color and usually has golden eyes. Its most notable feature is the "rexed" hair, which curls or waves over the body. There is a specific gene that controls this feature. The coat is a single coat with no guard hairs. All colors are acceptable except tortoiseshell and white. The body is hard and muscular. These are extremely playful and demanding animals.

EXOTIC OR EXOTIC SHORTHAIR

Think "Persian with short hair" and you have a pretty good idea what the

Adding Another Cat

It is certainly possible to add a kitten to a home already ennobled by an adult cat, but it may take some time to socialize them. The older they are when they meet, the less likely it is that they will become true friends. Also, it usually works out better if the second cat is of the opposite sex.

Cats and kittens come in all shapes, colors, and sizes. There are more than 40 cat breeds recognized by various registries.

Exotic is like. Indeed, other than coat length, it conforms exactly to the Persian breed standard. The coat is dense and needs a touchup a couple of times a week, but it doesn't cause nearly the trouble of a Persian's coat.

The Exotic is a sweet-tempered, quiet cat that is particularly good with children. The breed is quickly becoming more well-known and more popular.

JAPANESE BOBTAIL

The name says it all—almost. This is a breed with half a tail. It does come from Japan and was first imported to the United States in 1968.

The Japanese Bobtail is famous as a mouser. Medium-sized and muscular, it has a triangular head, and comes in solids, bi-color, and tri-color. In fact, any color pattern but pointed like a Siamese or ticked like an Abyssinian is permitted. These are talky cats, like the Siamese. Friendly, intelligent, and active, they make great pets and get along with other pets and kids.

MAINE COON CAT

This is the breed that I grew up with in Maine (before it became a recognized breed). The local theory was that these cats were "half raccoon," but of course that is not true. But they are big felines, with some individuals weighing as much as 25 pounds. They are sweet, gentle souls, and their long, weatherproof fur is easier to keep in order than that of a Persian. Maine Coons are famous for their big, tufted ears, feet, and tail. This is a slow maturing breed in which even teenagers act like kittens. They come in all colors except agouti and are pointed like a Siamese. The classic color, however, is tabby and white.

An excellent family pet, this breed gets along well with other animals. This is a feline meant for the owner who wants a lot of cat—and I mean that in every sense of the word. One of the largest of the cat breeds, the Maine Coon also makes its presence known (in the most charming way). And unlike most other cats, Main Coons seem to love water. In addition, the breed is renowned as mousers and has been prized by farmers for that very reason.

MANX

The Manx cat, a very ancient breed, is a tailless cat with high hindquarters. Otherwise it is fairly unremarkable, although it is quite rare. Some varieties of the Manx are: Rumpy, Stumpy, Tailed, (all of which are graded on the length or absence of tail) and Cymric (a rare longhaired variety of the Manx). The eyes are large and round, as is the head. The coat is short, with the color corresponding to the standard colors of a British Shorthair.

NORWEGIAN FOREST CAT

This cat shares many features with the Maine Coon Cat. After all, Norway and Maine have a lot in common, well in terms of weather. This may be the same cat that Norse legend calls the "fairy cat." It is an active and independent animal with a triangular head, straight nose, and high-set larger ears.

The Norwegian Forest Cat is famous for its climbing abilities, and truly enjoys being outdoors.

ORIENTAL

The Oriental is basically a Siamese cat wrapped in a rainbow. Every imaginable color is available, and their personality is equally colorful. There is also a longhaired and shorthaired variety available. The eye color can vary to complement the coat color.

Orientals have a slender body and fine-boned

A Cat of a Different Color

Cat breeders and fanciers have been more interested in the various colors of cats than in anything else. The basic color and pattern of cats is the tabby. In fact, all cats carry tabby genes, even though they may be hidden.

A tabby cat generally has a striped or brindled coat, with an M marking on the forehead. There are four tabby patterns, however: the standard tabby, the mackerel tabby, the spotted tabby, and the agouti tabby. The basic patterns can emerge in cream brown, blue, red, chocolate, lilac, golden, and cameo colors. Solid colors came later, and geneticists believe that the first solid color to appear was black. (The Phoenicians are credited with shipping these black beauties around the Mediterranean.) Other color combinations occurred later.

legs and tail, wedge-shaped head, and large ears. They are outgoing, active, and have a people-oriented temperament.

PERSIAN

The Persian is a breed known for its sweet, laid-back temperament and its beautiful silky flowing coat, which needs daily brushing. Without it, the coat can mat quickly and is too difficult even for this fastidious feline to manage all on her own. Under the heavy coat, the Persian is actually a rather small cat, although her bones are heavy. Persians come in many colors: black, blue, chocolate, cream, lilac, red, white, and various patterned colors such as bi-color, blue-cream, and chinchilla. Each color requires a slight modification of the breed standard, but all are recognizable as Persian.

More quiet and inactive than other breeds of cat, Persians are less likely to seek close contact than many other breeds (possibly because its long, heavy coat may make the cat hot), although they can be coaxed into playing for short periods of time. They also seem less interested in catching birds than most other cats. They can't be bothered with such trifles. While affectionate, Persians are perfectly capable of remaining home alone without complaint. They find themselves extremely entertaining.

RAGDOLL

The Ragdoll, which was bred in the United States in the 1960s, is probably the most domestic, affectionate, and easy-going of all the breeds. These are extremely affectionate, gentle animals, and their breed name is said to come from the fact that they will flop lazily in your arms like a doll. They are also a very silent cat, which can be a relief for someone who has owned Siamese. This easygoing feline loves to be cuddled and caressed and won't demand much from her owner, but she prefers quiet and peaceful surroundings.

Ragdolls have blue eyes, a plumy tail, and a medium to long coat (especially on the chest and abdomen), which does not easily mat, unlike a Persian's. These basic color patterns are available: bi-color, colorpoint, and mitted. For each pattern, Ragdolls may be pointed (in seal, blue, chocolate, blue, lilac, red, cream, or tortipoint).

SIAMESE

They are Siamese, if you please. These uniquely characteristic cats do indeed hail from Thailand, once known as Siam. The long-legged Siamese was first imported to England in 1884, and then brought to America in the early 20th century, where it achieved stunning popularity.

This is the world's most familiar, recognizable cat, with its trademark "points" and long, tubular body. The hind legs are slightly longer than the front ones. The head is long and well proportioned, and the eyes are a clear, deep blue. The Siamese is always pointed, in seal, chocolate, blue, or lilac. Kittens tend to be paler than the adults. No grooming is required.

The sleek Siamese is famous for its chattiness, playful nature, and wild antics. In the United States the tabby and red Siamese are sometimes known as Colorpoint Shorthairs by some associations.

SPHYNX

The Sphynx is best known for being "hairless," although many individuals have a peach-like down on their bodies. Their skin is said to feel like warm suede. Of course, this is a cat that needs to be kept warm in the winter and protected from the sun in the summer.

This is an intelligent, medium-sized cat with enormous ears and an alert, intelligent expression. Curious and energetic, the Sphynx will enjoy your undivided attention, and may even perform tricks for you to get it. These cats tend to bond strongly to their owners, and some people have even suggested that they are not unlike dogs in their interactivity with their humans and other pets.

TONKINESE

The Tonkinese breed is a cross between the Siamese and Burmese. It derives its color from the Siamese and its body type and affectionate nature from the Burmese. Colors come in sable brown, champagne, blue, mink, and platinum. Pointed varieties have blue eyes, mink cats have aqua eyes, while the solid colors have green or yellow-green eyes.

Playful and friendly, the Tonk has a medium-sized build and a soft, sleek coat. Their colorful personality makes them ideal, devoted pets.

Chapter Two

Preparing
for Your Cat's
Arrival

"A cat isn't fussy—just so long as
you remember he likes his milk in
the shallow, rose-patterned saucer
and his fish on the blue plate.
From which he will take it, and
eat it off the floor."
— Arthur Bridges

To invite a cat into your home is an act fraught with responsibility. Taking that responsibility seriously is the best guarantee that your cat-owning experience will be successful and joyful. Unfortunately, so many myths have accrued about cats that even the best intentioned people sometimes underestimate how much care is involved in cat ownership.

Myth #1: *Cats can take care of themselves.* While it is true that cats are more self-sufficient than dogs, modern cats are dependent upon their owners for food, companionship, and veterinary care. Nearly all other cat myths are somehow related to this one.

Myth #2: *Cats keep themselves clean and don't need grooming.* While shorthaired cats can generally avoid the brush and comb, longer haired varieties need regular brushing. And all cats can benefit from dental care, ear cleaning, and parasite prevention.

Myth #3: *It's not important to feed cats regularly. They can just go outside and kill something.* Many domestic cats are not particularly good hunters, and those who are may kill songbirds, not mice. They may also ingest mice that have been dosed with mouse poison. Your cat is safer indoors and on a regular diet provided by you.

Myth #4: *Cats can exercise themselves.* It is true that cats can exercise themselves, but like people, most won't unless given an incentive to do so. Giving your cat interesting, interactive toys and taking her for walks add interest and health to her life.

As you can see even from this short list, a cat has needs that you must supply. Being a cat owner to some extent means being a cat-servant. Luckily, buying the things your cat needs is actually kind of fun.

Before you bring a cat or kitten home, you need to make preparations for her arrival.

❧ Cat Accoutrements

Your new cat will need some basic supplies to meet her daily care needs. Having the proper accessories will not only ensure your pet's happiness and comfort, but her physical and mental well-being as well.

FOOD DISHES

Look for dishes that are easy to clean (dishwasher safe), sturdy, safe, and tip proof. Extra features on some include sealed feeders to preserve freshness for long-term feeding and a cooling element for canned foods. Some dishes have a rubber, skid-proof bottom. Don't use great big bowls; cats prefer smaller portions more frequently and will reject stale food just as you would.

It's best to have at least three bowls: one for water, one for canned food, and one for kibble (if you feed kibble). All bowls should be weighted to prevent tipping. Many cats have an aversion to deep dishes, even though they tend to keep food from scattering about.

For most people, the best choice is sturdy, easy to clean, nonbreakable metal. Ceramic bowls are pretty and also easily cleaned, but make sure that the glazes are nontoxic. Avoid plastic. It's not sanitary, and if your cat chews on it, it will develop tiny little indentations that make good homes for bacteria. Some cats are also allergic to plastic dishes and develop chin acne from them. All food containers should be cleaned with warm sudsy water every day.

If you will be gone for a while, consider a timed feeder. They are available for both canned and dry foods. Feeders should be as sturdy and tip-proof as the regular dishes you use.

LITTER BOXES

A litter box is a necessity. It is recommended that you have one more litter box than you have cats. The most important quality of a litter box is that your cat likes it enough to use it for its intended purpose. No matter how charming and appealing it is to you, it's the cat's opinion that must dictate your choice. Of

Feline Fountains

You might want to consider getting an automated "drinking fountain" for your favorite feline. This may sound like a luxury, but it's really important for your cat's health.

Research shows that one of the best ways to improve feline health is to get cats to drink more water. This is especially true for those who eat dry food. Most cats actually have a low thirst drive and tend not to drink enough. This is all right for cats who live solely on wet food, but not for others. In fact, it puts them at a risk of cystitis. A fountain of cool fresh water, however, is just the thing to tempt your pet to imbibe more freely. Some include a charcoal filter to improve the taste and quality of the water. Cats really enjoy drinking from it, and it has a very pleasant relaxing sound as well.

course, her taste in this matter may not be easy to predict, and different cats like different things (another reason to have more than one litter box). You may have to do some experimenting.

SIZE

Get a litter box large enough for your cat's comfort. If it's too small, your cat won't use it at all or else she will "miss" and deposit her leavings on the floor. The sides should be high enough to keep in the litter after your cat scratches around in it, but low enough that an old, arthritic cat or a small kitten can get over it. Unfortunately, many litter boxes are just too small, and the animal ends up "missing," much to her embarrassment and your displeasure.

SHAPE AND STYLE

Litter boxes come in several basic styles:

Flat With Sides: The traditional litter box is nothing more than a big, rectangular pan. These litter boxes come in a variety of colors, sizes, and depths. They are easy to clean and very cat-friendly. Some have rims under which you can place the kitty litter liner. These boxes are very durable. If this is the only kind of box your cat will use, you can keep the kitty litter from spilling all over the place by putting the pan in the bathtub. You can simply rinse the stray litter down the drain and easily clean the litter box at the same time.

Hooded: This is my personal favorite. I have one shaped like an igloo for my cats, although you can get rectangular ones too. These offer privacy for the cat and odor-relief for you. (Some cats feel nervous in them, however, and prefer to eliminate in a place where they can look around and see if anyone is coming.) Most of the hooded boxes have filtered vents to help with odor control—the bigger the vents the better. The truth is that most people (including myself) don't bother with the filters, and I am not sure they make much difference. Some covered litter boxes are hard to clean; check the model first. The tricky part is making sure the hood is firmly attached to the base after you finish cleaning out the litter. If it's shaky, it might fall off and scare the cat into not using it again.

Self-Cleaning: Yes, you can buy open, electric, self-cleaning litter boxes that can be used with scoopable litter. These have timed

The most important quality of a litter box is that your cat likes it enough to use it. Find out the type your new cat or kitten has been using and buy a similar one.

sensors that activate a cleaning cycle, scooping the feces into a well with a special rake. They have special sensors and are designed to begin the clean cycle only when the cat is not using the box. Cats like the continual (but imperfect) cleanliness of this box, but like all things electronic, there can be problems if the automatic rake becomes clogged.

Sifting Boxes: These litter boxes have two rectangular pans and a "sifter tray," and they can be used with any kind of litter. The two boxes stack onto each other, and the sifting tray sits inside the top pan. After the cat uses the box, lift the top sifting tray, and shake it slightly to separate the feces from the litter. Then simply discard the waste, place the sifting pan into the empty tray, and pour in clean litter from the full tray. Place the empty tray on the bottom. And so on, through an endless cycle.

Designer ("Hidden"): Yes, you can get litter boxes designed to look like part of the decor—perhaps a planter. Their usefulness depends on how big they are and whether or not you can convince your cat to use them.

Litter

Gone are the days when you just got some play sand and threw it in a box. Today, litter choices can leave even an educated consumer filled with wonder. There is no one best kind of litter because cats have their own preferences, which may not coincide with yours. And the best litter in the world turns into the worst if the cat won't use it. Some cats annoyingly will urinate but not defecate on certain kinds of litter, or vice versa.

So you'll have to experiment a little. Start with something that appeals to you and see if you can get your cat to agree to it. Litter can be clay or plant-based, fine or pelleted, clumping or nonclumping. Some are super at controlling odor; others are less likely to be tracked around the house. Some are friendly to the environment, some not so.

Clay: Clay litter is closest to a cat's natural preference (garden soil) and is good at controlling odor and moisture. The cheapest kind, the granular stuff, is very good at absorbing odor, but unfortunately allows the cat to track it everywhere. Traditional clay litter is not scoopable, and some kinds can be dusty.

Be Prepared

Before you bring your new cat home, be sure to have the following on hand:
- cat carrier or crate
- litter box and scoop
- cat litter
- food and water bowls
- cat food
- toys
- scratching post
- cat bed
- grooming tools (brush and comb)
- kitty first aid kit

Potty Etiquette

In colonies of feral cats, subordinate individuals cover up their feces while more dominant cats leave their feces uncovered. Pray for a submissive cat. Of course, all cats should be subordinate to all people. Unfortunately, it doesn't always work out that way.

If you like clay, I recommend the clumping litter, which makes for easy disposal and a very easy-to-clean litter box. Clumping litter should be cleaned twice a day. It too can be dusty, although you can get "low-dust" brands of both traditional and clumping litters.

Pelleted litter is easy to clean up, but some cats won't use it, preferring the fine sand litter, but this too will track all over the house.

Pellets: For the ecology-minded, recycled litter (from newspapers or materials that are biodegradable in landfills) is available. They come in both fine and pelleted form. They tend to be more expensive than other types.

Beads: One of the newest trends in litter is silica gel litter, which takes the form of clear plastic beads. It absorbs urine well (without the need to scoop) and is less unsightly than other litter—if you like looking at litter, that is. When the litter changes color, it's time to clean out the box. You will have to scoop feces as usual, though. The beads also make noise when the cat urinates; what you hear is the liquid getting soaked up. Another great thing about this litter is that is lasts up to a month before you need to change the whole box.

While my own cats are not fussy and will experiment with any kind of litter, some are much choosier and dislike any new litter on principle. If you decide to make a change, you'll have to do it gradually.

It's important to remove feces and wet litter every day. At your convenience, dump it all, wash the box with warm water and soap, rinse, and replace.

SCRATCHING POSTS

Installing a scratching post will keep your cat happy and protect your furniture. It should be steadily anchored and tall enough for your cat to stretch to her full height while using it (30 inches/76 cm is ideal). It should be covered with a fabric that will tear enough to satisfy her, making her feel that she is accomplishing something. Burlap, sisal, or carpet fabric that leaves visible marks is ideal. Place the post in an easy-to-find, obvious location, so your cat can show off her prowess. And the more scratching posts you have, the more likely it is your cat will use them.

To train your cat to use the post, rub catnip on it or put treats on the top. Do not try to force her to use it by putting her paws on it. That will only make her fearful. If she won't use a vertical post, try using a horizontal one encased in a box. You can easily make one yourself from some carpet or sisal weave and plywood. To really go all out, invest in a cat jungle gym.

TOYS

Cats love to play and toys (especially those supplied with catnip) make great fun; they are particularly critical for indoor cats, who have fewer natural diversions to satisfy their curiosity. They help exercise a fat or lazy cat, as well. Toys are also a great way for you to interact with you cat and bond to her. Perhaps the greatest benefit of cat toys, though, is for you. It's just plain fun to watch a cat pounce, carry, and stalk her "prey." If you do not provide your cat with toys, one of two things will happen: (1) Your cat will grow bored, fat, and unhappy. (2) Your cat will "make" her own toys, an activity you might not approve of. In the feline world, "making" often means "shredding" and "chewing." It's safer for you to provide the toys.

Cat toys come in several basics types:

- *Balls and spinners* give your cat plenty of opportunity to run and exercise.

- *Plush and furry toys* satisfy your cat's natural stalking drive. Cats know that they aren't real mice, but like to pretend anyway, just like a child with a doll.

- *Wands and teasers* are super for playing with your cat and thus helping the two of you to bond. They also give your feline plenty of opportunity to stretch and use those "boxing paws." Some mimic the flight of birds, which really turns a cat on.

- *Interactive toys* help develop your cat's natural brain power. Some are designed for the cat to use on her own; others require your participation as well. Get some of each! There are "peekaboo boxes" with crevices in which you can hide treats or catnip, an excellent activity for a bored home-alone cat. There are miniature "swing sets" that include a variety of toys. There are laser lights, which are as much fun for you as for the cat. One interesting toy is a kind of mitten that has extra long dangling fingers with pompoms at the ends. Cats love these, but there is a danger you might be encouraging her to scratch at your hand, something you definitely want to avoid.

All cats are compelled to scratch and stretch as part of their natural behavior. Installing a scratching post will keep your cat happy and protect your furniture.

39

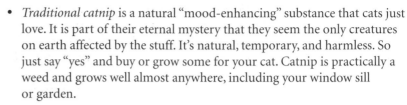

- *Traditional catnip* is a natural "mood-enhancing" substance that cats just love. It is part of their eternal mystery that they seem the only creatures on earth affected by the stuff. It's natural, temporary, and harmless. So just say "yes" and buy or grow some for your cat. Catnip is practically a weed and grows well almost anywhere, including your window sill or garden.

Of course the best toys in the world are useless if your cat ignores them. You have to experiment.

You can also make your own toys at home. A balled up sock or piece of aluminum foil is a simple delight that thrills many a cat. I once had a cat whose favorite toy was bottle tops.

CAT BEDS

This isn't a real necessity because some cats won't use one anyway, no matter how much you spend on them and how invitingly you display them. I had a cat whose preferred sleeping spot was a box of nails on the back porch. You never know. But if you want to experiment, pick a washable bed. You can even use some of your clothes or stuffed pillow cases. (A lot of cats like nothing better than to sleep in a basket of laundry.) Some cats, of course, enjoy sharing your bed. That's between you and her.

KITTY CONDOS, GYMS, AND PLAY TOWERS

You can combine some of the features of bed, toy, hiding place, exercise equipment, and scratching post with a piece of special cat furniture variously known as a kitty condo, kitty gym, or play tower. These are all variations on the same thing and are perfect for multi-cat households. Some companies will even build one for you and customize it to your specifications. Many include detachable ladders, sisal scratching posts, toys, lots of openings, and platforms. Many are so handsome that they provide interesting focus and charm to your living room, den, or bedroom. I have never known a cat who didn't love these.

OUTDOOR CAT ENCLOSURES

An outdoor cat enclosure solves every cat owner's dilemma. We all want to keep our cats safe, but we want them to have some experience in the "wild" as well, which they love. Cats are just like us; we want to be secure *and* we want to have fun, and sometimes it's hard to balance these needs. It is a fact that indoor cats live longer than do outdoor ones (5 years for outdoor cats, 15 for inside ones), but it is also true that they suffer much more mental stress. We don't want to kill our cats, but we don't want to drive them crazy either...what to do?

If you have the room and the means, an outdoor, screened and roofed cat enclosure is just the ticket for your indoor cat. (You can leave the ground uncovered, for ease of building and your cat's additional pleasure, or you can purchase one of many different floor materials. You can have one of any size, and for apartment dwellers there are enclosures that attach to a window. This is not just a "big cage," but a real chance for fun and adventure. When you're done, you may like it so well you'll spend more time in it than your cat will.

You can buy a ready-made enclosure (some can be custom designed), you can build one yourself, or you can take the middle path and buy a modular kit. Your choice depends on your time, funds, space, and, of course, your carpentry skills.

GROOMING TOOLS

Unlike dogs, cats are self-groomers, but that doesn't mean they can do the job in a completely satisfactory way. Self-grooming cats leave hair all over the house (or swallow it, creating hairballs), and longhaired cats simply have too much to handle on their own. That's where you come in.

A cat brush with soft nylon bristles, a flea comb, and nail trimmers or clippers (for indoor cats) are critical, especially for longhaired cats. During shedding periods, you might consider a cat shedding blade. These are great for removing dead hair; they also reduce the serious problem of hairballs. You may also want to buy a grooming glove to be used after brushing. Special mat removers can help with longhaired cats who get into a tangle.

Don't forget cat shampoos and conditioners. Not every cat needs a bath, but some do—at least sometimes, like when they make a mess or get into something they shouldn't have. You can also buy a dry powder or liquid "waterless" shampoo.

Toys provide your cat with necessary stimulation and exercise.

41

Rules of the Great Outdoors

Many caring pet owners believe that cats, regardless of how domesticated they have become, deserve the right to roam, play, and sleep outside amidst the glory of their natural habitats. However, there are real dangers to the well-being and survival of a small, helpless feline in the wide open spaces of that vast and great beyond more commonly known as the outdoors.

Being hit by a car is one of the major causes of death for a cat who ventures outside without supervision. Other dangers, such as disease, parasites, predatory animals (coyotes, dogs, raccoons, or other wild animals), weather hazards (sunburn and frostbite), getting stuck in a tree or caught in hunting traps, exposure to chemicals and pesticides, and freak accidents can prove hazardous to your feline's health and, quite possibly, her life.

As a responsible pet owner you, make sure that your cat is never allowed outdoors without constant supervision. Monitor her closely so that she doesn't get into any trouble and don't let her wander off. Safer options may include providing a safe outdoor enclosure or taking your cat out on a leash.

LEASH AND HARNESS

A few cooperative cats can be taught to walk on a leash, especially if you start them young enough. (This isn't a matter of a cat not being "smart enough" to walk on a leash. It's a matter of dignity. How would you like to walk on a leash?) Walking a cat on leash is a safe way of exposing your cat to the glories of the world without risking her being hit by a car, lost, or stolen. One of the newest types of leashes is the "bungee" leash, which is fun for both the owner and the cat!

A leash is useless unless attached to a harness. (Don't attempt to walk your cat on a collar; it puts too much pressure the neck, and cats just don't like that strangling feeling.) And, you get the additional control you need. The best kind of harness for many cats is an H-shaped or figure-eight adjustable harness. To correctly size the harness, measure your cat's girth just behind the front legs and add 2 or 3 inches (5.1 to 7.6 cm). Most harnesses are made of sturdy nylon and some have quick-release buckles.

Even better for many cats is a cat walking jacket. They are soft, flexible, and provide the additional reassurance that most cats require. Unlike dogs, cats are not natural leash walkers.

(See chapter 5 for more information on leash training.)

IDENTIFICATION

Like dogs, cats should wear visible identification tags. (In some counties it is mandatory.) An indoor cat can become an outdoor cat really fast when your roommate or child leaves the door open. Visible ID is the *single most important factor* in getting your cat returned to you if she becomes lost. In fact, many stray cats picked up by animal control are not strays at all but rather someone's household pet out for a stroll.

A proper ID tag should contain, at a minimum, your address, name, and phone numbers. The address is important because if someone finds the cat near your home, he can just carry her to your doorstep. You may also want to put your vet's phone number on the back and instruct him in advance that if your cat is injured and turned in to him, you'll pay the needed bills. However, collars are not perfect. They can break or be slipped out of. And over time, ID tags often become illegible.

You may also opt for a tattoo, usually placed on the inner thigh or ear. This must be done by your vet or a trained specialist. Several registries are available; they will provide numbers and assistance, or you can use your phone number (if you're sure it won't change). Tattoos are fairly permanent, but they can fade over time or can also become illegible. They can also be altered, if someone really wants to go to the trouble. However, their biggest disadvantage is that the finder will need to know where to look. Shelters usually will do so, but you can't count on a private individual to know about them. Because multiple registries exist, it may be hard to track down the owner.

You can also ask your vet to implant a microchip with your contact information on it. This is a simple, painless procedure that will help to ensure that you get your cat back. The vet will simply insert a rice-sized chip between your cat's shoulder blades. These are permanent chips. In fact, they have a lifetime of about 75 years—long enough to last through all your cat's nine lives. If your cat is lost and picked up by a shelter, the shelter has a universal scanner that will read the chip; you will be notified where your cat is. As with tattoos, however, a private person may not know about the existence of the chip and would need to take the cat to a shelter or vet for a reading. Even though multiple registries exist, the scanners now available can find the correct one and provide contact information.

If you choose to have a collar too, and you have an indoor cat, engrave a tag on it that says, "If I am outside, I am lost. Return me to (*name*)." Be sure to put your address as well as phone number on the tag. The collar to which the tags are attached should be a lightweight buckle collar. The only real reason to have a collar on your cat is to attach an ID to it. For your pet's sake, please select an expandable safety collar that, if it catches accidentally, will quickly release your cat from the possibility of choking.

TRAVELING CRATE OR CARRIER

Unlike dogs, cats don't just jump into the car and want to go wherever you go. Sometimes they seem positively relieved to have the house to themselves. If you insist on their company, you'll need a handy pet carrier to transport your cat to the vet, boarding kennel, or vacation house in the country.

43

Clean-Ups

To clean up pet-related "accidents," don't use any product with ammonia in it because it has the same basic ingredients as urine and can induce a cat to urinate in the spot where it was applied. The best products clean and control odor as well.

Because you never know when you'll need to be evacuated from your house, you should have a cat carrier for every cat you own. Dozens of varieties are available: soft and hard sided, plastic, wire, and fabric. You have only to consult your own needs and desires. Just make sure it is large enough for the cat to comfortably stand up and turn around in (if you plan on a long trip) and that it is small enough for comfort and convenience.

PET-FRIENDLY CLEANING PRODUCTS

Choose something cat-specific for getting rid of tough odors safely, which means an enzyme cleaner specifically formulated for cats. Ordinary household cleaners don't work well. Enzyme cleaners come in both powder and spray form. Cat urine stains are difficult to get rid of. And if the stains are old, you may have to use several applications. Follow directions carefully.

Cat urine contains five different bacteria strains, two of which are associated with the cat's marking scent. The other ones appear in cat spray and urine. Most of the bad smell is caused by uric acid, which contains insoluble crystal that bind tightly to the surface they are deposited on. They're activated by moisture, which is one reason why cat urine smells worse in hot humid weather.

Is Your Home Cat-Friendly?

Although it's not absolutely necessary to redecorate your entire home in anxious anticipation of your new arrival, it wouldn't hurt either. Take at least a quick look around the place and see how cat-friendly it is. And it doesn't hurt to inspect the environment at "cat-level" to see what's down there. Of course, cats being cats, they are equally likely to get into as much trouble above your head as down by your feet.

Your purpose is to save your cat's life. It sounds scary, but it is true. Cats can be drowned, shocked, burned, strangled, and poisoned by the most innocuous looking objects in your home. It's not nice to think of your home as a death trap, but accidents can happen. They can also be prevented.

HOUSEHOLD DANGERS

Cats are intelligent and curious animals, and the adage that curiosity can kill them is very true. While you can't go back to pre-Industrial Revolution days, you owe it to your cat to use common sense and keep her away from dangerous electrical appliances like hot stoves and whirring fans. Electrical wires are very attractive to kittens, who may attempt to chew them. Tape such cords closely to the wall or spray them with an aversive spray like bitter apple. Even charming, pre-electrical items like candles are very dangerous. Your cat can knock them over and set the house as well as herself on fire.

Also be sure to store sharp utensils properly in a drawer or cupboard.

Tiny Hazards: Cats like to play with all kinds of small dropped items—from paper clips to toothpicks to buttons. Items such as these can be choking hazards. If it looks like it could be dangerous, it probably is. Pick it up. Cats are wonderful at helping us be better housekeepers.

Stringy objects like yarn, roast-tie strings, rubber bands, twist-ties, sewing thread, tinsel, and dental floss can be extremely dangerous. Cats are very attracted to them and if ingested can cause terrible problems with the intestines.

Windows and Doors: Keep your doors and windows closed. At least put a screen on them. Cats often jump out of open windows or escape through open doors and are lost, injured, or killed. (No, cats do *not* always land on their feet.) Cats are also attracted by lace curtains, nettings, and blind cords. Change window treatments and move cords out of the way. (Kittens are especially likely to get tangled in cords and choke to death on them.)

ID tags can save your cat's life. Visible ID is the single most important factor in getting your cat returned to you if she becomes lost.

Because it's almost impossible to keep young kitten from climbing and ruining curtains, you can save the situation by installing vertical blinds instead. A cat can simply push them aside to sit on the windowsill.

Speaking of doors, keep the doors to the washer and dryer closed. More than one cat has ventured into a snug, clothes-filled washer or dryer and never emerged alive. And keep the lid to the toilet down. Kittens can drown in a toilet.

People Food: While most human, meat-based food is safe for cats if fresh, old food and dry splintery bones are definitely not. This is a matter of common sense. One thing that may not be intuitive is half-filled glasses. Your cat can get her head stuck in a half-full glass of milk trying to get a drink.

Finish the milk yourself or throw it way.

Poisons: Cats are much smarter than dogs and are unlikely to ingest chemical poisons, even if you do leave them around. Felines are just not that attracted by drain cleaners, although you shouldn't confine your cat to small areas where these items are found. And since they don't have a sweet tooth, they aren't too likely to munch down on a Hershey bar, although it has happened. They are more likely to get in trouble with plants.

While houseplants are beautiful, some are poisonous if ingested. The Easter lily is one of the most deadly to cats, but you should remove all toxic plants from your home for your cat's safety. Older cats will probably ignore most of them, but kittens are so curious they are willing to give anything a try once.

To prevent your cat from chewing on your houseplants, mist the leaves with water and then sprinkle a little cayenne pepper on them. Another option is to buy bitter apple spray or a similar plant-safe product and spray it on the leaves.

To keep your cat from digging up the soil around your houseplants, buy some plastic needlepoint mesh, and cut it to fit over the top of the pot, making a slit for the plant. Simply place it on top of the soil. Or soak a cotton ball in oil of clove and bury it just below the surface.

Ant, Snail, and Roach Traps: Remove them. Some of these can kill a cat.

BREAKABLE ITEMS

Cats are fond of knocking fragile, valuable items off shelves. Put them away before they get a chance to do so. Cats do this on purpose, by the way. They are not clumsy and don't make mistakes. If a cat does break something, it's because she wants your attention, she likes the sound of crashing, or the item was in hideous taste and she couldn't take it any more.

CARPETS

The key here is mix. Any solid color, light or dark, readily shows stains and stray fur. And of course, a textured carpet is going to hide things better than a smooth one. Expensive Oriental rugs should be rolled up and stored—at least until you're sure your new cat

Cats are intelligent and curious animals, so make sure you pet-proof your home to protect your feline companion from household dangers such as open windows and doors.

is not going to rip them to pieces or soil them. Even if you get them professionally cleaned, a tell-tale circle will remain.

My favorite pet-friendly floor covering is tile. Easy to clean and beautiful, it is perfectly cat-resistant. The next best thing is a hardwood floor, sealed with urethane, which has the same advantages. Both of these floor coverings can be slippery for an older, arthritic pet, however, and some people prefer plain old linoleum.

FURNITURE

If you have upholstered furniture, a floral or print pattern hides stray hair better than a solid color (either light or dark). If the upholstery fabric is easy to shred, throw some pretty, washable slipcovers over it. Anything wicker, rattan, or sisal is going to be too much of a temptation for your cat. These materials have "scratching post" written all over them.

GARAGE

The garage is full of toxic items such as antifreeze, paints, thinners, and gasoline. Keep your cat out of this area. Cats have also been known to creep inside warm, just-turned-off motors and have been killed in a horrible way the following day.

THE HUMAN FACTOR

I daresay one of the greatest dangers to cats may be the one closest to you—your toddler or young child. Children must be carefully supervised around pets. They may not intend to be cruel, but kids can step on, strangle, or otherwise injure a small cat faster than you might think. You can be dangerous yourself. My husband sat on our tiny kitten, Meadowsweet, (it was dark) by mistake and broke her femur. (She's fine now.)

Is Your Family Cat-Friendly?

Once the house is ready, you need to prepare your family for the big event. It should be clear to everyone what their responsibility will be: Who will feed the cat and brush her? And who will clean the litter box? As the grownup in the family, of course, the ultimate responsibility falls upon you to make sure the cat is well cared for. Your child may insist she will keep the water bowl filled and the litter box clean, but if she doesn't, you will

House Rules

Your new cat will have a lot to learn when she moves in. In addition to figuring out where the litter box is, what time she can expect to be fed, and where to find the best bird-watching spot, she will have to learn the "rules" of the household.

Teach your pet what is and isn't acceptable in your home. Show her where the scratching post is so she won't claw the sofa, instruct her to stay off the counter, but do allow her to jump onto a favorite windowsill or cat perch.

Pet-Proofing Tips

Aside from keeping hazardous items away from your cat, be sure to teach family members about pet-proofing the house and the importance of feline safety. Go to the ASPCA's website at www.aspca.org for guidelines on pet safety.

Bringing a pet into your home is a serious commitment because your cat will rely on you to provide for all of her needs for the rest her life.

have to do these chores yourself. A pet should not suffer because of a forgetful youngster.

Make sure your family knows what to expect when you bring home your new pet, especially if you've never had a cat before. Although youngsters will be curious about the new pet, they should not be left alone with her for any length of time. Quite often a young child may accidentally do something to cause the animal to scratch or bite. Older children who have been taught to respect pets can help the recent arrival adjust to life in her new home by playing with her and helping out during feeding time. This not only benefits the cat but also lets the child know what is required to take care of the new feline friend.

Family members will also need to learn all the rules for cohabitating with a cat, which include responsible daily care as well as constant attention to keeping the house pet-proofed.

TIMING

Timing is important. You want to introduce your new cat during a period that allows household members ample time to spend with her, but it may be unwise to choose a holiday such as Christmas when everyone is frantic and there is a lot more "dangerous stuff" around, like Christmas trees. If possible, bring her home on a weekend or arrange to have time off from work to stay with your pet so that you don't have to leave her alone in a strange place. The more time you spend with your cat, the stronger the bond will be between the two of you.

The Right Start

Introduce your feline friend to her new home slowly and with patience. In time, you will learn all about her personality, her likes, and her dislikes. Spend quality time getting to know each other. The first few days you spend with your cat may be the most important ones because these are the days during which your kitten or cat learns to trust you and see you as her new family and protector.

The following is a partial list of plants that are toxic to cats:

arrowhead vine (all parts)
asparagus fern
azalea
bird of paradise (fruit, seeds)
Boston ivy (all parts)
caladium (all parts)
calla lily
Christmas rose
chrysanthemum
creeping charlie (all parts)
creeping fig
crown of thorns
daffodil
dieffenbachia
dumbcane (all parts)
Easter lily
elephant ears
emerald duke (all parts)
English holly

English and glacier ivy (leaves, berries)
geranium
heartleaf (all parts)
ivy (hedera)
Jerusalem cherry
lily of the valley (all parts)
majesty (all parts)
marble queen (all parts)
mistletoe
nephthytis (all parts)
parlor ivy (all parts)
philodendron (all parts)
poinsettia (leaves, flowers)
pothos (all parts)
pot mum
red princess (all parts)
saddleleaf (all parts)
schefflera
spider mum

sprengeri fern
swiss cheese plant
tulip (bulbs)
umbrella plant (all parts)
weeping fig (ficus)

However, you don't have to go plantless! Here are some safe plants to have around cats:

african violet
aluminum plant
any of the true ferns (boston fern, maidenhair, etc.)
cacti (but make sure they are real cacti, not just a succulent)
catnip
coleus
gloxinia
goldfish plant
grape ivy
hanging african violet

lipstick vine
miniature roses
pepperomia
prayer plant
shrimp plant
spider plant
swedish ivy
sweet potatoes
variegated philodendron leaf
wandering jew
wax begonias

Chapter Three

At Home
and on the Road

"As every cat owner knows,

nobody owns a cat."

—Ellen Perry Berkeley

Okay, so the house and family are cat-ready, but you still have some decisions to make about your cat's comfort and safety.

Naming Your Cat

In *Old Possum's Book of Practical Cats*, T.S. Eliot said, *"The naming of cats is a difficult matter. It isn't just one of your holiday games."*

Naturally, before the introductions begin, you'll need to name your new pet. In case you've forgotten, here are some of Eliot's famous feline character's names: Growltiger, Rum Tum Tugger, Mungojerrie, Rumpelteazer, Old Deuteronomy, Mr. Mistoffelees, Macavity, Bustopher Jones, Skimbleshanks, and (apparently running out of ideas)—Gus. (Remember that long-lived Broadway show, *Cats*? Well, it was based on his poetry from a book called *Old Possum's Book of Practical Cats*...Just thought you'd like to know.)

In some ways it doesn't matter what you call your cat, since she probably won't deign to respond to her name anyway. Your best bet is "Kitty," a name cats seem to like better than any other, but I am sure you want to be more creative than that. My two current cats are Hollyhock and Meadowsweet, and I have had cats named Isis, Osiris, Eiger, Streak, Tonto, Folpet, Pansy, Orange Bowl, Katzenbach, and more.

If you want to go with a trend (or avoid one), the most popular names of late for male cats are: Max, Sam, Simba, Charlie, and Oliver. For females, the most popular names are Sassy, Misty, Princess, Samantha, and Lucy.

Perhaps it doesn't matter. As Eliot well noted, cats have secret names, a one true mystical name that you will never find out:

"When you notice a cat in profound meditation,
the reason I tell you is always the same:
His mind is engaged in a rapt contemplation
of the thought, of the thought, of the thought of his name..."

Settling In

Keep in mind that once your new kitten or cat arrives, she will need time to adjust to her new surroundings. Your house, family members, and other pets will all seem strange to her. Be patient with her for the first few weeks until she becomes used to living in her new home.

New arrivals are often a little afraid and anxious when you first bring them home. A young kitten will miss her littermates and may cry for her mother. She won't know what to expect in an unfamiliar place and may be startled by anything loud and different. An adult cat will not be familiar with the sights

When your new cat or kitten first arrives, give her time to adjust to her new surroundings.

and smells of the new home. It is therefore important to be patient and to do all you can to make your cat or kitten feel as comfortable and secure as possible until she has settled in. Spend extra time with your new kitten or cat for the first few days until she has started adjusting to her new surroundings. However, keep visits to a minimum, especially from kids and curious friends.

To ease this transition, you may want to prepare a room or a special quiet area away from too much activity where your cat can spend her first day or two, perhaps a spare room or bedroom. Provide her with a soft, warm bed or sleeping area, some toys, a litter box, food, and water.

While she is still in this stress-free area, the most important thing is to show her where the litter box is and how to get to it. Most kittens are pretty much self-trained, so your kitty will just need to learn where it is. It's best to begin using the same kind of litter that the breeder or previous owner used so that your kitten doesn't have to learn too many new things at once. The same goes for her new dining and sleeping areas. She may decide not to sleep in the place or bed you've chosen for her, but you can at least give it a fair shot.

Let her live in this special room until she has adjusted to being on her own. A quiet, safe place will help your cat settle in faster. Check in on her often and talk to her calmly as you pet and play with her.

53

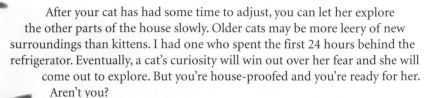

After your cat has had some time to adjust, you can let her explore the other parts of the house slowly. Older cats may be more leery of new surroundings than kittens. I had one who spent the first 24 hours behind the refrigerator. Eventually, a cat's curiosity will win out over her fear and she will come out to explore. But you're house-proofed and you're ready for her. Aren't you?

At this point you can begin to introduce your new feline friend to younger family members and guests.

Picking Up Your New Cat Safely (for Both of You)

Everyone will be excited to meet your new pet. Family members and friends will be anxious to hold her and play with her. However, it's important that this be done in an appropriate manner, both for their sake as well as that of your cat.

The safest way to pick up a cat is to approach her from the side. One hand goes palm up right beneath her front legs. The other hand crosses over the cat's back and holds the cat under the belly in front of the hind legs. Hold the cat close to you. Some cats enjoy being held on their back, legs up.

Never pick up a cat, even a kitten, by the scruff of her neck. Mother cats carry their kittens this way, but they have no other choice. Never pick up a cat by the tail or legs, and do not allow young children to hold a cat unsupervised. If a child wishes to pet the cat, it's better that you hold the animal for him.

Making Friends With the Incumbents

Most cats don't require feline company, especially if they have an enriching life of their own. However, young kittens brought up together do seem to have extra fun, and many older cats may enjoy their company. Unfortunately there's no real way to tell. Obviously, the cat's not going to say anything, so it can be cause for guessing.

Whether or not your cat can learn to live with your other pets depends on three factors: the particular cat, the other pets, and you. There is more to this statement than might be apparent at first. Some cats will get along with any pet that doesn't try to kill them. Some pets will consistently try to kill a cat. And you are the one who is going to have to figure out what the heck is going on and find a way to manage it all.

CATS AND CATS

Cats are not social by nature, and while they can and do live together in harmony, it's easier to attain a peaceful accord by starting with littermates or at least two kittens near in age rather than introducing a new cat into the household.

Unlike dogs, cats don't suffer from a lack of company with their own species. Many of them couldn't care less if they ever see another cat (unless the breeding instinct takes over). In fact, for most felines, meeting another cat is a rather stressful experience. And while a majority will eventually accommodate themselves to a newcomer, some never will. In fact, the more cats you acquire, the greater the probability that some severe fighting may occur among them from time to time.

That said, it's perfectly possible to keep two or more cats in a single household. Cats do not have a social hierarchy like dogs do (they are not pack animals). They usually arrange themselves in such a way that there is one "lead" cat, with the rest on sort of an equal standing with each other, somewhat like the sun and solar system. There isn't much social interaction among group members (compared to dogs), so if the newcomer can avoid outright hostilities, things will usually work out, with the circle gradually widening. However—and this is important— research shows that a *single* hostile encounter between two unfamiliar cats can set the tone for their relationship for a long time. Getting off on the right paw, so to speak, is critically important. (Dogs seem to be more forgiving in this regard.) Even if the worst happens, though, and your cats hate each other, the results almost never result in the kind of damage dogs can do to each other. Yet it is true that one cat can bully and terrorize another one beyond bearing. If possible, match the personalities of the newcomer and the resident cat as best you can.

Energetic cats do better with an animal of the same lively temperament; the reverse is true as well. While you can never tell about individual cats, certain breeds such as Siamese are more likely to be energetic than Persians or British Shorthairs for example.

Before you ever set foot in the door with your new cat, be sure your established cats are protected from any

Properly Introduced

Introduce your new cat to other household pets before you allow her to explore your home freely. You can use a crate or cat carrier to let them see and sniff each other (the crate will keep them from fighting), or allow them to meet by sniffing each other under a closed door.

Cats are territorial, and, more than likely, the established cat might not take kindly to a new individual wandering around. Be aware that cats may fight, hiss, or growl at each other until they learn to get along. Never leave cats alone together until you are certain they will not fight. Most cats are extremely adaptable, and problems are usually minor and temporary. However, if you have a dog, make the introductions slowly, and be sure the cat has an escape route. Again, don't leave the dog and cat alone together until you are sure they are good friends. Pets that sleep together can usually be trusted not to kill each other while you are gone.

If you have other pets, introduce them to your new cat slowly so they have time to get to know each other.

diseases or parasites the newcomer may be harboring. If you got your new pet from a shelter, be aware that various kinds of upper respiratory infections are rampant there, even if you don't see any obvious signs of illness. Keep your new cat isolated from other pets for a week or two. This has the added benefit of gradually letting them become accustomed to the smell and sound of the new pet.

Also, it's advisable that a new pet be taken to the vet as soon as possible, usually even before you bring her home. Your vet will want to test for potentially lethal diseases like feline leukemia virus (FeLV), feline immunodeficiency virus (FIV), and feline infectious peritonitis (FIP). Cats with no clinical signs can still be carriers of disease. Your vet will also do a fecal exam to test for internal parasites.

When the "quarantine" period has lapsed, let the curious felines meet briefly. Open the door to the new cat's room and allow them access to one another. If a poor interaction occurs, shut the door and try again later. You might try getting them to accept a small, tasty, high-value treat beforehand so they'll associate something good with meeting each other. Maybe. You can also put the newcomer in a crate and let them meet that way. Or, you can first isolate one cat, and then have them switch places so that they get used to one another's scent. Switching their bedding will also accomplish the same thing.

Eventually, you can leave the crate door open and let them get acquainted. Let them eat in different rooms or opposite sides of the same room for a while. Some nasty back chat is to be expected, but they will probably eventually learn to live amicably together.

It's also important to know that in order to encourage the best transition possible, you must provide your new cat with her own feeding bowls, toys, and scratching poles.

CATS AND DOGS

Both cats and dogs are predators. That is their natural heritage. Because most dogs are bigger than most cats, a dog may regard a cat as fair game—especially a cat who runs away from him. In addition, some dog breeds have a very high prey drive. This can be somewhat eradicated if you bring up a puppy among cats, but there is absolutely no guarantee. My Gordon Setter was brought up with cats and he still chases them. I don't think he would hurt them, but the cats don't share my view and have asked me repeatedly to give the dog away. If you already have a dog who has an anti-cat track record, do the feline world a favor and do not add a cat to your household. It would be very unfair to both animals.

To help your pets become friends (or at least to not become enemies), introduce them to each other from a distance at first, with your dog under good control. (It's probably a good idea to have him on leash.) Repeat the process frequently until the animals seem more relaxed around each other. You can then decrease the distance between them gradually. Always make sure your cat has a safe high place to which she can escape from the dog. Never allow a dog to rush at a cat, even if you are sure the dog is "only playing." A playful dog can kill a cat in a heartbeat.

Always supervise dog and cat interactions until you are absolutely positive they are good friends or at least not enemies. Getting puppies and kitten at about the same time adds to the chances of success. The critical learning period for social acceptability is between 3 and 12 weeks of age in dogs and between 2 and 7 weeks in cats.

CATS AND SMALL ANIMAL PETS

If you have a cat, small pets like hamsters must be kept caged, and that's all there is to it. Cats kill mice and other small rodents by instinct. If you like your little pet, protect him by keeping him in a cage that has very closely spaced bars or wires. The cage should also be heavily built or sturdily attached to a table—you don't want to take the chance that your cat could knock it over and terrify the critters within. (And in poorly constructed cages, the door may fly off. Guess what happens next.)

CATS AND BIRDS

Birds, especially smaller and more delicate ones, can literally be scared to death by cats. A cat will stare at a caged bird until the latter has a heart attack. They must be kept in a separate room for their safety and well-being.

The younger the cat, the more easily she will adapt to a new companion.

The age at which children should be allowed to interact with a pet depends on their maturity level and the personality of the pet.

CATS AND FISH

Fish seem oblivious to cats, but you must keep the aquarium covered and secure to prevent your adventurous feline from dipping in a paw, or worse, knocking the whole thing over. I have an outside fishpond, and while my cats may watch the goldfish, I have never seen any of them try to catch one. I am not saying they haven't. I am just saying I haven't seen it.

CATS AND REPTILES

These species are not natural friends. They must be kept apart. Big cats can kill small snakes and vice versa.

CATS AND KIDS

I think by now we all know, don't we, that cats do *not* suck away the breath of babies. Cats and children can get long just fine if the kids are gentle and respectful of them. It's your job to teach your child not to chase the cat, yank her tail, cut off her whiskers, or put her in the dryer. Little girls especially like to dress cats up in doll clothes, and some very good-natured ones may allow this indignity. Whatever the case may be with your particular pet, always supervise playtime—and make sure the clothes are removed from your cat after you take the picture! Some cats will play short games of fetch, but generally prefer it if you allow them to make the first overture.

Unwelcoming Behaviors

If you have a dog, you know that dogs can make peace with each other by exhibiting certain appeasement behaviors such as rolling, exposing their necks, and so on. Cats don't display these types of behaviors. On the other hand, hisses and growls can only mean one thing—your cat is really annoyed about something. When this happens, retreat and leave your cat alone. Even if you're just playing with or petting your cat, when she growls or hisses at you, the best move you can make is to back away from the apparent fury of your feline.

Maybe cats were meant to live alone...

On the Road With Your Feline Companion

"Would you tell me, please, which way I ought to go from here?"
"That depends a good deal on where you want to get to," said the Cat.
"I don't much care where" said Alice.
"Then it doesn't matter which way you go," said the Cat.
"As long as I get somewhere," Alice added as an explanation.
"Oh, you're sure to do that," said the Cat, "if you only walk long enough."
—from *Alice in Wonderland* by Lewis Carroll

While traveling with a cat is never a picnic, sometimes (like when you are moving or taking the cat to the vet), it's plain inevitable. Good luck.

There may be an occasion in which you suddenly become a mother—even if you are a guy—because a cat has abandoned her newborns or dies soon after their birth. Don't worry—you can do this. It just takes some determination.

Housing: The first thing you will need to do is provide a safe, warm place for the kittens to live away from drafts and the direct blast from heaters. A cozy box is just fine, with plenty of soft, absorbent bedding. (Change it frequently.) You can buy a warming plate just for this kind of thing to place below the bedding. Kittens do best in an environment of 92°F (33°C), so keep them snuggly. By the time they are two weeks old, they can generate enough body heat to make it on their own. At that time the air temperature is less critical.

Diet: Brand new kittens require a mommy milk replacer like KMR. You'll need to feed it with an eye dropper or a kitten nursing bottle (which you will have to squeeze because most kittens can't suck the liquid through the nipple). If the kitten won't suck at the nipple, use an eyedropper to squeeze the milk in. Warm the bottle up under some hot running water.

If it's an emergency and you can't obtain the right milk formula, you can use a can of evaporated milk (not sweetened or condensed) with an egg yolk mixed into it. Get the real replacement milk as soon as you can, though.

Feed the kittens every couple of hours. They won't eat much—maybe a teaspoonful (5 cc's) at each feeding. Contact your vet as soon as possible for more advice and directions.

When the kittens are about three weeks old, you can start weaning them by providing some canned kitten food that is watered down at first. If you feed kibble to your other cats, you can gradually start switching them over to dry food.

Clean Up: Mother cats keep their kittens' digestive system running and the litter box clean by stimulating them to eliminate waste and then eating the results. So much for feline fastidiousness. You can accomplish the same thing by taking a warm, damp paper towel and massaging the anal and urinary openings. The kittens should immediately urinate or defecate. Dry the area gently. At about three weeks of age, they will be able to accomplish this on their own. You can then provide them with their first litter box (low sides, please), which kittens generally learn to use on their own.

Vet Care: Have your vet see the kittens as soon as would be convenient. If there are no problems, a good time to take them for their first checkup is when they are about four weeks old. Your vet will advise you about vaccinations, parasites, and other needs. Signs of serious health problems include inappetence, weakness, respiratory distress, and so on.

HITTING THE ROAD

Nowhere does the difference between cats and dogs show up more clearly than in the area of travel. Dogs can't wait to get into the car with you. Cats are smarter than that. They know odds are you're just hauling them to the vet and, even if you're not, they aren't convinced that any place on earth is better than home sweet home. There are a few exceptions, of course. I had a childhood cat who loved to ride, and later, when we lived in Maine, we had a cat who liked nothing better than to climb into the neighbor's snow plow and ride around while he was clearing roads.

In some cases, you can condition your cat to enjoying a car ride. You can put her in the car and have a treat ready for her. The motor will be off, of course. If she gets used to that, you can try the same with the motor on. Eventually, you can take her for small trips around the block and then bring her right back home. Obviously, if every trip she takes ends up at the vet's office, she will not want any part of the car. Don't hurry this process, and make sure that your cat is secured safely in a traveling crate for every ride.

The sad truth is that most cats have to be coerced into riding. Buy a carrier and see if you can get your cat into it without too much fuss. (They even make seat belts for cats, but I think you're better off with a crate.) Some cats can be lured into the crate with a treat, but others know something bad is up and would rather starve themselves first. It helps if your cat will wear a harness. You can use it to gently pull the cat into the crate. I think it helps to position the crate so the door is on top, and then place the cat in it rear end first. Then shut the door and return the crate to its normal position.

Many cats sort of "hide out" silently while they are trapped in the crate; others yowl plaintively but insistently for the entire ride. Unless it is a very long or hot trip, don't put any food or water in the crate. It will just create a mess, and the cat will probably be too nervous to eat. If your cat is a victim of car sickness, talk to your vet about giving her the proper dose of motion sickness medication. Most are quite safe

Foreign Travel With Pets

If you are traveling to a foreign country for vacation, you might not be allowed to bring animals into the country for various health reasons. Customs regulations may require your cat to remain in quarantine anywhere from several weeks to several months. Be sure to investigate the rules and regulations of traveling with a pet with your travel agent before making final arrangements.

When traveling in a car with your cat, make sure she is always secured in a carrier for her safety as well as yours.

for cats. Bring some paper towels just in case. To help keep the carrier clean, line the bottom with newspaper and put an old blanket or towel on top.

Of course, you will never leave your cat alone in a car during warm weather. If the car is in direct sunlight, the temperature can climb 40 degrees in a matter of minutes. The inside of a car can overheat during any season, actually. The cat's own warm breathing can also intensify the effect. If you absolutely must leave your cat alone in the car during the summer, leave the air conditioner running, and don't do this for more than a brief period of time. By the way, this also applies to bitterly cold weather as well when it's important to leave the heater on.

When you open the crate after reaching your destination, one of two things will happen. Either the cat will hunker down in there and refuse to get out until you turn the crate upside down, or she'll come charging out, her claws ready to slash at anything in the way. The "way" is usually to the top of some inaccessible part of the room. The chance that she will quietly and sedately emerge is very, very low. (If your cat has a harness, it may provide some needed purchase for you.)

If you are just going on a trip, it may help to medicate your cat. Don't do this on the way to the vet, however; he'll need to see her unmedicated. Plus, if your cat is sick, using a sedative may complicate the illness. Otherwise, medication may make the trip more comfortable for both of you. It is certainly kinder to a terrified cat. Give it to her well before the trip begins. Talk to your vet about your options; never give your pet any medications without first discussing it with a professional.

When traveling, be sure your cat wears visible ID. It's easier to lose a cat while you're on a trip than at any other time. I acquired a lovely cat who had been left at a rest stop along the interstate. I am willing to bet that she leaped out of the car when the owners stopped, and ran off to hide in the bushes, where we found her yowling piteously. And it was raining, too.

PLANE TRIPS

Every airline has its own rules about traveling with pets. So please check with each individual airline before you finalize your plans. It's also worth noting that these rules *can* change without notice, so have a backup plan. A few airlines do not allow animals to fly at any time.

Your cat must travel in a commercial pet carrier—not a basket or a blanket. Label the carrier "Live Animal," and mark "up" arrows on all sides of the crate. Also, write your home address and telephone number clearly on the crate, as well as any other vital contact information at your destination. All kennels must have fixed food and water bowls clipped onto the door.

Also keep in mind the nature of your destination. Many airlines wisely have temperature restrictions. For example, if the temperature of the destination or arrival airport is over 85°F (29.4°C) or less than 10°F (-12.2°C), your pet may not be allowed to fly cargo or baggage that day. Some airlines won't fly pets as baggage in the summer.

Traveling With a Senior Cat

Older adult cats or seniors often have a harder time adjusting to travel because they are accustomed to their routine home life. When forced to travel, they may become anxious or stressed. Because of this, be mindful of the temperature in the car (and in the place where you'll be staying). Older cats are sensitive to temperature changes, and your cat could easily become too warm or too cold. If she has a special diet or is on any medications, pack enough supplies to last until you come home from the trip.

Many senior cats do not like to travel (especially if they've never traveled in their younger years) and may prefer to be left home with a trusted family member. Consider the stress and strain that traveling will put on your senior cat, and do what's best for her.

For your pet's safety, take it upon yourself to research this before making reservations. Many animals have perished when the cargo compartments are not properly monitored.

All airlines require a health certificate issued within ten days of your departure. Your veterinarian will have to examine your cat and issue a certificate certifying that she is free of disease and healthy enough to travel. Animals must be at least eight weeks old to travel by plane. It is strongly recommended that older cats have a heart examination and bloodwork done to make sure no underlying liver or kidney damage is present before flying because the stress of flying can make it worse.

Most airlines, like Continental, allow cats to travel in the cabin with you as a carry-on. This is the best plan if you can arrange it! They usually require that the kennel fit under the seat, and your cat must remain in the carrier until the plane lands. In some cases, you can use a soft carrier as a carry-on. Inquire. There will probably be an added charge of course.

Continental has brought in a new program called PetSafe QuickPak Cargo. Under this program, they do not accept pets as checked baggage. The plan provides cargo service with same-day, airport-to-airport delivery that includes features designed to ensure an animal's comfort and safety.

Whatever plan you select, it is important to reserve as far ahead as possible and to confirm those reservations 24 hours before takeoff. Get to the airport early enough to navigate the possible bureaucratic hassles.

Lodging

There are now lots of great places designed to cater to people vacationing with their pets. If you'd like to take your cat with you on your travels, check out PetTravel.com or another pet-related database.

Always call ahead to make sure the hotel you'll be staying at will accept pets, and check to see if vaccinations or a health certificate is needed. Bring your cat's carrier, toys, and food, so that there aren't too many changes in her routine and she can feel a sense of comfort having a few things from home around her. When you leave your accommodations, put out the "Do Not Disturb" sign to discourage staff from entering and frightening your cat. It may also relax her if you turn on her favorite TV show for entertainment and company.

Boarding or Petsitting Your Cat

If the idea of traveling with your cat or doesn't thrill you or her, you may be able to board her. Consider a cat-boarding kennel that caters only to felines.

Most dog-boarding kennels are loud and frightening for a cat. An even better idea is to enlist the services of a petsitter who will come to your home and care for your cat in her own environment.

There are more than nine-thousand boarding kennels in this country. A good one is near you. You can ask your trusted vet, groomer, or a neighbor if they have any recommendations. When you get one that sounds promising, call the kennel and ask to visit. Not all kennel owners will let you wander around the place, both for your own protection and that of the animals (you could be tracking in something), but there should be a viewing area where you can check out the activity areas and observe the animal guests.

A good kennel looks and smells clean. Some kennels have indoor/outdoor runs, others have totally enclosed facilities for cats. Most cats do enjoy an outdoor run, however. The kennel should also be secure, with plenty of supervision for all the animals. Fire extinguishers should be plainly visible.

Food and Water: Each boarded animal should have individual containers filled with clean fresh drinking water. Feeding policies differ from kennel to kennel; most allow you to provide any special diet information or feeding instructions if medically necessary.

65

Temperature Control: The kennel should be able to maintain temperatures within a comfortable range all year long. Older pets are especially sensitive to hot or cold temperatures. All units should be individually heated and cooled.

Quarantine: There should be no chance for cats inside the kennel (other than those from the same household in the same unit) coming into direct contact with one another or with any other animals. Each area should be insulated and lined with an impervious material like fiberglass or polypropylene and enclosed to facilitate heating. It should allow the cats free access to their run through a cat door.

Ventilation: Check for good ventilation; it is critical for your cat's health and comfort by reducing the spread of airborne pathogens.

Sleeping Quarters and Bedding: Most kennels allow you to bring your own bedding; others supply their own. Cats generally like a shelf to lie on and not the floor.

Vaccination Policy: A good kennel has a vaccination policy to protect its feline boarders. Cats should be vaccinated against rabies, panleukopenia or distemper, feline rhinotracheitis, calicivirus, and pneumonitis (FVRCPP). If your cat is on medication, be sure to explain what it is, what it is for, and how it should be given. Inquire if there is an additional charge for medicating.

Parasite Control: Good kennels control parasites. Be sure to ask how this is done at the kennel you are considering.

Bathing or Grooming Services: These may be added at any extra cost.

Remember to book your kennel facility early during peak periods.

Luxury Pet Hotels and Inns

When shopping for temporary quarters for your special feline friend, you might want to consider more luxurious accommodations: imagine spacious suites with plenty of catnip, toys, and personal attention. Yes, say goodbye to yesterday's version of plain old kennels. Hotels, inns, and even spas for pets are the latest rage among traveling pet owners. In fact, some of the places you can book your cat into just might be nicer than where you end up staying on your getaway!

Worrying about your cat while you're on vacation is the last thing you want to do. That's why the concept of special boarding facilities specifically designed for felines is quickly rising in popularity. Knowing your favorite kitty is in a luxurious setting, being pampered and played with, brushed, fed, petted and consistently monitored will, without a doubt, make your time away less stressful and more enjoyable.

Many of these new pet hotels and inns include guest rooms of differing

Technically, a boarding kennel for a cat is a "cattery," but that is a word that makes people stare.

sizes to accommodate one cat or a family of multiple cats who are used to being together. In addition to the minimal requirement of feeding and medicating cats, these feline resorts cater to your cat's every whim and include grooming time and even play time to avoid boredom and relieve the stress associated with being in an unusual place. A wide range of accommodations is available, so be sure to check out all the options.

Petsitters

Undoubtedly, if you must travel, the best solution for your cat is to enlist the services of a petsitter. By choosing this option, your cat can luxuriate in the comfort of her own home while someone waits on her hand and foot. And because cats like a routine, familiar food, and their regular surroundings, your pet will be much less stressed.

If you are lucky enough, you can press a trusted friend or neighbor into service, but if that doesn't work out, you can hire a petsitter. If you must hire a stranger, your best bet is to arrange for the services of a member of Petsitters International or a similar organization. Petsitters is a nonprofit group that certifies and screens petsitters for knowledge and integrity. To find a member near you, visit http://www.petsitters.org/ or call them toll-free at 1-800-296-PETS.

A good petsitter should:
- Have commercial liability coverage insurance (and provide proof).
- Be bonded (so you are protected against theft).
- Keep written records of your cat's special needs, habits, diet, routine, and medicine.
- Be able and willing to transport your cat to your vet or an emergency clinic if the need arises.
- Have a backup for herself in case of an emergency on her end (and be able to provide you with that information upon request).
- Provide a written contract that

Kennel Certification

Although nothing is foolproof, one sign a kennel operator is keeping standards up-to-date is membership in the American Boarding Kennel Association (ABKA). (Look for a plaque on the office wall.) An even higher bar is the CKO (Certified Kennel Operator) designation by ABKA. This affirms that the kennel has been inspected and accredited by the Association. Over 200 standards of excellence must be met to receive this designation. You can also look for approval by the Feline Advisory Bureau, which has its own *Standard for Construction and Management of Boarding Catteries.*

clearly specifies her responsibilities, including medicating or grooming your cat.

- Provide references and contact information.

Make arrangements to meet with the petsitter before you hire her and check out how she responds to your cat and vice versa. If anything about the arrangement makes you uncomfortable, trust your instincts and find another sitter.

If you like what you see, make arrangements as early as possible. Make sure your cat is up-to-date on vaccinations (it's a good idea to get her a wellness check before you leave); check her visible ID, and buy extra supplies. Leave the petsitter some extra money in case of any emergency and arrange with your vet to keep your credit card number on file. Finally, make sure your petsitter knows all your contact numbers and is aware of the location of important features of

Most cats don't like changes in their routine, so the best solution when you travel may be to leave your feline at home and enlist the services of a petsitter.

your home such as circuit breakers, furnace, water valves, and so on.

As an added bonus, many petsitters will pick up your mail, water your plants, or do other chores while you are away. They may charge you extra for these services, or they may throw in a few things gratis. Always check first, and make sure all responsibilities are listed in the contract.

Moving With Your Cat

If you're planning a permanent move with your feline partner, you'll have to consider more than the trip to get there. Prepare for the fact that your cat will not be enthusiastic about the move or the new home, even if it's for her benefit. Cats like things the way they are and the way they have always been.

On moving day, crate your cat. With people charging in and out of the house, yelling and carrying boxes, your cat is going to be miserable. Confining her will keep her from getting lost or running away in the process, and if she is used to her crate, it will give her a degree of comfort as well.

Try to make the new house as inviting as possible. Moving the old furniture in first will provide some familiarity. Make sure doors and windows are securely shut before allowing your cat out of her crate. You might even lay a catnip trail around the house to encourage exploration or spray some cat-appeasing pheromones such as Feliway in different spots. This comforting scent will calm her. You can get

Change

Cats don't tend to like changes in their routine; they are creatures of habit. For example, a major change in environment, such as a move to a new home or the addition or removal of another pet, or the loss of a family member, can make your cat insecure and lead to stress and separation anxiety, and at times even illness. Stress may also contribute to many problem behaviors.

Try to make your cat as comfortable as possible whenever it becomes necessary to introduce change. There are several ways in which you can help her feel more at ease. A comforting scent will often calm her as will having her favorite toys nearby. Rubbing your cat well with a towel and then transferring that scent to key parts of an unfamiliar space often settles a nervous cat. More importantly, be patient. If your cat is stressed, give her lots of extra attention and love. Treat her gently and talk to her in a soothing, reassuring voice. Let her know that everything will be fine, and in time she will calm down and settle into the new circumstances.

something of the same effect by rubbing your cat well with a towel before leaving your former home and then transferring that scent to objects in key parts of the new house. You might be able to fool your cat into thinking, "Hmmm…smells familiar. I've probably been here before." Tranquilizing a hyper cat is also not a bad idea, but talk to your vet first.

Put your cat in one room with her litter box and dinner and shut the door. Cats like to get to know their new surroundings gradually. Over the course of the next couple of weeks, let her explore larger and larger areas. She should soon feel at home. If she is an indoor/outdoor cat, give her another three weeks or so in the house to "claim" it before you let her out. You don't want her stalking back to the old place. (If you'd like to make your formerly outside cat an inside cat, this is a good time to transition to that.)

It's possible that once you are all moved in your traumatized cat may soil or urinate in the house, or that she may become depressed or destructive. Be patient. This too shall pass.

❮ The Lost Cat

One of the most traumatic events a pet owner can experience is the disappearance of a beloved cat. Begin by searching the area—and I mean your entire house. Cats can get stuck in some unexpected places like pipes, appliances, and crawl spaces, or trapped in garages, sheds, barns, closets, and attics. Look behind things and under things. Don't make the assumption that your cat would never crawl into some little space and get stuck or locked in there. It happens. If your cat is scared or injured, she will hide in a dark place. She will not respond to you. You'll have to find her.

Check also with your immediate neighbors. Cats are most likely to be observed in the early morning and evening when they are most active. Hand out copies of photographs and put out flyers. Everywhere. Talk to everyone you meet. Advertise a reward for your pet's safe return. Call the shelter and all the local animal hospitals. After 5 pm, call veterinary emergency clinics. Your cat may have been hit by a car and taken to an animal hospital.

Don't wait to contact a shelter. Government animal control agencies usually keep an animal for only three days and then they either adopt it out or euthanize it. Actually go to the facility and look at the animals in person. Don't rely on the observations of the attendants. And don't give up. Leave a picture of your cat at every shelter and clinic with your contact information clearly listed on it. Lost cats have been reunited with their owners even months later.

However, there is a growing problem of lost-pet fraud and other related scams. People have been known to steal pets and then hold them for ransom. Others pretend to find your pet, but have actually abducted them trying to get a reward. Some will claim that your pet jumped into their car, but they didn't notice until they were 200 miles away. And, of course, they need money to send your cat back to you. Don't fall for this. Ask them to describe the cat in detail. You can put a ringer in the questions, too, like, "Does the cat have a white tip on the tail?" when of course your cat does not . . .or ask about the eye color or any other identifying marks that you did not publicize. I am sorry to relate all of this to you, but it's a sad world we live in. You need to be prepared.

Cat Politics and Controversies

The world of cats is not as peaceful and issue-free as one might like. There are plenty of debates revolving around ethical care, and good-intentioned people are not always in agreement. Here are two of them.

INDOORS OR OUT?

Sadly, many outdoor cats are struck by cars, killed by dogs, or poisoned accidentally—or even deliberately. Cats also fight with other cats and are exposed to disease and parasites outside the home. But the reality is that all cats are safer when kept indoors. And, as a result of their more controlled living conditions, they will live much longer and probably be healthier in the long run. Also, an outdoor cat who isn't spayed or neutered will likely contribute to the serious homeless cat overpopulation problem.

That being said, there is a case for an indoor-outdoor cat. Indoor-outdoor cats tend to be leaner and more active than their indoor cousins. They exhibit fewer behavioral problems, especially the kinds of psychogenic obsessive disorders that can have their roots in boredom. They also keep the yard and environs free of vermin. However, and this is a big "however," your cat is safer when she is indoors and so are the little songbirds. Some people believe that cats have had a detrimental affect on the songbird population in this country. And the number of diseases an outdoor cat can contract is really pretty frightening.

This is a personal decision that will have to be based on the dangers of your neighborhood, the number of other cats and animals around, local regulations, and other important factors. If you keep an indoor-only cat, you must make a concerted effort

Going Indoors

If you have adopted an outdoor cat and want to make her an indoor cat, or if you have just decided that the indoors is safer for your cat, you can do it. The cat will complain, sulk, whine, and may become out and out hostile, but it's possible. Provide her with plenty of enrichment and exciting toys, play with her often, and most importantly, don't give in. After a couple of weeks she will adjust to her new lifestyle. Try not to feel guilty.

If your cat becomes lost, act quickly. Any delay in searching for your pet will make her harder to locate and may sometimes result in dire circumstances.

to provide her with everything she needs to be physically and mentally fit, which includes activities that will stimulate and entertain her when you are away from home, as well as spending lots of daily quality time with her when you are at home.

DECLAWING

Please do not declaw your cat, even if she is a totally indoor pet. The surgery involves the removal not just of the claw itself, but the nail bed and a good portion of the digit. The claw of the cat is not just a toenail like that of other animals. It's a movable digit attached to muscle by powerful tendons and ligaments that permit the cat to extend and retract her claws. Only cats have this ability! Without claws, your cat cannot grasp, hold, or establish proper footing.

Do not kid yourself. This is one of the most intensely painful of all surgeries. In fact, the pain is so bad that declawing surgery is often used to investigate the efficacy of various kinds of pain relief in pets. Many of the nerves are cut or destroyed as well during this procedure, which can produce paralysis and lack of function.

With regard to the laser surgery alternative, while using lasers to declaw a cat may slightly reduce the pain of the procedure, it doesn't change in the least what the procedure actually does.

After surgery, your cat must still hobble around painfully, use the litter box, and try to adjust to a clawless life. Although most cats do return to normal afterwards, some cats never get over it and hobble around forever. And because you are depriving them of their best means of defense, declawed cats often become quite aggressive—they may resort to biting. Seventy percent of cats turned into pounds and shelters for behavioral problems are declawed cats. If you wouldn't yank your dog's teeth out because he chews things he shouldn't, you shouldn't declaw your cat because she may shred some fabric.

Twenty countries have already made this procedure illegal or consider it so unethical that it can be done only under extreme circumstances. These countries include: The United Kingdom, Italy, France, Germany, Austria, Switzerland, Norway, Sweden, the Netherlands, Ireland, Denmark, Finland, Slovenia, Portugal, Belgium, Brazil, Australia, New Zealand, Yugoslavia, and Japan. It's a sad state of affairs that a country as presumably progressive as ours hasn't figured this out, too.

Both the Cat Fanciers' Association (CFA) and the American Animal Hospital Association (AAHA) strongly disapprove of declawing, and for basically the same reasons:

- Declawed cats are defenseless.
- Declawing surgery (onychectomy) is painful and traumatic. It can have both physical and psychological effects.
- Damage to furniture can be kept to a minimum by trimming the cat's claws or by purchasing tips to place on them.

The American Veterinary Association basically concurs, saying: "Declawing of domestic cats should be considered only after attempts have been made to prevent the cat from using its claws destructively or when its clawing presents a zoonotic risk for its owner."

Declawing Alternative

If you feel you must do something about your cat's claws, try Soft Paws or Sticky Claws. Soft Paws are vinyl nail caps that glue on to your cat's claws. Believe it or not, they come in different colors. Sticky Paws are water-based medical grade transparent adhesive strips that are applied directly to a piece of furniture (or wherever you want). Cats hate the tacky feeling and won't scratch it. If you must declaw your cat, the cat needs to be kept indoors at all times. Only the front feet need to be declawed.

TENECTOMY

A technique known as a "tenectomy" (or tendonectomy) is becoming a common alternative to declawing. Instead of amputating the cat's claw, the surgeon removes the portion of the tendon that controls the cat's ability to flex and extend her claws; as a result, they remain permanently extended. Most cats who undergo this surgery can still use their claws at least somewhat, but cannot retract them. Some people feel this surgery is even worse than the one it was designed to replace! Cats who have undergone this procedure must have their claws trimmed constantly. If they don't, the claws will grow into the foot. I can't see the advantage in this procedure.

Chapter Four

Feline Behavior & Communication

"Way down deep, we're all motivated by the same urges. Cats have the courage to live by them."

—Jim Davis

Cat Language

To understand cats, it's important to understand their language. While cats may not have the range of expression available to dogs, they have enough to tell you what's on their mind—if you only pay attention. Most of their vocabulary is basic enough that you don't need a dictionary. They also have that wonderful purr—not in a dog's vocabulary at all.

Language serves many purposes in addition to direct, information transfer. It is actually a social bond that can indicate trust, love, fear, and uncertainty. Knowing your cat's language, which is written in body, voice, and gesture, is an excellent way to become a better cat owner.

BODY

Cats use body language and scent to communicate with each other. Although your own sniffer isn't sophisticated enough to read the scent messages cats send to other cats, you can learn their body language. If you can figure out what that universal set of body postures mean, you may get to know what your feline companion is thinking or feeling and learn to interpret her many moods.

Cats use body language and scent to communicate with each other. Knowing your cat's language helps you to become a better pet owner.

You've seen all the moves:

- Hostile cats generally walk with their heads slightly down and moving from side to side. This means, "Get out of the way before I kill you."
- A cat on the defensive has her back up and her head held to the side. She may hunker down if she can't run away.
- A fearful cat may have an arched back.
- A crouching cat with a sawing rear end is about to attack something.
- Trapped cats often exhibit piloerection, a neat trick where their hair stands up straight. This makes the cat look larger (and apparently more frightening) to other animals than she really is.
- A bend in the forelegs means the cat will try to avoid a confrontation, but will defend herself if the need arises.
- A bend in the hind legs signals uncertainty about how to proceed.
- Lying on the back may mean she is inviting you for a game, but be careful—it's also the position that makes scratching most effective.
- The head butt is a sign of affection and trust.
- Face rubbing—your cat is telling you that she owns you. Cats have special glands around the nose, cheek, chin, and chest area that secrete oil with a scent unique to your cat. Your cat is imbuing you with her special fragrance. You can't smell it, but other felines can. Your cat is warning them to stay away.
- Lifting and shaking paws may indicate complete disgust—almost as if the cat has "stepped in it."
- Kneading, which comes from the days when the cat drew milk from her mother, signifies contentment. Kneading is usually accompanied by purring.

TAIL

The primary purpose of a cat's tail is to keep her balanced. A cheetah uses her tail almost like a gyroscope to keep from falling over while chasing game. However, cats can also use their tails to communicate. A feline will swish her tail when she's mad, tuck it when she's scared, and hold it straight up when she's happy to see you. A straight-up tail curved to one side may be an invitation to play.

CAT'S-EYE

Cats are notable for their amazing vision. Physically, their eyes are very large considering the size of their head. If our eyes were as big as theirs, relatively speaking, they each would be 8 inches long. Cats' eyes also bulge slightly, which provides them with excellent peripheral vision.

Cats are fond of staring at people, and while their unblinking (and somewhat unnerving) stare may indicate they are mad about something, it's just as likely that they're thinking about how wonderful you are. At least that's how I choose to interpret it. Other eye shapes and movements can mean different things:

- If the pupils are just slits, you can be pretty sure your cat is contented.
- Dilated pupils, especially in bright light, may indicate fear, distress, or pain.
- Slowly blinking eyes signal relaxation

SMELLING

Cats can't smell as well as dogs (the super-sniffers of the world) do. However, they can use their sense of smell a lot better than humans can, having twice the amount of "sniffing surface" on the inside of their noses. Like dogs, however, their sniffing receptacle is located toward the back of the oral cavity and, as a result, the cat has to make an effort to analyze scents. They don't just float into their noses. Their nose and upper lip are also sensitive to temperature.

MOUTH MOTIONS AND THE FLEHMEN RESPONSE

Beneath the floor of the nasal cavity, cats and certain other animals (including dogs) have a special organ called the vomeronasal or Jacobson's organ. It connects to tiny openings behind the upper incisor teeth, and allows a cat to literally "taste" a scent if she gapes with open jaws. This organ is present in humans too, but only in a rudimentary form. If you see your cat sniffing another cat's urine, for instance, and making this characteristic expression, you can be sure that she is carefully evaluating the scent to glean important information about the urinator. If your cat looks calm and is just sitting around with her mouth open, she may be tasting the pheromones floating in the air.

Can Cats See in Color?

Cats have color vision, but not to the degree that human beings do. It's a fact of physiology that, in general, one can see well at night or one can see well in color, but not both. Cats have decided that they would rather see at night and therefore have many more rods (for low-light vision) than cones (for color vision). The color cats can see best (apparently) is green. They can also see a little blue.

HEARING

Like most night hunters, cats have superb hearing and highly mobile ears. In fact, a cat has 20 working muscles in the pinna (ear "leather") that allows the ear to turn to an extraordinary degree. Animals with pricked ears, like cats, still have a lot of "wild" in them; floppy ears are a sign of domestication. You never run into any floppy-eared cats, although there is a breed called the American curl, with very strangely shaped ears. That's different.

- The normal position for a cat's ear is up and forward, which indicates normal attentiveness.
- Ears to the side may signal hostility, pressed back ears may indicate extreme fear, and rapidly rotating ears mean your cat is very focused on the environment. Check the back door. Somebody might be trying to break in.
- Flattened ears signal that the cat feels threatened.

Cats can also hear higher pitched sounds than dogs can, maybe because they are used to hunting things with squeaky little voices.

THE CAT'S MEOW: VOCALIZATION IN CATS

A cat's meow is truly her attempt to communicate with us. Cats do not usually meow to other cats, only to us humans!

As for the purr, cats purr for about the same reason people smile—mostly because they are happy, but sometimes for other reasons such as when they are distressed or afraid. Think about the nervous smile people have in a dentist's office. It's much the same thing. Queens also purr while giving birth, and kittens purr while suckling. Some experts believe this is a self-comforting sound.

In case you're wondering, the measurable frequency of a cat's purr lies between 25 and 150 Hz. The "how" of the purr is somewhat controversial. One study found that purring involves activation of nerves inside the larynx. These nerve signals make the vocal cords vibrate, with the diaphragm acting as a piston pump pushing air in and out of the vibrating cords, thus creating "a musical hum." Another theory is that, rather than something vibrating in the cat's larynx, it is the vibration of the blood vessels that causes the purr.

By the way, big roaring cats like tigers and lions cannot purr, although smaller wild cats such as cougars can. It even appears that raccoons can purr, although I have never observed this. Perhaps the raccoons I've caught invading

What's That Funny "Pocket" on the Outside of the Ear?

Ah, that's the bursa, and no one is sure what its function is, if any. It may help the ear fold, and it may help the cat localize where sounds are coming from. But that's just a guess.

You can often interpret what your cat may be thinking or feeling based on her vocalizations and the position of her ears, eyes, whiskers, and tail.

our trash cans weren't that happy to see me standing out there waving a flashlight and screaming at them. As far as the simple meow goes, this is a sound seldom uttered by a wild or feral cat because other cats don't seem to respond to it. But human beings do. So cats meow when they are hungry, want to go in or out, or otherwise need your attention.

Cats also growl when they are angry, yowl when they are upset or in season, and hiss when they are threatened. In fact, hissing is always purely defensive. It is almost always a defensive rather than offensive strategy. A hissing cat is *scared*. Remember that. The same is true with snakes, by the way. A hissing snake is trying to scare you away, not attack you. Is a cat's hiss mimicking a snake's hiss? I suppose we will never know, but I wouldn't be surprised. Because cats are solitary animals, they never evolved the kind of appeasement behaviors that are common in dog packs, such as tail wagging or lowering the head in submission.

Behavior Problems

Once you understand cat behavior, you can make life happier and healthier for your feline friend. But there's an advantage in it for you as well: Having this information at your disposal is like having the secret to successful cat training, which will enable you to deal with any behavior problems you may be faced with. It's pretty simple really. The key is to reinforce good behaviors and to discourage negative habits. Some behaviors are just instinctual and you will not be able stop them, but you will be able to curb or shape them. You'll never get your cat to do anything that's totally outside of her natural behaviors, but you can teach her how to adapt those behaviors so that both of you can live happily together.

All complex animals can exhibit behavior problems. (I suppose less complex creatures like fleas do not have behavior problems, although I would not know. Their very existence is a problem in my opinion.) However, most of these problems can be prevented or solved.

One of the most difficult things to work out about cat behavior is that cats walk a fine line between boredom and being distressed because things are just *too* exciting for them. Cats enjoy consistency in meal times, your comings and goings, and attention to the litter box, but they are also highly intelligent, intensely curious (but cautious) animals who need appropriate stimulation. Outside cats get plenty of this on their own, but indoor cats will need you to supply them with a reason for being happy.

Exercise: You can help in both regards by giving your cat plenty of exercise. Outdoor cats are less likely to display the neurotic behavior of their indoor sisters, but even indoor cats can be kept sufficiently busy.

Healthful Diet: Nutritional deficiencies or oversupplementation can ruin even the best cat's disposition.

Attention: Not only should you keep your cat company, but it's also important to "listen" to your cat. Her signs of distress might be subtle, but if you catch trouble brewing before it erupts, you'll both be better off.

Toys and Adventures: Cats are intelligent creatures who like interesting things to do. Help them by giving them plenty of interactive toys and an opportunity to explore the world "outside the box," even if it's limited to a window through which they can see.

Health Care: Certain diseases can make cats act wacko. Make sure your cat has frequent checkups. And if necessary don't pooh-pooh the idea of modern pharmacology. It can help cats experiencing serious psychological difficulties.

AGGRESSION

While the word "aggression" often brings to mind a raging pit bull, cat owners know that even our elegant felines can have a few bad moments. In many cases, aggression in cats is caused by a medical problem rather than by environmental stressors. Aggression is manifested in violence or the threat of violence. It can be directed against people, dogs, or other cats. Mark Twain once wrote: "You may say a cat uses good grammar. Well, a cat does—but you let a cat get excited once; you let a cat get to pulling fur with another cat on a shed nights, and you'll hear grammar that will give you the lockjaw. Ignorant people think it's the noise which fighting cats make that is so aggravating, but it ain't so; it's the sickening grammar they use."

Medical conditions associated with feline aggression include:

Brain tumor: In this case the aggression may be accompanied by other signs of odd behavior. Confirmation can be made by CT scan or MRI. In some cases it may be possible to remove the tumor surgically.

Pheromones

Pheromones are special hormones that provide information. Cats can read each other's pheromones, even if we can't. Some of these special hormones are secreted by sebaceous glands in the skin of the cat's forehead, and when a cat rubs against us, she is telling the world not that she loves us, but that we are her possessions. Which is true in a way, I suppose. After your cat rubs up against you, you may notice her carefully grooming and licking herself. Perhaps this is to assimilate your own odor. Or, perhaps she is trying to cleanse herself of it.

Head trauma: Trauma could cause a subdural hematoma, which may often be drained.

Hyperthyroidism: Suspect hyperthyroidism if your senior cat suddenly develops an aggressive attitude, especially when combined with weight loss and excessive thirst. Your vet can have a hormone (T_4) test performed to confirm the diagnosis. Medication can treat the condition.

Ischemic encephalopathy: This condition is caused by a parasite affecting younger or middle-aged cats who spend time outside. The culprit is the Cuterebra larva (and there is nothing cute about it, believe me). The cat may also experience sudden blindness and strange circling behavior. Ivermectin and supportive therapy may eliminate the problem.

Thiamine deficiency: This condition can occur if you feed your cat uncooked freshwater fish. I don't know anyone who does this, but it can happen. Raw fish has lots of thiaminase, an enzyme that destroys thiamine. In addition to aggression, a cat with a thiamine deficiency may have a poor coat and assume a hunched-up stance. The cure, as you might suspect, is thiamine supplementation—and a change of diet, for heaven's sake.

NONMEDICAL CAUSES OF AGGRESSION

Other than physical illness, most kinds of aggression are the expression of normal feline frustrations, irritations, and being just plain ornery. Commonly, feline aggression is displayed toward other cats or dogs in the house.

Aggression can be divided into offensive and defensive acts. Both types are connected to a stressor of some sort. Cats who are about to attack another cat (or rarely a dog or person) pitch their ears forward or sideways. They may growl in a low-pitched tone, and their pupils will become narrow slits, focused intently on the object of the aggression. The cat may crouch slightly and move her head from side to side. The tail swishes. She is ready to strike.

The defensive cat, on the other hand, will have ears pasted back against her head, and her pupils will become enlarged. You may notice the hairs on her body standing out all over. This is called "piloerection," and it is nature's way to help a cat on the defensive look much bigger than she is—and nothing to tangle with. She may arch her back or cower with her tail at her side or curled under her body. She will probably hiss and spit. And her claws will be at the ready just in case.

Ain't Misbehaving!

Cats don't usually misbehave out of spite. They just do what seems natural or makes sense to them. To correct unwanted behaviors, you have to first figure out what your feline is trying to communicate and then redirect these behaviors toward an acceptable positive behavior. With patience and consistent reinforcement, your cat will make the "good" connection and the "bad" behavior will be changed.

Territorial Aggression

Two or more cats may compete for the same territory, such as a prized windowsill or a comfortable chair. This is classic territorial aggression. Behavior such as this is much more common in house cats than it is in cats allowed outside. Cats permitted to venture outdoors seem to be relaxed by the experience, using up their bad tempers in arguing with the neighborhood cats (not yours), hunting, and just taking a breather. The more cats you have in a house, the more likely it is that aggression will break out among them. Adding a new cat is a particular stressor. Aggressive behavior may erupt all at once or it may build up over time, with the more dominant cat gradually striking out to guard her resources or to antagonize the weaker cat. (This ranking is not dependent on gender, size, or strength, but rather in some unidentifiable realm of psychological one-upmanship.)

Nonrecognition Aggression

Some cases of aggression are labeled nonrecognition aggression. This occurs when one cat who previously got along fine in the household has been away, even for a short trip to the veterinarian. The resident cats either do not recognize the "newcomer" (perhaps she smells strange), or they believe that the old cat has relinquished her place in the hierarchy by her absence. Or, it may be that the cat who has been away is simply exuding stress. At any rate, the period of aggression is usually very brief and is over when the cat resettles.

Redirected Aggression

Redirected aggression occurs when one cat has been stressed by something other than her roommate. It could be the sight of another rival cat. Or, maybe the household dog made her mad. Instead of deciding to attack the Rottweiler, the cat goes after her feline housemate—a petty, but safer decision.

Petting Aggression

Another annoying type of aggression, called petting aggression, causes the cat to go after people during petting. Some cats seem to put up with and even enjoy being petted. But then they suddenly turn on the owner and bite him. The situation is worse if the cat has been held or restrained in some way.

Cats exhibiting this sort of behavior are often termed alpha cats, but I think they're just ornery. The attack, however, is not as unexpected as you may at first think. Your cat is giving you definite signs—swishing her tail perhaps or glaring. The truth is that many cats, even though they seek out petting, actually have limited tolerance for it. If your cat does this, unceremoniously dump her on the floor and don't let her back up on your lap for a while. When you finally give in, just sit there, don't pet her. You can eventually begin very light and brief petting, but always keep a careful eye out for a sudden turn.

PREY AGGRESSION

Some aggression in cats is perfectly natural. This type is called *prey aggression* or *predatory aggression*, which is simply the natural urge to stalk and kill prey, usually a small animal or bird. Not a very pretty picture, but there it is. No stressor is involved, and cats appear to be at their very happiest when stalking or killing. I am very sorry that cats are like this, but it is their nature. You can't change it. And if you have a mouse infestation in the house, you may not want to!

Kittens first start showing this kind of behavior at about five weeks of age, usually with their littermates. It continues through kittenhood, usually peaking at about four months. Cats who grow up in a home without other kittens may attack their owners instead, usually but not always with gloved claws. It's just practice. Because cats are genetically programmed to be hunters, you cannot train them not to kill mice or birds. Your only option is to protect birds or small pets by never allowing your cats to have access to them.

Cats who do not get enough mental or physical stimulation can become bored, restless, and develop behavior problems.

Kittens around four months of age often start to engage in very rough, aggressive play either with a housemate or with an owner. This is also normal behavior—the kitten is rehearsing her adult role as hunter. The behavior usually stops by the time the cat is a year old. If she does this with you, you should be flattered because it means that the cat trusts you enough to engage in this sort behavior with you. If you put her down or at least "freeze" when she tries it, she may eventually give up. If you want to play back by waggling your foot, be prepared for the consequences. Otherwise, try giving her some interactive toys to kill instead of your foot.

MATERNAL AGGRESSION

Maternal aggression is another natural kind of aggression, but unlike prey aggression, it's accompanied by high levels of stress. When kittens are born, a special hormone called oxytocin, the "bonding hormone," is released. In response, progesterone (the pregnancy hormone) drops and is replaced by estrogen. So what? Well, progesterone is a hormone that encourages calm in the mother-to-be, while estrogen is an activating hormone. (No jokes about PMS, please.) The new protective mom may act very strangely, and even her owners should be careful not to upset her and get on the wrong end of her claws. I well remember Pansy, a childhood cat, who managed to run off a Standard Poodle, a Newfoundland, and a Beagle that came too close to her kittens.

If a catfight occurs for any reason, don't be a fool and try to stop it. They won't kill each other, but they could give you some nasty scratches. Spray them with water or startle with them by making a loud noise and then separate them for a few hours.

TREATING AGGRESSION

The best way to handle cases of aggression between cats is to neuter them, encourage plenty of exercise, and, if necessary, even put bells on them. Bells of different tones will warn undercats that their dominant housemates are around. It will give them time to hide. Some people suggest rubbing all the household cats every day with a towel imbued with the scent of the others, especially facial pheromones, which have a calming effect.

PLAYING OR FIGHTING: HOW CAN YOU TELL?

Cats like to tussle, so how do you know if they're just joshing or if a serious disagreement has broken out? Here are a few simple rules:
- Playing is usually silent. If your cats are screaming, they are fighting.

Play can escalate into a fight, of course, in which case, there's usually one scream and then the cats walk off in a huff to cool down.

- Playing cats switch roles from chaser to chasee. If one cat is doing all the chasing, she is being a bully.
- Lots of hissing on the part of one cat means she is constantly being put on the defensive and is being bullied.
- No physical harm results from playing. Fighting draws blood.

THE DEPRESSED CAT

Like people, animals can become depressed. We don't necessarily have to ascribe human causes, such as "The cat is sad because mommy and daddy are getting a divorce," but it is true that they don't like change in routine, and they can sense stress and tension in the family. Even changing the cat food or kitty litter can set it off. New pets, the death of old pets, a human who moves away, gets sick, or just changes working hours can cause anxiety and depression also.

Obviously your cat is too proud to come up and tell you she is depressed. But the signs will be there: loss of appetite, change in sleeping habits, neglect of appearance, meowing excessively, and loss of housetraining can all be indications of a problem.

Another cause of depression is plain out-and-out boredom, a common ailment of indoor cats. Cats who are allowed outside might be in mortal danger, but they are never bored. Indoor cats need many more toys and much more human interaction to keep them interested.

If simple things like more interaction and a consistent routine don't work, a trip to the vet is in order.

Misdirected Play

Never use your hands or fingers as cat toys. That sounds like common sense, but you'd be surprised how many people do this. If your cat bites you while you're playing with her, hiss at her or howl in agony. Next time, be gentler. Biting usually occurs when a cat gets overly excited.

THE FEARFUL CAT

The expression "scaredy cat" has its roots in our common experience. Cats haven't survived this long in the world by living with reckless abandon. They are cautious to a fault. Cats are sensitive critters and, like other highly-evolved mammals, can develop phobias or seemingly irrational fears about strangers, restraint, noise, and other stressors. Some fear is natural and self-protecting; it's only a phobia when it's irrational and out of hand. Some cats are just inherently shy.

It's generally accepted that there is genetic component to feline fearfulness as well as the influence of environmental stressors, particularly those that occur during the "sensitive period" between two and seven weeks of age. Cats who have a bad experience during this time may be fearful ever after, especially if it's coupled with a "shy gene."

These cats run away, hide under the bed or in a closet, freeze, hiss, or even exhibit thigmotaxia. (Isn't that a fabulous word? It means that the cats presses herself against the wall. I would memorize this word if I were you. You never know when it may come in handy.)

In some cases your cat can overcome these fears with gradual desensitization. This works if you accurately pinpoint just what your cat is afraid of (not always as easy as it seems) and also can control her exposure to it.

The classic way to "cure" a phobia is to present it to the cat in a controlled setting at a low intensity that does not produce anxiety, and then gradually increase the length or intensity of the exposure. The goal is for the cat to learn to associate pleasure rather than fear with the stimulus. Each step of the retraining program process should include highly palatable food treats; this is called *counter-conditioning*. For example, reward the cat for sitting quietly. However, I should say that most truly phobic cats are too terrified to eat.

For less serious cases, cats may get over a fear stimulus if they are constantly exposed (flooded) to it. For example, cats in a boarding facility will usually get used to it.

It is a serious mistake to try to calm or reassure a phobic cat; this will only reinforce the anxiety. For example, carrying a nervous cat to a "stranger" or something else the cat is afraid of will only make the animal feel trapped. Trapped cats get even more fearful and aggressive.

In some cases, anti-anxiety medication has proven helpful. These medications can sometimes reduce the anxiety to the point at which desensitization can take place.

Sadly, some owners don't recognize how serious a phobia can be. After all, the cat is hiding under the bed, so you may not recognize the problem. Still,

Understanding why your cat is misbehaving and getting to the root of the problem is the best way to correct unwanted behaviors.

How to Restrain a Cat

From time to time you may have to restrain your cat. If you have no pillow case, towel, or other restraining implements, you can rely on the simple, tried-and-true method the mama cat uses: the old scruff-of-the neck tactic.

Oddly enough, most cats are rather resigned to this technique and seldom put up a fuss. To do it right, simply grab the scruff with your dominant hand and hang on. Do not let go. With your other hand, hold your cat in a sitting position. If you think she may attempt to scratch you, hold on to her front legs instead so she can't, but keep cradling her. I hope you're still holding on to the scruff. That's important. And don't forget about the teeth—they can do a surprising amount of damage. Cat teeth are sized and spaced just so they insert neatly beneath the vertebrae of a mouse to kill it instantly. The same teeth slide very easily between your finger joints.

the cat is experiencing terror. If desensitization and counter-conditioning don't work, do your best to provide a very safe private place for your cat. Often she will return to her usual sane self once the fear-inducing stimulus is removed.

In any case, use caution around a terrified animal. Once we had a fire in our home, and a rescue worker reached under the couch to drag out our terrified cat, Isis. The distraught animal bit him as he hauled her out. Even though there were sirens screaming, a houseful of noise, and smoke and strangers—one of whom yanked her from the only hiding place she could find—the authorities labeled the bite as an "unprovoked attack," and we had to keep her in quarantine for ten days.

Some people have had good luck using flower essence therapy for their scaredy cats. I have seen no evidence at all that these actually work. (I put them in the same class as homeopathy, but flower essences have their defenders.) Here are some of the more commonly used "anti-phobia" flower essences:

- **aspen** — vague or unconscious fears
- **garlic** — nervous fear
- **cherry plum** — extreme stress, trapped feeling
- **filaree** — anxiety and obsessions
- **impatiens** — nervousness
- **mimulus** — nervousness, shyness, travel-phobia
- **penstemon** — trauma, for inner strength
- **poison oak** — fear aggression
- **red clover** — hysteria
- **rock rose** — total terror
- **snapdragon** — fear aggression

Mix up to five essences (four drops each) in a dropper bottle with water and shake gently. You can try to drop them directly into the mouth, but if that doesn't work, apply to the ears. Several doses may be required. You can also put the essences in a spray bottle and use a mist. Take note that most flower essences are preserved in alcohol. However, I think you'll have much better luck with feline pheromones.

The same is true of homeopathy. I have yet to see any real evidence that it works; however, it has powerful proponents. Homeopathic remedies that are

said to work with fearful cats include:

- *Aconitum napellus* — terror to the point of hysteria and difficult breathing
- *Natrum muriaticum* — fearful vomiting
- *Cocculus indicus* (**Cocc**) — fearful panting and drooling
- **Phosphorus** — noise fears
- *Arsenicum album* — separation anxiety and exhausted fear
- *Gelsemium sempervirens* — quiet trembling fear

Choose a strength lower than 30 C. A combination homeopathic remedy called Calms Fort is also said to be helpful. Again, it may be necessary to apply the remedy to the animal's ear. Trying to force open a cat's mouth to squeeze in a medication is going to hurt.

For an herbal remedy for anxiety, try chamomile tea sneaked into your cat's food. This really does work, but it's not going to be easy to convince your cat to imbibe the stuff.

CATS WHO PESTER STRANGERS—ESPECIALLY ONES WHO DON'T LIKE CATS

It's happened to us all. A cat walks into a roomful of company, looks around, and picks out the one person who doesn't like cats to sit on, all the while ignoring the encouraging looks from the cat lovers. Is this just orneriness on the cat's part?

Probably not. Researchers theorize that people who fear or dislike cats won't look at them (or at least not very much) when they come into the room. Because staring is a threat in the animal world, the cat misinterprets not looking as a friendly sign. And bingo, she's on the enemy's lap. One of my friends had a true terror of cats. Every time she came over to my house, our cat Malachi would jump on her lap. Sharon would scream in terror and freeze in place until someone removed the errant cat. One day, though, everything changed. Sharon stopped by, casually picked up the cat, put her on her lap and starting petting him. "Sharon," I said in amazement. "I thought you were terrified of cats." "Not any more," she said. "Mike and I are getting a divorce. I'm going through too much stress in my personal life right now to put any energy into being afraid of cats."

NAIL BITING

Oddly enough, cats can nervously bite their nails the same as humans do. It seems to stem from anxiety. It's not usually serious enough to do anything about, so don't bite your own nails over it.

SEPARATION ANXIETY

Here's one of the biggest myths in the pet world. "You're too busy for a dog. Get a cat. Cats don't require company." What a lie. Like dogs, cats crave human companionship. If they didn't, they wouldn't sit on you or just "hang around." I admit, they often pretend that their interests lie elsewhere, but we know better.

And while cats are certainly more independent and self-reliant than dogs, they can still suffer loneliness if neglected or left alone for long hours. Breeds most susceptible include Siamese, Burmese, and other highly social cats. "Tougher" breeds like Maine Coon Cats are less affected. Animals who have been left in shelters, weaned too early, or had other painful experiences are also most likely to be affected.

Signs of feline separation anxiety are more low-key than those shown by dogs. Your cat won't chew her way out the door or keep the neighborhood on edge with ceaseless vocalizing. But it doesn't mean she's not miserable all the same. Signs of separation anxiety include "Velcro" behavior on the part of the cat when you are home, and vocalization or depression when you leave. The cat may also urinate or defecate on the floor after you have left—not because she is trying to "get back" at you, but because she is truly distressed to the point of losing control. Some cats even vomit out of nervousness. A physically ill cat, of course, will vomit whether you are home or not. A cat with separation anxiety will vomit only in your absence. Some cats will claw at the door, apparently in an effort to get out and join you.

This is a hard condition to address using behavior modification training (it's much easier in dogs), but you might be able to help by providing your cat with a view of the world outside, especially if it includes birdfeeders. Enrich her environment in other ways with catnip toys and a radio or TV tuned to talk not music. This seems to be soothing, for some reason. In severe cases, you may want to resort to medication like Clomicalm (clomipramine). While this medication has been officially approved for dogs only, it gets similarly good results with cats, but check with your vet first.

Fear and Anxiety

Moderate fear or anxiety isn't usually a serious problem, and it may sometimes be temporary due to a change in environment or circumstances that your cat may eventually adjust to. If the fear becomes excessive or irrational, however, she may have developed a phobia and will require professional help to overcome the problem. Some cats who seem to always be in a state of dread are victims of what is called "global fear." These animals will benefit most from pharmacology.

CATNIP BUZZ

Okay, what is it about this stuff that makes cats go crazy? It's a mystery. Catnip (*Nepeta cataria*) belongs to the mint family. Its active ingredient, as far as cats go, is nepetalactone, part of a group of chemicals called terpenoids. Other animals are immune to the stuff. To confuse things even more, only about half of cats seem to be affected by it. (It's genetically determined whether a cat will respond to it or not.) Those who are, sniff, roll, shake their heads, run around the house like mad, and sometimes act as if they are falling-down drunk. But they do seem to enjoy it. Certainly, any plant that had this effect on people would probably be declared illegal. In fact, it's already happened. Oddly, kittens have to be three or four months old before they will respond to catnip.

Some recent studies suggest that the molecular structure of nepetalactone resembles opium and may produce similar effects. Only in cats though, and even in them it is not addictive. Here's a practical use for catnip: Give it to rival or feuding cats. It seems to settle them down and lets them tolerate each other's company.

You can buy catnip in spray or even in bubble form. Your cat will chase the bubbles all around the house. It's hysterical.

CHATTY CATS: HYPERVOCALIZATION

While a mewing cat is not nearly as aggravating as a constantly barking dog, it can be irritating enough. People who have a low tolerance for chitchat should avoid vocal breeds like Siamese and other Orientals. Persians are much quieter.

If you find that your cat is making much more noise than usual, the cause may be a learned behavior (it gets her what she wants), something biological, or even a pathological condition. The most common behavioral cause of hypervocalization is simply the act of seeking attention, although fear or anxiety may also be responsible. Biological reasons can include estrus, pain, or hunger, and medical causes range from hyperthyroidism to a brain tumor. If you cannot figure out the cause on your own, it's time to take your cat to the vet.

Although you can't change your cat's natural, instinctive behaviors, you can teach her how to adapt those behaviors so that both of you can live happily together.

THE WAKE-UP CALL

"Cats come at dawn to sit on your bed. They may not nip your nose or inhale your breath or make a sound. They simply sit there and stare at you until you open one eyelid and spy them there about to drop dead for need of feeding." — Ray Bradbury

It's happened to us all: We are peacefully asleep on a Saturday morning, and it's one second past 6:00 am. "Yao! M'Yaio! Maw-o!" (or variations thereof). It's your custom-designed (although not by you) alarm clock, also known as your cat, and it has given you the wake-up call. Your feline companion is unconcerned that your internal clock does not match her own. How can you handle this?

Well, you can close your door and ignore her. Do not reward her carrying on with the slightest attention, even a "Cool it, Missy! You make one more sound and there will be no catnip." No, that doesn't work. You know it doesn't because you've tried it. Several times.

You do have to understand that your cat can't help waking up when she does. It's part of her heritage. Cats are crepuscular. That means that they are most active in the twilight hours of evening and early (very early) morning. Once she's up, she wants you up too. She has no stamp collection, comic books, or Saturday morning cartoons to beguile her. She has only you. And *any* response you give her will delight her.

Before you retire in the evening, provide your cat with plenty of toys and hope for the best. If you continue to ignore her, she may give up and resort to other activities such as hunting for mice or something.

THE GIFT-GIVING CAT

Last week I went out on my front porch and found a dead bat. There was also a meadow vole at the back door. Yes, my cats have been honoring me again with the unfortunate fruits of their night hunts. They are trophies of sorts, the kind of thing a mother cat brings to her kittens to show them the ropes. Sometimes the poor victim is still alive, leaving you with the dilemma of trying to rehabilitate it, returning it to the wild, or else figuring out the best way to put it out of its misery.

The only way to put a stop to this behavior is to keep your cat indoors (although if you have a mouse problem, a hunting cat will soon clear it up). Outdoor cats can be somewhat foiled by wearing a bell. And while feeding your cat well may slow her down, it won't really affect her hunting urges; cats are programmed to hunt and kill whether they are hungry or not. In the wild, only one out of ten strikes is successful, so if cats waited until they were hungry to hunt, they might starve to death.

COMPULSIVE BEHAVIOR

The more you look at cats, the more you realize they are creepily close to being just like us, and that includes compulsive behavior. Obsessively repetitive

Morning Cat

If you feed your cat first thing when you get up, you will find that she rouses you from sleep much earlier than you'd like. Unless she free-feeds, provide meals only after your morning is well underway if you can.

actions may begin as a response to emotional pressure, but can soon escalate out of control. Your cat will keep on doing them even when these actions are self-destructive or mutilating.

The most common of such behaviors are wool-sucking, over-grooming to the point of pulling out hair, and feline hyperesthesia.

WOOL SUCKING

Wool sucking is easily the most common compulsive behavior, although a cat may prefer another fabric or even plastic or wood. This behavior probably originally stems from nursing behavior that somehow got misdirected. It usually starts right after weaning, although no one knows why. As the affected cat matures, wool sucking may evolve into pica (compulsive eating of nonfood items). One of my cats (whom I found as a young kitten in my barn) exhibited this behavior for more than a year before finally stopping. Not only is it damaging to the material, but ingesting carpet is not good for a cat's digestive system either. This behavior is seen most frequently in Siamese and Siamese crosses, possibly because these breeds have a longer weaning period than other breeds.

Some wool-sucking cats show improved behavior if fed a high-fiber dry food (although I believe that dry food is worse for your cat than wool sucking). Others have had luck going the all-natural route. If your cat has a favorite spot to chew on, you can spray the area with bitter apple or some cayenne pepper.

EXCESSIVE GROOMING (PSYCHOGENIC ALOPECIA)

It is normal for cats to groom themselves when feeling stressed, and chronic stress can result in over-grooming. Cats with this condition will lick, chew, and even pull out their fur. They may also exhibit other anxiety-related behaviors such as eating disorders and hiding. Females around the age of puberty seem more prone than males. It always is a stressful time. Before starting treatment, a proper veterinary diagnosis must be made because parasites can cause similar symptoms.

HAIR PULLING

The fancy name for this awful behavior is trichotillomania. In humans, this type of behavior is recognized as an obsessive-compulsive disorder (OCD). And if it goes on long enough, you'll have a bald cat. The veterinary term for this hairless condition is *psychogenic alopecia*, which is defined as baldness caused by psychological problems usually identified as some form of chronic frustration or anxiety.

Are You Talking to Me?!

Cats often pester people when they are talking on the phone. Because your cat can't see whom you are talking to, she may naturally assume you are speaking to her!

Hair pulling seems to be more common in the Oriental breeds, possibly because they are more high strung, although it's possible there's a more specific genetic component involved. One of my cats is a hair-puller. Except she pulls *my* hair. With her teeth.

Before jumping on the OCD bandwagon, however, it's important to rule out possible medical causes of this condition such as fleas, mites, fungal infections, hormonal problems, and allergies. The typical OCD cat is overstressed, with baldness across the belly and inside the legs. There are no obvious skin lesions (usually) or parasites. You may also notice the cat grooming excessively.

Treatment includes eliminating environmental stressors wherever possible (separating rival cats, for instance), and enriching the cat's environment. In some cases, medications to reduce anxiety and compulsive behavior may be necessary. The most successful drugs are the selective serotonin reuptake inhibitors like fluoxetine (Prozac) and others in that class. They usually bring results in three to six weeks. Cats who don't respond may respond to anti-anxiety drugs like buspirone (BuSpar), which usually takes about two weeks to achieve its effects.

Catnip Caution

Washington County, Maryland, where I live, is considered the catnip capital of the world. The stuff grows positively rampant around here. Catnip is the common name for a perennial herb of the mint family. Given to the right cat, it can cause a rather curious reaction. The cat will rub it, roll over it, kick at it, lick it, and generally go bonkers for several minutes. Then she'll just lose interest and walk away.

Even the most fickle feline cannot resist the lure of catnip. For the most part, catnip has few negative side effects. However, some cats become overly excited when exposed to it, so aging or obese cats with heart problems should be kept away from it. A diabetic cat can also experience complications.

TREATING FELINE COMPULSIVE BEHAVIORS

The first step in dealing with compulsive behavior is to identify any emotional or environmental factors that may be causing stress. The most common are separation anxiety, a new person or pet in the home, a change of environment, boredom, being weaned too early, and loud noises. If the stressor can be removed, do so promptly. If not, you may be able to counter-condition the cat to the presence of the stressor by gradually exposing her to it when she is most comfortable, and then increasing the exposure until she is comfortable with it. It is also beneficial to enrich her environment as much as you can by providing her with toys, climbing apparatus, and exercise. Medication should be a last resort.

FURNITURE SCRATCHING

Cats need to scratch, and they don't care about the difference between a cheap scratching post and your recently reupholstered heirloom. Cats scratch first of all to make their presence known. In the wild, they leave telltale markings

on trees to warn rivals to stay clear—the territory is occupied. Scratching also releases a subtle pheromonal gland-odor that is undetectable to us. Thankfully. I bet if we could smell it, we wouldn't like it.

By the way, it's probably not true that your cat is actually sharpening her claws. Cat claws come plenty sharp. Your cat is, however, giving the muscles and tendons of her paws a good workout as well as shucking off the husks of her old nails. She is also leaving her scent on the furniture as a notice to other pets.

Don't even consider declawing your cat—it's an awful practice. To keep a cat from marking on new furniture, try rubbing some of the cat's familiar bedding all over it. Once imbued with the cat's own scent, the object will cease to seem "strange" to the cat. If your cat persists in scratching the sofa arms, you may need to cover them in heavy fabric available from your furniture store. Encourage your cat to use scratching posts, and make them convenient to use. One in every room is a good idea. Some are available that are designed to fit around couch corners and other areas that are attractive to scratching cats. You may also want to try a deterrent such as a moth repellent aerosol on valuable furniture. Some people also have good luck using two-sided sticky tape applied around the scratched areas.

Cats are crepuscular, which means they are most active in the twilight hours of evening and very early morning.

You can even purchase nail covers for your cat, which are basically plastic nail caps that can be glued on after a nail trim. You can replace them as they fall off. These things really work. It also helps just to keep your cat's nails clipped.

HOARDING

Some cats are natural collectors. Pieces of aluminum foil, lost jewelry, and other items may suddenly appear in a hiding place used by your feline. Not all cats acquire this hobby, and the reasons for it are not clear. Certainly, it's instinctive for mother cats to bring home prey items for her babies, but kittens can't digest foil or coins. The Munchkin cat seems especially prone to this type of behavior, and cat breeders think that an aberrant gene may be involved. So, if your favorite big shiny earring goes missing, check under the bed. The cat probably took it. Maybe she is trying to tell you something.

COUNTER CRUISING

Cats are curious. They like heights, are good jumpers, and don't really care what you think. Put all these things together, and you have a recipe for counter cruising. It's a nasty thought because cats track all the remains of their litter box and its contents right onto the counter. They also will steal anything to their liking you have left there. This habit is not only annoying, but it can be dangerous to your cat, especially if she decides to jump on the stove when the burners are on!

Frankly, this problem is difficult to treat. You can offer your cat other places to go. You can put cookie pans full of water on the counter and hope that when she jumps in them and gets her feet soaked, she'll think twice. (Be sure to tape the cookie sheets down so your floor doesn't get soaked, though.) You can try scat mats, which give your cat a mild electric buzz if she jumps on them. Still, cats seem preternaturally able to tell when something bad is on the counter and when it is not. Some people booby-trap the counter with mouse traps and coin-filled bottles or even more elaborate ruses. You can also stack metal pans precariously near the edge. The clatter they produce may keep your cat off the counter for quite a while. Or, try attaching Velcro strips temporarily to the counter surface. The sticky feeling is not pleasant. However, these solutions are probably more trouble than they are worth.

Is It Emotional or Physical? If your cat is acting up and you cannot understand why, take her to the vet for a complete physical. In some cases, behavior problems (such as housesoiling) are caused by a medical problem. If the vet cannot find a physical reason for the behavior, then it is likely to be caused by an emotional upset, and you may want to contact a professional animal behaviorist for advice. Don't just give up on your cat—do everything you can to help her through this difficult time.

An older cat who engages in an unwanted behavior will need extra time and patience to correct the problem.

You can chase your cat off the counter whenever she gets up there and even toss something noisy in her direction. But unless you deny access to the kitchen, she'll be on the counter again when you are not home. I promise you that. Cats like to be high up where they can survey their world.

Keep tempting stuff off the counter, and scrub it down after preparing any food there. If it's super clean and disinfectant smelling, your cat may decide for herself she doesn't like the smell of the thing.

INAPPROPRIATE SEXUAL BEHAVIOR

Some cats will masturbate or attempt to copulate with ordinary household objects, perhaps including your foot. Spaying or neutering will usually solve this unpleasant problem. If that doesn't work, it may help to get an additional cat. Some people have had luck with serotonin reuptake inhibitor interventions like clomipramine and fluoxetine.

SENIORS AND FELINE COGNITIVE DYSFUNCTION

None of us can turn back the clock and, like people and dogs, older cats may exhibit distressing behavioral changes. Some of these changes are quite normal. Your senior cat will be less active, partly because her joints are stiffening up and partly because her brain is also changing. (It actually shrinks, and, in addition, fewer functioning nerve cells are present.) She will sleep more, be less attentive to her surroundings, and may even be less particular about her grooming.

None of this is cause for alarm. Sometimes, however, something more serious is going on. Feline cognitive dysfunction, a condition resembling Alzheimer's disease in people and a similar disease in elderly dogs, can cause difficult problems in your cat's daily activities. One acronym frequently used to describe signs of this condition is DISH, which stands for disorientation, reduced social interactions, interrupted sleep/wake patterns, and loss of housetraining.

No one knows exactly how this happens, and treatment is still being researched. The same condition in dogs is helped by selegiline (Anipryl), and it is hypothesized that it may work equally well for cats, with about two-thirds showing marked improvement. In the old days you never heard of cats getting "senile," but in the old days cats didn't live as long as they do today.

The Veterinary Behaviorist

For serious behavioral problems, you may wish to consult an animal behaviorist. It's no use looking under "cat trainers" in the Yellow Pages. Even professional animal trainers know when to fold.

A veterinary behaviorist is someone who has completed an approved residency training program in veterinary animal behavior, and subsequently passed a certifying examination approved by the examinations committee of the American College of Veterinary Behaviorists (ACVB). The successful candidate is then a diplomate of the ACVB—a formally certified specialist. Currently, only thirty-five veterinarians hold this title in the United States, so your chances of finding one are slim. But all is not lost. Veterinarians who specialize in animal behavior, but are not diplomates, are referred to as "veterinary animal behaviorists."

Either professional can assess your cat's condition and suggest treatment options. Bear in mind that qualified veterinarians are able to prescribe any medication that might be needed.

Another professional who may also deal with your cat's problems is someone certified by the Animal Behavior Society. These folks are not vets, but they do work with them to provide treatment.

Getting Professional Help

Aside from accredited veterinary behaviorists, there are currently some animal behaviorists who practiced this specialty before there were any formal requirements for it. They have been admitted into the American College of Veterinary Behaviorists (ACVB) on the basis of founder status ("grandfathering").

If you feel that you need to employ the services of an animal behaviorist, speak with your veterinarian. He can most likely refer you to a trained professional who specializes in cats. Behaviorists are experts in animal behavior and motivation and will be able to give you advice on how to solve your pet's problem.

Make an appointment to talk with the behaviorist and explain your cat's behavior issues and any methods that you've used to try to solve the problem on your own. Be sure to get references, find out how many treatment sessions your cat may need, and ask what follow-up training (if any) you will have to do on your own at home. Many behaviorists make house calls and may want to observe your cat in her natural surroundings to better understand the unwanted behavior.

Part 2
GOOD DAILY CARE

Chapter Five

Training Your Cat

"Of all God's creatures, there is only one that cannot be made the slave of the leash. That one is the cat. If man could be crossed with the cat it would improve man, but it would deteriorate the cat."

—Mark Twain

Despite what many people tend to believe, you *can* train a cat. Anyone who has ever lived with cats is well aware of how intelligent and independent they are—not to mention how so many owners have somehow allowed themselves to become trained by their own cat (like getting up to feed them at the crack of dawn)! Cats learn your routines and figure out just how to get what they want from you. Despite their independence, however, few cats prefer to live solitary lives. It should come as no surprise, then, that your feline companion can learn a multitude of positive behaviors that will not only improve her health and the daily quality of her life, but may even enhance her relationship with you.

Litter Box Training—Where Cats Really Shine

Although cats are not as trainable as dogs, they surpass them easily in one area, and that's basic housetraining. Cats can train themselves to use the litter box almost immediately; all you need to do is provide them with the opportunity to do so.

PLACEMENT

Like you, cats don't want to eliminate near where they sleep or eat. If you separate the litter box from their "living quarters," you are more likely to win easy compliance from your cat about its use.

A quiet, low-traffic area is best, such as a spare bathroom or "lumber room." Situate the box in a corner for privacy and security. (Cats feel vulnerable during the elimination process. Besides, they are very modest—at least in this respect.)

LITTER DEPTH

Believe it or not, cats have different preferences when it comes to the depth of the litter. Some like more, some less. If you tilt the litter box when filling it so that there's more on one side than another, you may be able to figure out what depth of litter your cat prefers.

NUMBER OF BOXES

The general rule is one litter box for each cat plus one. So, if you have two cats, get three litter boxes. If you have 13 cats, well, I just don't know what to tell you. Arrange the litter boxes in different places

Trainability Vs. Intelligence

Contrary to what many pet owners believe, trainability and intelligence are not the same thing. Many supremely intelligent animals are actually too smart to be trained. Trainability merely indicates the degree of cooperation an animal is willing to show. Cats may be less cooperative than dogs, but they are certainly not dumber.

throughout the house—some upstairs and some down. Make special considerations for the very occasional or elderly cat who won't be bothered climbing up or down stairs.

CONSISTENCY

Once your cat gets used to a box, be chary about changing styles. First, simply add the new box without removing the old one. Make sure the cat will really use the new box before you take away the former one.

If you change litter, again the trick is to do it gradually, mixing in a little of the new with the old until the cat accepts the new litter entirely.

REMOVING WASTE

Put feces and clumped urine into a plastic bag, then knot it and toss it in a sealable kitchen trash can with a foot pedal. That will keep the odors way down. Keep the can near the litter box.

 ## Housetraining Gone Awry

While cats are famously easy to housetrain or litter train (usually training themselves), there are exceptions. Some kittens just don't seem to "get it" and some older cats suddenly acquire the distasteful habit of eliminating in unapproved places.

Your cat can learn a multitude of positive behaviors that will not only improve her health and the daily quality of her life, but may even enhance her relationship with you.

HOUSESOILING

If your cat is urinating in the home, she may simply have an aversion to the litter box for some reason. It happens usually because the litter box is not cleaned frequently enough. (Have you ever started to use a public stall and then immediately backed out when you saw the last visitor neglected to flush? Then you know how it feels….) Try cleaning the box once or even twice a day. On the other hand, if you are too scrupulous in this regard, like scrubbing the cat box with bleach or other harsh chemicals several times a week, the cat may also decide to go elsewhere. The smell alone might be enough to discourage her. Be sure also that you have poured in a sufficient amount of litter.

The type of litter you are using might also be at fault. Some felines positively hate coarse clay or scoopable litter. Others dislike the chlorophyll-based litter. In addition, cats can be pretty picky about where their little box is placed. If it's too high or located in a nasty or inconvenient place, don't expect your cat to use it.

Some cats respond to utter boredom by experimenting with inappropriate "bathrooms." In many cases, simply more attention will solve the housetraining difficulty. Some cats just won't share their bathroom with another individual. They prefer their own space. Some won't use another cat's box, and some actually "guard" their litter boxes to prevent other cats from using them. That's another good reason to have extra litter boxes.

Never Punish Your Cat

It is absolutely reprehensible to rub your feline's nose or face in her accidents (as some people have done in the past) to try to stop this behavior. Cats do not understand punishments such as this, and scolding your cat will only encourage her to hide her accidents to avoid further punishment.

No cat, no matter how wily, can guard more than one at a time. And yet in other cases your cat may be marking her territory.

Of course, ill health could also result in inappropriate elimination. It is possible that your cat has a urinary tract infection or bladder/urethra stones. Many felines with this condition suddenly seem to develop a dislike for the box, possibly because they find it painful to urinate and decide that it's the box's fault. Cats with arthritis might actually find it painful to climb into one. Internal parasites can be responsible for a cat's defecating outside the litter box.

Sometimes it helps to place the cat's food on the spot where she has taken to eliminating. If you can't solve the problem this easily, talk to your vet. She can do urine, blood, and fecal tests to see if there a medical problem is present.

Housesoiling can even be caused simply by anxiety, which can now be treated with a variety of pet-safe medications such as buspirone (Buspar) and fluoxetine (Prozac).

URINE MARKING

Urine marking, or spraying, is probably the most annoying behavior a cat can develop; in fact, it is the main reason why people surrender their cats to shelters and rescues. If your cat suddenly begins urine marking, have her evaluated for physical problems before attempting to correct the behavior in other ways. Tests may include urine analysis and culture, blood panels, or X-rays. More than one case of cystitis has been deemed a behavior problem.

Urine marking is an extreme form of scent marking in cats. It can be a response to a new and threatening object in the home, or a general sense of feeling lost or out of control.

The problem usually arises in intact cats over the age of six months. It occurs in both males and females (the latter may mark around the beginning of estrus), and in many cases the problem can be resolved simply by spaying

Housetraining Help

To address housetraining problems, first make sure all the litter boxes in the house are clean. If they aren't, some cats will let their owners know of their discontent in the most direct way they can. If your cat is housesoiling, it's possible she is sending you a message about your cleaning habits. You will probably be scrubbing down the walls and rugs, if nothing else.

When dealing with "accidents, " use an enzymatic odor neutralizer to do the job best. Don't use any product with ammonia. It smells like urine to a cat and actually encourages her to reuse the spot. If you don't know where the urine is, you can use a blacklight stain detector to search out urine marks.

Of course, ill health could also result in inappropriate elimination. If you have multiple cats and don't know which one is causing the problem, there are special dyes you can put in a particular cat's food to make her urine turn color under the blacklight as well.

If you can't solve the problem, talk to your vet. She can do urine, blood, and fecal tests to confirm if your cat's problem is physical or behavioral.

Cats can train themselves to use the litter box almost immediately. If your cat is housesoiling, she may simply have an aversion to the litter box for some reason.

or neutering your pet. Males, even neutered ones, are more prone to displaying this behavior than females. However, although testosterone levels drop after castration, the behavioral cure won't be instantaneous; the problem may not resolve for a few months. It's much better to neuter the animal before the behavior starts.

When a neutered cat sprays, it's usually the result of stressors such as inattention, overcrowding, or the addition of an unknown cat. In some cases, just having the new cat visit the yard is enough to get it started. If you move to a new home in which a previous cat has left a scent (even if you can't smell it), your cat may mark over those areas.

Sometimes the location of the spraying may give you a hint as to its cause. Spraying around doorways and windows suggests there may be a strange cat outside (who may be taunting your cat). Spraying on inside surfaces suggests a negative response to a housemate. The more cats you have, the more likely it is that they will spray.

Some cats void an enormous amount of urine during the process, others only a few drops. A male may anoint a wall, while a female may soak a carpet. Unlike elimination urination, a marking male cat will back up against the wall, shake his tail and spray the evil smelling stuff against a convenient surface. Females can spray also, although it's rather uncommon. Cats are not content with spraying in one place, either—they often have a pattern they use to "own" the whole house.

If the urine spraying is truly behavioral and not medical in nature, the problem can be difficult to address. However, keep in mind that your cat is not trying to spite you. Cats are too dignified to "get back" at you in such a childish way. Disgruntled cats reprogram your computer; they don't resort to spraying urine on the walls. However, stress can drive her to it.

One solution is to isolate the cat in one room (where she should sleep also). This will provide reassurance and comfort to her. Reducing a cat's territory reduces stress. Such cats will also tend to use their litter boxes more because it's better than peeing all over the room they eat in.

The herb valerian is a sleep-promoting substance that relaxes many cats.

You can get a commercial product called Pet Calm that contains it. However, for unknown reasons, some react in the opposite way to valerian and become overstimulated. Cats seem to like the smell of the stuff, but I think it's hideous. I took a valerian capsule once as a sleep aid and thought I would die. I prefer insomnia.

Those who prefer a homeopathic approach may try Calms Fort, a remedy available at many health food stores. Crush and dissolve a couple of tablets into a dropper bottle and give it to your cat every couple of hours during a stressful time.

A more effective treatment might be to use Feliway, a synthetic analogue of a pheromone secreted by the facial glands of cats. If this product is applied in households, the frequency of urine marking may be significantly reduced.

Once a cat has marked an area with her urine, the scent must be completely and immediately removed with an enzyme cleaner or she will return to the spot again and again.

🐈 That's Right, *Toilet* Training Your Cat

Of course cats can use the toilet. Being so much more intelligent and cleaner than dogs, they'd probably prefer it. And so should you. Forget the smelly litter box and the chore of dragging urine soaked litter to the trash every day. Send the cat poop to the same place human waste goes—the waste disposal plant—and let the professionals take care of it.

By instinct, cats like to hide their waste from sight and smell, so the toilet has an innate attraction for them (once they overcome their nervousness about the water).

The whole training process may take a month, although lots of cats learn it sooner. It depends on how amiable your cat is about trying new things. Just be patient. If she is reluctant, go back to the previous step.

Start with a cat over the age of six months, or one that is well litter trained. You can actually buy a kit to aid you in the process, or you can take the simple way out and use a cheap tin roasting pan and some duct tape (the savior of the contemporary world).

Tissue Tantrums

While we are on the subject of toilets (sort of), you may have noticed that kittens enjoy unrolling toilet paper and running around the house with it. You can usually get them to stop by installing the roll so that the paper hangs against the wall. If your cat tears up tissues, put the box upside down.

Begin by putting your cat's litter box near the toilet. Let her get used to its location there. Gradually start replacing the litter with flushable litter. Then s-l-o-w-l-y raise the height of the litter box by putting it on a sturdy stack of magazines or phone books, or whatever works best for you. It's essential that nothing wobbles, though. If it does, your cat will get really angry and take her revenge in an obvious fashion—by abandoning the litter box altogether.

When that strategy is successful, move the litter box to toilet height. Once your cat is used to this, replace the litter box with the roasting pan and a small amount of flushable litter, and then tape it in place on the toilet seat. Make a small hole in the center of the pan, and gradually enlarge it. You should eventually be able to remove the pan completely. Voila! Your cat is toilet trained. But you'll have to flush it yourself. Sorry.

Trick and Obedience Training

While cats will never rival Golden Retrievers in the training department, they do respond well to certain basic training techniques. After all, professional animal trainers train cats all the time for movie roles and other ventures. In addition, training—especially if you own an indoor-only cat—is an enriching activity that will help keep her from getting bored.

However, it takes much longer and requires much more patience to train a cat than to train a dog. In addition, because they are so well-behaved on their own anyway, do you really wish to take several weeks to train your cat to fetch the paper? It's a lot easier to go get it yourself. However, if you insist, there are a couple things you can do to train your cat without stressing yourself out too much. Just remember not to expect too much.

The only way to train a cat is through positive reinforcement. Professional cat trainers (now there's job for you) use clickers and cat treats to achieve their results.

Using clicker training, it's actually possible to teach a cat to sit, lie down, or jump up onto or off a chair. Even more complicated routines can be learned if you want to devote your life to the task. The biggest benefit from training your cat lies in the fact that the simple amount of time you put into it creates a stronger bond between the two of you, and you'll end up better friends.

WALKING ON A LEASH

Some cats will consent to accompany you on the end of a leash. An H-shaped harness (not a collar) works well if the fit is snug enough. Go slow and use plenty of encouragement and treats.

To begin leash training, you need to get your cat used to the idea of the harness and leash by leaving them around her sleeping area. Once she is accustomed to them being around, place the harness on her around mealtime (you can even offer her something really special) when she is very hungry and not as likely to pay attention to it. Let her wear it for a day or two without trying to attach the leash (which is restraining) to it. Then practice putting the harness on and taking it off for several days.

When your cat seems completely used to the harness, attach a short leash to it and let her walk around the house with it on. She will probably try to "kill" the leash, but will eventually accept it as an annoying but bearable appendage. Don't let the cat walk around unsupervised, however, because the leash could get tangled and possibly injure

Keep training sessions short (five minutes or less) and fun. A bored cat is an angry cat.

Using clicker training and treats, it's actually possible to teach a cat to sit, lie down, or come when called.

her. Then try picking up the leash yourself and following (not leading) your cat around. To try leading your cat, use a small, delicious, smelly treat. You are now ready to take her out into the world of the great outdoors.

If your cat will accept the idea, it's wonderful to expose your indoor cat to the adventurous world of the backyard or even a careful stroll around the block. The important thing to remember is that cats are not dogs. They are not natural "followers" and while they are extraordinarily quick, they don't have the endurance of dogs or people. A feline jogging partner is out of the question.

No Heels, Please!

Don't bother trying to teach your cat to heel. There is no advantage for either of you in this. The purpose of leash-training a cat is to allow her to safely explore the great outdoors with her protector (you) at her side.

COMING WHEN CALLED—OR RATHER, REQUESTING YOUR CAT'S PRESENCE

You can't yell at a cat and expect her to come trembling to your side the way some dogs will. Cats don't respond well to orders, loud voices, punishment, or even a superior attitude. They must be cajoled, begged, lured, or tempted. That is the way nature made them, and if you try to do anything against their nature, the result will be failure.

Although cats are not naturally obedient, you can often get a feline to come to you if you speak in a soft, high-pitched tone and reward her with gentle stroking or a treat.

It's best to start training your cat to come when called at meal time, when she is hungry and more likely to work for a reward. If you are in the habit of free-feeding your cat, use a special, delectable reward like fresh chicken. Speak your cat's name, or just say "kitty." (For some reason *all* cats respond to "kitty" as well as to their names. There is no exception to this rule.) Let her see the treat and feed it to her when she approaches. It won't hurt to praise her, but cats really aren't suckers for praise the way dogs are. Cats want concrete rewards.

SHAKE HANDS!

Because cats are accustomed to using their delicate paws to explore things and extract objects, you can easily teach your kitty to "shake" if you are patient and gentle with her. When your cat is in a calm, agreeable mood, and sitting quietly in front of you, touch her paw and say, "Shake" or another appropriate cue word. She will probably raise her paw, and you can shake it gently. Give her a tiny (pea-sized) treat when she complies. This must be a high-value, preferably smelly treat, something she really enjoys. A piece of stale kibble won't cut it. When she becomes reliable at this command you can gradually make your rewards less consistent.

SIT UP!

Wait until your cat is in a normal sitting position. Then hold a highly desirable treat over her head and say "Up!" When she reaches up correctly, give her the treat. Repeat.

WAVE!

In this exercise, you're taking advantage of a cat's normal instinct to grab at prey. When your cat is sitting, place a small treat directly in front of her, but out of her reach. Move the treat slowly and temptingly in the air just in front of her. As she reaches for the food, it will look as if she is waving. She is not, of course. She is trying to kill something. Always remember that.

PM Activity

The best time to play with your cat is between 7pm and 9pm. That is the time of day when cats are most active, and it seems to be when their "play-buzzer" goes off. You can combine cat activities with watching TV, which is healthier than making yourself a snack.

The easiest way to train your cat is to make it worth her while, so always practice when your cat is alert and hungry.

 Regular Playtime

Most indoor pet cats are understimulated and thrive best by playing interactively with you. This is especially true for adult cats. Kittens are fairly active on their own, but as cats grow older and edge into a more sedentary lifestyle, you may need to help them recover their former zest for activity. This doesn't mean that cats don't want to play or can't be coaxed into it. It means that most won't come to you with a toy in their mouth begging you to play with them. Playing with your cat (even as little as 5 minutes a day) will not only help your cat, but save your house. Bored cats are much more likely to damage furniture and engage in house-spoiling. This is a win-win situation.

You can combine playing with training (above), or you can just opt to engage in a few fun activities together. Playing with a cat relies upon provoking their highly developed prey drive. By the way, playing with your cat does not require that you buy an expensive jungle gym or join a cat yoga class. Not at all. While cats do enjoy playing in jungle gyms and other "cathouses," you and your cat can have just as much fun tossing a piece of crumpled paper (as a writer I have a lot of that) or, to get slightly more high-tech, using a pole with a feather or ball attached. Catnip stuffed toys, laser lights, and shiny aluminum balls are also highly attractive to felines. You can make a loose "ball" with some pipecleaners. Your cat will not only chase the ball, but also try to take it apart after the capture, the way she would do with a mouse. One of the most classic toys of all time is a simple paper bag large enough for your cat to crawl into. Put the open bag on the floor and watch her pounce on it, tear at it, "kill it," and eventually crawl into it and go to sleep.

Interactive play not only makes your pet socialized, but it's a great way to give her the exercise she needs while keeping her mind and instincts sharp.

The point is that you do not have to spend hundreds of dollars on "toys" for your cat. You can make them yourself and enter into the spirit of the game.

Cat Sports

Cat agility is fast becoming a popular sport for cats and their owners. An organization called the International Cat Agility Tournaments (ICAT) has created a new category of cat competition in which felines negotiate an agility course designed to display their speed, coordination, beauty of movement, physical condition, intelligence, training, and the quality and depth of their relationship with their owners who train with them and guide them through the course.

The sport of agility offers all the elements necessary to make any cat a happier, healthier companion animal. Like a playground for your cat, an agility course also exercises all of her natural instincts while keeping her stimulated and in top physical condition. In addition to strengthening the bond between cat and owner, it can be a lot of fun. For more information, you can contact them at www.catagility.com.

Daily Interaction

All cats and kittens need daily playtime. Cats who do not get enough play or interaction with their owners can become bored, restless, and develop behavior problems. Set aside 10 to 15 minutes every day to play with your feline friend. Your cat will look forward to your scheduled playtime and will miss it if you skip a day. Play not only makes your pet socialized, but it's a great way to give her the exercise she needs while keeping her mind and instincts sharp.

She-Cats

Why are cats often called "she?" No one really knows, but presumably it's because of their grace, elegance, and indefinable feminine qualities. Not to mention their craftiness, charm, and sheer intelligence. Dogs who are clumsy, gullible, and easily tricked into being trained are called "he."

Chapter Six

Diet & Nutrition

"When the tea is brought at five
o'clock, and all the neat curtains
are drawn with care,
the little black cat with bright green
eyes is suddenly purring there."
— Harold Munro

Good nutrition is one of the most important factors affecting your cat's health. That seems obvious, but it has taken a long time for us to draw the right conclusions.

Cats are obligate carnivores. That means that they must eat meat. Dogs and people generally like meat too, but we can get along without it if we get properly balanced and good quality plant protein. Cats don't have that option. They must have animal-derived protein to survive.

Cats as Carnivores

Cats must be on a feline version of the Atkins diet—dare we call it the Catkins diet? (The American Veterinary Medicine Association does!) The modern cat has changed very little in behavior and physical type from her wild ancestors. Wild cats eat mice, and here's the nutrient content of a nice healthy mouse: 3 percent carbohydrates, 40 percent protein, and 50 percent fat. You heard me right.

I will bet anything your cat is not eating like this, even though she should be. Cats are special in the way they process protein, carbohydrates, and fat. As strict carnivores, they have a tremendous ability to produce glucose from protein, but they have difficulty processing carbohydrates. (The technical way of saying this is that the feline liver has normal hexokinase activity, but no glucokinase activity.) Cats are limited in their ability to mop up excess glucose and store it as glycogen (a ready reserve of glucose in a form resembling starch). That leftover glucose turns to fat. It also predisposes cats to diabetes. (See Chapter 7 for details.)

Before commercial diets came into the picture, most cat owners fed their cats leftover organ meats that they didn't want themselves. These foods were too low in calcium and too high in phosphorus. This led to nutritional secondary hyperparathyroidism, which causes calcium to be taken out of the bone to maintain the correct calcium level in the blood and other tissues. Commercial foods also presented similar issues; by the 1980s, it was clear that the high pH levels in pet foods were leading to struvite bladder stones.

Pet food companies scrambled to "acidify" their products, and then cats began developing oxalate stones. It finally occurred to someone to check the pH found in a mouse, which is about 6.5. Commercial diets conformed, and the stone problem seems to be disappearing. (The mouse standard never fails us!)

Another problem people began noticing in cats was a heart problem called dilated cardiomyopathy, which was eventually linked to taurine deficiency. Other diets too low in potassium led to hypokalemic nephropathy, a condition that results from kidney damage.

Commercial companies were having a hard time—not in figuring out what cats needed, but how to get it into a box of kibble. Kibble is inexpensive, not smelly, and convenient to serve, but it is not the best-quality nutrition for a cat. You just can't get enough protein and fat (without the carbs) in kibble. In addition, cats love the stuff and will nibble on dry kibble all day long and get fat, something they are less likely to do with canned food. Some people think their cats don't like a canned diet. They do, they just stop eating when they have had enough. Carbs don't trigger the same "I-have-had-enough" signal that protein and fats do.

The ideal cat food is moist, high in protein, high in fat, and low in carbohydrates—just like a you-know-what. EEK!

To keep your cat or kitten at optimum health, feed her a balanced diet of good-quality food.

 Dietary Requirements

As a responsible pet owner, it's your job to ensure that your cat is fed a balanced diet of appropriate, good-quality food. That means making sure she eats the best food possible and receives all the vitamins, minerals, and nutrients necessary to live a long and healthy life. It's also important to feed your pet a diet that is suitable for her physical condition and stage of life, so understanding feline nutrition is a must.

PROTEIN

Protein is critical for growth and to boost the immune system. Proteins comprise twenty-two amino acids, but each protein source contains different levels of each amino acid. Cats can synthesize some of these amino acids in their bodies, but they have to consume the rest in their food. These "essential" or dietary amino acids are arginine, histidine, isoleucine, leucine, lysine, methionine, phenylalanine, threonine, tryptophan, valine, and taurine. (Dogs can synthesize taurine to some extent, but perhaps not as well as people used to think.) One job of arginine is to eliminate protein waste. Cats can't make arginine on their own as dogs can, and so need it every day in their diet. Taurine helps the heart, retina, and bile. Taurine is found in the greatest quantity in animal products.

Then there's felinine, a very weird compound made from the sulfur-containing amino acid cysteine. No one knows exactly what felinine is good for, but there's a lot of it in the urine of male cats. Researchers suspect it may part of the pheromonal signaling process of the male cat. Cats need a lot more cysteine than any other mammal as well.

Cats need lots and lots of protein, more than we do and more than dogs do. Kittens require a diet of 30 percent protein, and adult cats between 15 and 20 percent. They cannot be vegetarians because plant protein is just not good enough for cats. Any food based on plant products such as corn, wheat, rice, or other grains is not protein-rich enough for your favorite feline. Not all proteins are equal, either. Egg protein has the highest "biological value" and is given a score of 100. On this scale, fish meal has a value of 92. Beef is around 78, while soybean meal is 67. Corn is a pathetic 45. Surely you don't expect your cat to live on "failing grade" proteins like that!

Wild cats dine upon mice, rats, and baby rabbits, not leaves and berries. Cats will however, chomp on grass from time to time, possibly to obtain cellulose fibers to aid digestion. But that's just a guess. No one really knows. Some experts note that wild carnivores eat the intestines of the grass-eating prey first and that this provides necessary nutrients. You can buy some grazing grass for your cat at the pet supply store.

Proper Nutrition

Cats have very special dietary requirements separate from dogs. Over time, a cat could die if fed nothing but dog food because it may be missing important vitamins, amino acids, and proteins that cats need. Also, kittens and adult cats have different feeding requirements, so it's important that you provide your pet with a healthy diet suitable for her life stage.

At any rate, the bad thing is that, while the cat food label will tell you the percent of protein, it won't tell you where the protein came from. That's not good because cats thrive best on high-quality animal protein, not the inferior stuff we get from plants.

Cats with healthy kidneys cannot get too much protein; they will just excrete what they don't use. However, cats with kidney failure need a special diet.

FAT

Fats are extremely important to the feline diet. These concentrated forms of energy not only fuel the body but add taste to food. They also carry fat-soluble vitamins. Cats get fat in their diet from lard, tallow, and vegetable oils.

Kittens need a diet of about 20 percent fat, while adult cats need a diet of 15 to 20 percent. Lucky dogs. I mean cats. The minimum fat requirement for a cat is 5 percent; it's 8 percent for a kitten.

ESSENTIAL FATTY ACIDS

Altogether there are over seventy fatty acids. They work very hard in a variety of bodily functions, especially with cell structure components and chemical reactions, including hormonal and energy activities. They also help make a lipid block in the skin to keep out infections and irritants. But not all fatty acids are essential, although they are all very important! What's the difference?

When we use the word "essential" we mean that this required nutrient cannot be made by the body and must be added in the diet. Some substances are essential for one species but not for another. The three most important fatty acids are linoleic, alpha-linolenic, and arachidonic. Essential fatty acids should constitute at least 2 percent of the daily caloric intake to prevent deficiencies. Half of that (1 percent) should be linoleic fatty acid. That's true for everybody, by the way, not just cats. Without enough fatty acids, wounds heal more slowly, the coat looks bad, and skin infections are more likely.

Lipidosis

Cats are really bad at mobilizing body fat to produce energy. If put on a "starvation diet," a cat can develop a condition called hepatic lipidosis, or feline fatty liver disease. This is the most common form of liver disease in cats in North America.

The condition is triggered when a cat stops eating due to stress, another disease, or for any other reason. After a few days without food, the cat's body will begin to use fat for energy. Cats do not metabolize fat well; therefore, the fat cells build up in the liver and eventually prevent it from functioning normally. FHL is very dangerous for cats and can be life-threatening if left untreated.

Kittens won't grow right, and breeding cats will have trouble reproducing.

Dogs can make arachidonic acid from linoleic acid, so it is not "essential" for them. Cats can't synthesize arachidonic from linoleic acid, however, so it must be supplied in their diet, along with linoleic and alpha-linolenic acids. The liver of the cat is missing the delta-6-desaturase enzyme, which performs this neat little trick, in case you were wondering.

CARBOHYDRATES

A carbohydrate is any member of a group of organic compounds that includes sugars, starches, celluloses, and gums. Carbohydrates are a major energy source, but they are not essential in the feline diet because cats can make carbohydrates on their own from fat and protein. However, most commercial pet foods are loaded with carbohydrates (between 30 and 70 percent) because they are an inexpensive source of energy—much cheaper than fat or protein. In addition, carbohydrates give dry food texture and structure. The problem is that felines in their natural state do not eat nearly that amount of carbohydrates, even though they can make use of them.

Canned foods could be made carb-free, although that would make the product more expensive. The most common carbohydrates in pet foods are rice and corn, although wheat, barley, and oats are also used. Too many carbohydrates in cat food can cause obesity and poor digestion. (Carbs are easily converted to glucose, and cats weren't really designed to eat them. My own feeling is that carbs in cats should be avoided whenever possible.)

FIBER

Technically, fiber is a subcategory of carbohydrates, but for nutritional purposes it is usually treated separately (and listed separately on a pet food label). Unlike most carbohydrates, a lot of fiber is considered insoluble, meaning that the enzymes in the small intestine fail to digest them. The most common fibers include cellulose, hemicellulose, pectin, gums, and resistant starches. Most of the fiber in pet food comes from the cell walls of plants—especially those found in rice hulls, beet pulp, bran, and the like.

Fiber is not considered an essential nutrient, even though all pet foods have it. It doesn't provide energy or build muscle or anything like that. It does help colon health by increasing the bulk and water in the intestines. In some way not completely understood, it aids the intestine in achieving normalcy by helping both diarrhea (slowly fermenting fibers) and constipation (rapidly fermenting fibers). Most pet foods contain both slowly fermenting and rapidly fermenting fiber. Pectin is a rapidly fermenting fiber, while cellulose is a slow one.

Fiber is also helpful in controlling obesity: Because it is indigestible it doesn't add to the caloric intake, but eating it makes the cat feel full. In addition, many medications work better with an adequate amount of fiber in the diet. It is well recognized that a higher-fiber diet may be important in managing diabetes because it controls swings in blood sugar levels. Fiber may reduce the chances of colon cancer in your cat as well.

VITAMINS

We know vitamins mostly by their letter names (A, B complex, C, D, E, K… don't ask me what happened to F), although they have real names too (retinol, thiamin, niacin, etc.). Vitamins A, D, E, and K are the fat-soluble vitamins, which are stored in the body. Because of this, fat-soluble vitamins can be dangerous if oversupplemented. Vitamin C and B complex are water soluble, and any excess is excreted through the urine. Consequently, water soluble vitamins are safer to supplement.

VITAMIN A (RETINOL)

Vitamin A is an important essential nutrient for most creatures, including cats and people. It is important for growth, mucous membranes, vision, bone growth, and reproduction. Increased vitamin A is needed during growth and pregnancy. Cats lacking sufficient vitamin A are more susceptible to infections, stress-related disorders, and the formation of stones that can cause urinary tract problems.

The main dietary sources of vitamin A are found in liver, other animal tissue, and fish liver oils. About 90 percent of the body's vitamin A is stored in the liver, which is why liver is an excellent source of vitamin A; on the other hand, too much liver can cause vitamin A toxicity. This toxicity is common in cats fed fresh liver and can cause new and abnormal bone to form around joints. This is painful and causes lameness.

Vitamin A itself is not found in plant material, although its

Beet Pulp and Fiber

Many commercial foods contain beet pulp, which does not come from the garden beet, but from sugar beets that are grown to produce—you guessed it—sugar. Beet pulp, a by-product of the extraction process, is an insoluble, moderately fermentable fiber. It adds bulk and moisture to animal stools and may improve the health of the large intestine.

precursor, carotene is. Dogs, buffalos, sheep, rats, goats, and pigs have the necessary enzymes to turn plant-derived beta-carotene right into vitamin A. Cats (and minks) cannot. Cats need vitamin A in its preformed state, which is one reason they cannot be vegetarians. Cats must be fed vitamin A already in the "liver storage form" as retinyl palmitate. Most commercial cat foods have sufficient vitamin A included. Supplementation is unnecessary and may be dangerous.

B Vitamins

The B vitamins occur in many forms (vitamin B complex), including thiamin, niacin, riboflavin, pantothenic acid, pyridoxine, folic acid, cobalamin, and biotin. All are water-soluble, and toxicity is not believed to occur, even if your cat eats very large amounts of them. However, because these vitamins are not stored within the body, your cat must have enough of them every day. Since many B vitamins are destroyed by heat, pet food manufacturers add them in after processing. The most important B vitamins are:

- **Thiamin (B_1):** Thiamin converts glucose to energy and is needed for normal muscle and nerve function. It is found in plants, fruits, milk, fish, and other meats. However, eating raw fish (especially herring, smelt, and catfish) as a sole source of food will make felines become thiamin deficient because these foods contain thiaminase, which destroys thiamin. Cooking the fish solves the problem. Too little thiamin causes appetite loss, weakness, loss of reflexes, loss of nerve control, and eventually death.

- **Niacin (B_3):** Niacin helps enzymes function properly. Niacin is found in meats and meat by-products. Niacin is a B vitamin cats must have in a preformed, animal-derived form. They can't convert plant-derived tryptophan to niacin the way dogs can. Cats suffering from a loss of niacin are said to have "black tongue" or "sore mouth disease," in which they lose weight, won't eat, and have red, inflamed gums, lips, and inner cheeks. Bloody diarrhea and death may follow. This condition can occur in cats whose owners try to force them to become vegetarians.

- **Riboflavin (B_2):** Riboflavin is important for normal growth, muscle development, and coat health. It is found in organ meats and dairy products. Cats lacking sufficient riboflavin may suffer from poor growth, eye abnormalities, weakness in the hind legs, and eventual heart failure. Deficient patients usually have periodic episodes of fainting.

- **Pantothenic acid (B_5):** This B vitamin enables the body to make energy from carbohydrates, fats, and proteins. It is found in most raw foodstuffs including meats. Processing foods reduces the amount of pantothenic acid available to the cat. Pantothenic acid deficiency causes hair loss, diarrhea, and gastric upsets. It has also been associated with abnormal graying, particularly in black-coated animals.

- **Pyridoxine (B_6):** Pyridoxine, which is important for the utilization of amino acids, is found in many foods. Processing destroys it. It is absolutely essential for life. Pyridoxine deficiencies cause anemia, poor growth, kidney stones, tooth cavities, skin lesions, and death.

- **Folic acid (B_9) and cobalamin (B_{12}):** Folic acid and cobalamin (also called cyanocobalamin) are two closely related B-complex vitamins necessary for bone marrow to produce red blood cells. A deficiency of either can cause anemia. Both vitamins are usually included in the diet and are found in organ meats.

- **Biotin (B_7):** Biotin helps maintain healthy skin and hair, and is important for growth, digestion, and muscle function. Deficiencies have been reported following the ingestion of raw egg whites, which contain an enzyme called avidin that destroys biotin. Cooking inactivates avidin. In addition, the egg yolk is very high in biotin and, if the whole egg is fed, the avidin in the white and the high biotin in the yolk cancel each other out. A cat lacking biotin may have poor hair, skin lesions, dried eye discharge, diarrhea, decreased litter size and, in advanced cases, a paralysis of the limbs. Beef liver and brewer's yeast are the richest sources.

Vitamin C

Vitamin C exists in two forms, dehydroascorbic acid and ascorbic acid. Ascorbic acid is easily hydrolyzed

Your cat's daily diet should contain the proper amount of proteins, vitamins, minerals, and other essential nutrients such as taurine.

There has been a lot of talk in some circles about vitamin C curing feline leukemia and preventing urinary tract infections, but the evidence is spotty. However, it does appear that, because vitamin C is excreted totally unchanged, it can acidify the urine, which makes the bladder a less pleasant place for the bacteria that cause cystitis to live (most bacteria love an alkaline environment).

(mixed with water) and therefore it is readily absorbed through the intestinal wall. Very little is stored in the body (except for a small amount in the adrenal gland). Ascorbic acid is important for bone formation. Unlike us, cats can manufacture their own vitamin C. Dogs can too, but cats are much better at it.

VITAMIN D

As we all know, vitamin D is the sunshine vitamin. That's because cats, dogs, and people use ultraviolet radiation from the sun to convert vitamin D precursors into the active form of the vitamin. The skin is where it all happens and, because of this, some experts think vitamin D is more like a hormone than a vitamin. We don't need to quibble over labels, though.

Vitamin D helps regulate calcium and phosphorous levels in the bloodstream and stimulates the kidney to conserve calcium, which therefore helps the body to retain it. Cats can also obtain some vitamin D directly through meat or fish oil. If your cat never goes outside, she's not getting enough sunshine, even if she sun bathes in the window, because glass blocks ultraviolet rays from reaching your pet. She won't get sunburn, but she won't get any vitamin D from that source either. Low levels of vitamin D will cause rickets, a bone deformity.

VITAMIN E

This fat-soluble vitamin helps with cell functioning, especially in the eyes and intestines. It is an antioxidant, and also helps metabolize fats. Vitamin E is found in plant oils (like sunflower oil), liver, and fatty meats. A deficiency of this vitamin can cause something called *brown bowel syndrome*, or ulcerated bowels. Cats fed an all-fish diet can get something called *yellow fat disease*, referring to a condition in which the animal has trouble metabolizing fat.

VITAMIN K

Vitamin K is essential for normal blood functions. Animals need it especially to help blood clot. (Animals who have eaten rat poison must have large amounts of vitamin K to combat the poison, which causes internal hemorrhaging.)

However, because the intestinal bacteria can make quite a bit of vitamin K on their own, little or none is actually needed in the diet.

MINERALS

Twelve minerals are known to be essential for cats. Calcium and phosphorus are crucial to making strong bones and teeth. Other minerals like magnesium, potassium, and sodium are necessary for nerve impulse transmission, muscle contraction, and cell signaling. Many minerals are only present in minute amounts in the body; these are the so-called "trace minerals" like selenium, copper, and molybdenum. Following is a list of dietary minerals, with their function and symptoms of deficiency and excess (those needed in the greatest proportions by the body are presented first).

CALCIUM

As well as being needed to form bones and teeth, calcium is also important for blood coagulation, nerve impulse transmission, muscle contraction, and cell signaling. Of all the minerals, calcium is required in the greatest amount. It is found in bones and dairy products. High-calcium diets without adequate phosphorous cause problems in young, rapidly growing dogs. However, no studies have been done in cats to see if the same conditions apply.

Taurine

Taurine is one essential amino acid that all cat foods should include. Cats who do not get enough taurine in their diets can suffer severe eye problems, possibly leading to blindness. The latest studies have shown that taurine also prevents heart disease in felines. It is interesting to note that because canines do not need taurine, it's not usually present in commercial dog foods. Never feed your cat a diet of dog food. It doesn't contain that feline-necessary protein, taurine, or at least not the amount a cat requires.

PHOSPHORUS

Phosphorus is needed for the skeleton, DNA and RNA structure, metabolism, movement, and acid–base balance. Animals need almost as much phosphorous as calcium. Oddly, many foods that are low in calcium are high in phosphorous. On the other hand, many foods that are high in calcium are equally high in phosphorous. Phosphorus is pretty easy to find, being very common in meat, which however lacks calcium. The most important thing about calcium and phosphorus is the balance between them. They should be fed at the correct ratio of around 1.2 parts of calcium for each 1 part of phosphorous (1.2:1). Quality commercial foods do this for you. However, a meat-only diet (without bone) provides too much unbalanced phosphorus, which draws calcium from the cat's bones and can result in a number of diseases.

MAGNESIUM

Magnesium controls many enzyme functions, boosts muscle and nerve-cell membrane stability, aids hormone secretion, and adds to the mineral structure of bones and teeth. Magnesium is found in raw wheat germ, whole grains, soybeans, milk, and fish. Cooking at high temperatures can remove magnesium from the food. But too much can lead to bladder or kidney stones. This is a major concern for commercial dry foods, which seem to be full of the stuff.

SODIUM AND CHLORIDE

Sodium and chloride are electrolytes that help regulate acid–base balance, osmotic pressure, and nerve-impulse transmission. They are found in practically all foods; in fact, they are hard to avoid. Sodium is even added to pet food to improve the flavor. (Salt does not just make food more salty; it actually releases the flavor in the food, which is why it is often included in recipes.)

POTASSIUM

Like sodium and chlorine, potassium is an electrolyte that helps maintain acid–base balance, muscle function, nerve-impulse transmission, and enzymatic reactions. It is found widely in foods. Cat foods should contain at least 0.6 percent potassium (on a dry matter basis). Additional potassium may need to be supplemented in certain disease conditions like chronic diarrhea or in animals on diuretics. Signs of potassium deficiency include cardiac arrest, nervous disorders, loss of appetite, poor growth, and weakness.

Understanding the basic requirements of proper feline nutrition helps you to protect your cat's health and increases her longevity.

IRON

Iron combines with copper and protein to make hemoglobin, the molecule in red blood cells that carries oxygen. Iron also is necessary for some enzymes to work properly. The body needs a constant supply of iron because red blood cells only live about 110 days and then die and must be replaced.

Iron is found in liver, lean meats, and fish. Cats need 36.4 mg of iron daily for every pound of food they eat (on a dry matter basis). The iron should be in a form other than iron oxide or iron carbonate. Most commercial diets supply it in abundance. Iron is absorbed in the small intestine, and iron deficiency results in anemia. Too much iron can interfere with the absorption of phosphorus.

COPPER

Copper is critical for many body functions, including the formation of collagen, bone, and connective tissue; iron absorption; the development of red blood cells; and pigmentation of the hair. Copper is found in liver and fish. High-quality commercial cat foods are supplemented with copper. It should be in a form other than copper oxide. Copper is absorbed in the stomach and small intestine and stored in the liver, kidneys, and brain.

The recommended daily requirement for a kitten or a pregnant or nursing cat is 2.3 mg of copper for every pound of canned cat food eaten (on a dry matter basis). Animals on kibble need more, about 7 mg per pound. This is because copper may not be so easily absorbed in that form by pregnant animals. For adult, nonpregnant, or lactating cats the requirements is 2.3 mg per pound of food (on a dry matter basis), regardless of the type of food. Copper deficiency or excess is rare in cats.

ZINC

Zinc is important for enzyme reactions, cell replication, protein and carbohydrate metabolism, and wound healing. Zinc is found in meat and bone. The weird thing about zinc is that it is hard to absorb—only between 5 and 50 percent of what is eaten actually gets into the body. Cats with inflammatory bowel disease may develop zinc deficiency because of their failure to absorb it properly. Toxicity is very rare.

MANGANESE

Manganese is important for enzyme function, bone development, reproduction, neurological function, protein and carbohydrate management, and in making fatty acids. Manganese is present in whole grains, seeds, nuts, eggs, and green vegetables. The daily requirement for an adult cat is 3.4 mg of manganese for every pound of cat food eaten (on a dry matter basis). Manganese deficiency is very rare in cats, and manganese toxicity is unknown. It just doesn't happen, so you can cross that off the worry list.

SELENIUM

Selenium is a trace mineral important as a defense against oxidation. It works in conjunction with vitamin E to do this job. The daily requirement for selenium is less than the requirement for any of the other trace elements and, perhaps not incidentally, it's also the most toxic. In fact, before it was understood to be necessary as a nutrient, it was regarded as a poison! Selenium is found in most meats. Cats need 0.05 mg of selenium daily for every pound of food they eat (on a dry matter basis). While selenium deficiency is unknown, an excess ingested over a long period can be toxic, so be careful about supplementation.

IODINE (IODIDE)

Iodine is essential for thyroid hormone synthesis and cell differentiation. It also regulates the metabolic rate and aids in normal growth. Iodine is found in fish and iodized salt (salt with iodine added). Commercial pet foods supplement iodine by adding potassium iodide, potassium iodate, sodium iodide, or calcium iodate. The daily requirement for an adult cat is 0.16 mg of iodine for every pound of cat food eaten (on a dry matter basis). Iodine deficiency results in abnormally low levels the thyroid hormones, which means poor growth, hair loss, weight gain, and weakness.

WATER

Of all the nutrients needed for maintaining good health, water is the most critical. It is necessary for almost every bodily function. While a cat can survive if she loses half her fat and protein intake, a 10 percent loss of water will make her very sick. Your cat needs about 2.5 times as much water as food, and you should always make sure she has a constant and fresh supply. Heat, exertion, and lactation increase the need for water.

Cats don't have a high thirst drive and are designed to get most of their

Supplements

A high-quality, commercially prepared cat or kitten food will provide all the necessary vitamins, minerals, and other nutrients that your cat needs.

If you're feeding your cat a home-cooked diet, you must add vitamin supplements to the food. You can purchase feline vitamin supplements from a veterinarian or at a pet supply store. These vitamins come either in a tablet form that can be crushed up and mixed with the food or in a liquid that can be given directly or added to the food.

Adding extra vitamins to your cat's diet can be dangerous, so don't add them unless your veterinarian specifically instructs you to do so. The vet will tell you what type, dosage, and frequency of supplementation that your pet needs, if any.

Of all the nutrients needed for maintaining good health, water is the most critical because it is necessary for almost every bodily function.

water needs from fresh meat. (The natural prey diet of the cat, a mouse, contains between 65 and 75 percent water.) Dry food is only about 10 percent moisture, and that's enough of a difference to be serious. In fact, the average cat on kibble must consume about 8 ounces of water a day to make up the difference. If your cat does not get enough water, she is at risk for feline lower urinary tract disease (FLUTD) and crystal in her urine.

So, if your cat is on a kibble diet, she may not be getting enough water, unless you make it very attractive to her by keeping it cool and clean. Animals eating canned food usually get their water needs met through their dinner, just like a wild cat raw meat. It is all right to offer more than enough water (it is simply excreted), but less than enough can be a disaster.

Quantity is not the only consideration. Your cat should get high-quality water, the same as you do (one hopes). Untreated water is dangerous; it contains bacteria, viruses, and organisms like giardia. If you drink your own tap water, it's probably okay for your cat, but if you doubt its purity, you may want to consider bottled water for Fluffy. You can also help keep your cat's water clean by washing out her bowls every day.

Commercial Diets

Many different types of food are on the market today, and the price and quality varies widely. When selecting a commercial food for your cat, choose a high-quality brand that contains all the necessary nutrients.

DRY FOODS

If price is the most important consideration, as it may be with people who own a number of cats, dry food (kibble) is the only choice. And the bigger the bag, the cheaper it is. A 40-pound (18 kg) bag can cost half as much per pound (kg) as a 5-pound (2 kg) bag of the same stuff. High-quality kibble can supply your cat's dietary needs well.

Because of its low cost and convenience (not to mention its lack of smelliness), kibble makes up the bulk of pet food sales. Kibble can be baked, pelleted, or extruded, with the latter being the most commonly used today. There's not really much difference between them, except in the final pressing and cooking process.

CANNED FOODS

Canned foods may be up to 80 percent water, while dry food has a moisture content of only 6 to 10 percent. Obviously, you don't want to pay for water, but that's the nature of canned foods.

Contrary to some popular lore, there is no indication at all that cats on a canned diet have more problems with their teeth than those on kibble.

How to Choose

Select a food formulated for your cat's life stage: kitten, adult, or senior. Your best bet is to offer an Association of American Feed Control Officials (AAFCO) approved food or one that adheres to or surpasses its standards. The label will say, "Formulated to meet the AAFCO Cat Food Nutrient Profile for Kittens/Adults/Seniors." AAFCO develops guidelines for the production, labeling, and sale of animal foods. Pet foods that meet the AAFCO's requirements will include one of two statements on their label.

The first and lower standard states "formulated to meet AAFCO's nutrient requirement." This means the food was tested in the laboratory and was found to have the recommended amounts of protein, fat, and so on.

The second, higher standard states that the product was actually

Diet and Teeth

Contrary to conventional wisdom, kibble is not beneficial to keeping a cat's teeth healthy. Cats don't grind their food; they swallow it whole. The grainy kibble dissolves in the saliva and forms a sticky mess that coats the teeth with a starchy film, encouraging plaque growth. This is one reason why it is very necessary to brush a cat's teeth if she lives solely on a diet of kibble.

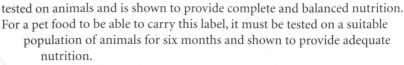

tested on animals and is shown to provide complete and balanced nutrition. For a pet food to be able to carry this label, it must be tested on a suitable population of animals for six months and shown to provide adequate nutrition.

Labeling problems have occurred, however. Companies complained that if they made the slightest change to a product (like substituting turkey for chicken), they'd have to run the entire test all over again, and this would become an expensive proposition that would be passed onto the consumer. So, eventually, it came to pass that if a product in a manufacturer's line passed the test, the company could include the same statement on other products in the same "family," as long as those products provided equal or greater concentrations of all the nutrients.

Milk Myth

Cats are known to love milk, but many are lactose intolerant because they don't have the enzyme to process it. As a result, the milk remains undigested and can cause diarrhea. However, you can now purchase commercial "cat milk" with low levels of lactose. Some products include the important amino acid taurine.

GUARANTEED ANALYSIS

All commercial food labels include a guaranteed analysis. This information lists the minimum levels of crude protein and fat, as well as the maximum levels of fiber and water. Notice that they are listed as "crude." That means the label doesn't take into consideration the digestibility of the protein. Proteins from animals and eggs are highly digestible, those from plants are less so.

INGREDIENTS LIST

AAFCO-approved foods list ingredients according to weight. However, some manufacturers get around that requirement by a dubious practice known as "splitting." They know that consumers want to see meat products as the first ingredient listed. But let's say they manufacture a food with more corn than meat. They can still list meat first, if they "split" the grain component into various components like corn, corn gluten, corn bran, and so on. It's a deplorable tactic, but it exists. Common ingredients you'll find on cat food labels, with their own special AAFCO approved definitions, include:

- **Meat:** Meat is the clean flesh of slaughtered animals (like chicken, cattle, lamb, and turkey). The flesh can include striated skeletal muscle, tongue, diaphragm, heart, esophagus, overlying fat and the skin, sinew, nerves, and blood vessels normally found with that flesh.
- **Meat By-Products:** Meat by-products are clean parts of slaughtered animals, not including meat. These include lungs, spleen, kidneys, brain, liver, blood, bone, and stomach and intestines freed of their contents. It does not include hair, horns, teeth, or hooves.
- **Poultry By-Products:** Poultry by-products are clean parts of slaughtered

poultry such as heads, feet, and internal organs. It does not include feathers.

- **Chicken Liver Meal:** This meal is made from chicken livers that have been ground or otherwise reduced in particle size.
- **Fish Meal:** Fish meal is the clean ground tissue of undecomposed whole fish or fish cuttings.
- **Beef Tallow:** Beef tallow is fat derived from beef.
- **Ground Corn:** Ground corn is the whole ground or chopped corn kernel.
- **Corn Gluten Meal:** Corn gluten meal is the by-product after the manufacture of corn syrup or starch, and it is the dried residue after the removal of the bran, germ, and starch.
- **Brewers Rice:** Brewers rice is the small fragments of rice kernels that have been separated from larger kernels of milled rice.
- **Feeding Instructions:** Feeding instructions or guidelines are usually included, but they are only estimates. Every cat is an individual.

Commercially prepared foods come in canned, moist, and dry varieties. Be sure to choose one that meets AAFCO requirements for the best possible nutrition.

OTHER INGREDIENTS

Along with the more common ingredients, manufacturers sometimes add healthy fillers or supplements to their products.

Antioxidants: All dry cat foods contain antioxidants; their purpose is to keep fats and fat-soluble vitamins nutritious and tasty. (Canned foods are tightly sealed and preserve freshness without the need of antioxidants.) Both natural and artificial antioxidants are used. Artificial antioxidants include butylated hydroxytoluene (BHT) and butylated hydroxyanisole (BHA). While it was charged that these substances cause cancer, research showed the contrary—they may actually protect against cancer. Ethoxyquin (ethyoxyquin) was once widely used in fairly high amounts; however, because of safety concerns, most pet foods now contain none or little of it. If you are feeding kibble, select one without artificial preservatives; canned food does not usually contain any preservatives. Popular natural antioxidants include tocopherols (vitamin E), ascorbic acid (vitamin C), citric acid, and rosemary.

You may not want to hear this, but the artificial antioxidants keep ingredients fresher longer. If you prefer natural antioxidants, be sure to buy smaller amounts of dry cat food.

Supplements: Supplements are sometimes added to enhance food quality:

- **Chicory (*Cichorium intybus*):** Chicory is added to some pet foods as an aid to the growth of healthy bacteria in the intestine. The plant contains the dietary fiber inulin, which in turn contains oligosaccharides that are said to be helpful to the intestinal bacteria.

- **Probiotics:** Probiotics are cultures of microorganisms such as *Lactobacillus acidophilus* and *Lactobacillus casei*, similar to the active

cultures found in yogurt. They are supposed to help promote the growth of friendly bacteria in the large intestine. Some pet foods contain them.

- **Kelp and Algae:** These seaweeds are good sources of iron, iodine, potassium, and trace minerals.
- **Yeast:** Brewer's yeast (which is different from the active yeast used in baking) is rich in protein and B vitamins.

SUPPLEMENTING THE COAT

A good diet can make the difference between a clean, shiny coat and a dry or flaky one. Not all skin problems are due to diet, of course—air quality, parasites, allergies, and skin disease can also be at fault. But a good diet will help every cat handle every other obstacle. And the good news is that you can control it. Or at least offer it.

The skin benefits mightily from the proper oils in the diet. Fish oils and flax seed oil add omega-3 fatty acids, while safflower oil adds omega-6. Some people swear by B vitamins, others by kelp, acidophilus, burdock root, dandelion, sage, jojoba oil, lecithin, and digestive enzyme. While it's not a good idea to add all this stuff at once, it won't hurt to experiment with a few things and see what happens. Start with the fatty acids. They will make the most difference, I think.

Ingredients: Do the Math

Unfortunately, pet food labels rate the protein content and other important information by the food as-is, not on a "dry matter basis," which would be more accurate. If you really want this information, you'll have to do a little elementary math. The label will tell you what percent of the food is moisture. So, if your kibble has a 10 percent moisture content, and it claims to have a 20 percent protein content, divide the 20 percent protein by the 90 percent "dry matter" (20 divided by 0.9). My calculator tells me that comes to 22 percent. So that's the real protein level. If we do the same thing with a canned food that contains 80 percent moisture (20 percent dry matter) but also claims 10 percent protein, and we do the same math (10 divided by 0.2), we find that the canned food is 50 percent protein per dry matter basis. (You can do the same kind of calculation for the other ingredients as well.)

Natural, Raw, and Homecooked Diets

By now, everyone has heard of the melamine contamination of commercial pet foods, a catastrophe that killed hundreds, if not thousands, of cats. Although commercial foods are generally safe, the possibility of mass contamination always exists. This problem can be avoided by feeding your cat a properly prepared home diet. The emphasis is on *properly prepared*. A bad diet, whether homemade or commercial, can kill your cat.

Some owners prefer to make their cats' meals because they can control exactly what goes into their pets' food, and they know and trust what they are consuming. The ingredients are often natural and fresh and, depending on the food that you prepare for your cat, you can choose a nonorganic or organic home-cooked diet or a raw diet. Practically anything humans eat can go into a home-cooked or homemade diet.

Be aware that preparing meals for your feline friend can be very expensive and time-consuming. If you want to feed a home-cooked diet, talk to your veterinarian first. He will be able to educate you on nutritional requirements and can give you a few basic recipes to follow. As an added bonus, some cats with diseases and allergies have had good results and improved health when switched to a homemade meal plan.

HOMEMADE DIETS

The basic principles of a homemade diet are the same as those for a high-quality commercial diet: It should contain all the nutritional components necessary for a fully functioning animal.

It is well known that most commercial diets are far too high in carbohydrates for a cat's ultimate health. Cats are not cows. They are obligate carnivores and must have their protein in the form of meat. Too many carbohydrates take away from the protein component of the diet, and plant protein is just not an acceptable substitute for cats.

A good natural or homemade diet must be scientifically planned and not something you just throw together. Throw-together diets work all right (sort of) for omnivores like people, but obligate, specialist carnivores like cats have unique nutritional needs that are met by whole mice, birds, very high grade commercial foods (with low carbohydrate content), or a specialized home diet. Dogs are specialists too, but not to the degree that cats are.

The FDA and Pet Food

At the federal level, pet foods are subject to the Food and Drug Administration (FDA), the United States Department of Agriculture (USDA), and the Federal Trade Commission (FTC). The Federal Food, Drug, and Cosmetic Act requires that pet foods, like human foods, be pure and wholesome, contain no harmful or deleterious substances, and be truthfully labeled.

THE RIGHT BALANCE

Although you must be careful to provide the proper balance of all essential vitamins and minerals when offering homemade diets, one of the trickiest things to get right is the calcium/phosphorus ratio. Cats need both, but if you provide them in the wrong balance, the results can be disastrous, especially for kittens. Nature is very funny about these two

elements. Meat contains little calcium, but plenty of phosphorus. Bones have calcium but little phosphorus. Eggs have phosphorus; eggs shells have calcium, and so on. Most dairy products (aside for cottage cheese, which leans heavily on the phosphorus side) are balanced, but when you add them to meat, they don't provide enough calcium to overcome the overloaded phosphorus in meat.

A NATURAL DIET

A good natural diet for cats should be at least 60 percent protein in the form of ground beef, chicken, cooked fish, eggs (once a week or so), and occasionally and in small quantities (a teaspoon or so), some organ meat. Meat is probably best lightly steamed, broiled, or boiled. If your cat will eat vegetables or fruits, you can add them to the diet as well (about 20 percent). I once owned a cat who was mad about mango. Some cats like cucumbers. You never know. The other 2 percent of the diet can be grains, in the form of steamed or boiled brown rice. Providing a vitamin-mineral supplement is important to make sure your cat is getting everything she needs.

Even better, according to many, is a diet composed of 90 percent meat,

Unhealthy or Toxic Foods

A number of foods are harmful or just plain toxic to cats. The following is a list of foods that cats should never eat:

Onions, Garlic, and Related Root Vegetables: Onions and garlic can produce a dangerous though temporary anemia in cats by damaging the red blood cells.

Tomatoes and Green (Raw) Potatoes: These foods contain a bitter, poisonous alkaloid that can cause violent lower gastrointestinal symptoms.

Chocolate: It's becoming more widely known that chocolate is very toxic to both cats and dogs. Theobromine is the offending substance.

Grapes and Raisins: The ASPCA advises that, although many unknowns still persist about the toxic potential of grapes and raisins, you should not give grapes or raisins to pets in any amount.

Milk: Although milk is not toxic to cats, it may have adverse effects. Adult cats fed a nutritious diet don't need milk, and many are lactose-intolerant, which means that milk and milk products produce stomach upset, cramps, and gassiness. If your cat loves milk, and begs for it, a small amount of cream is acceptable two or three times a week. (The more fat in the milk, the less lactose it has.) Another compromise is a product called CatSip, which made from skim milk with an enzyme added to help the digestion of lactose. It is available in some supermarkets and pet stores.

If you think your cat has been poisoned by one of these food items, contact your veterinarian or the ASPCA's National Animal Poison Control Center immediately at one of the numbers below:
1-900-443-0000
1-888-426-4435

organ, and bone products. Some commercial products you can buy contain these ingredients in the correct balance, thus providing a way to combine the convenience of store bought with the wholesomeness of homemade, which is my top recommendation.

RAW FOODS

The raw food movement was pioneered during the 1930s and 1940s by Dr. Francis M. Pottenger, Jr., who studied the effects of heat-processed foods on cats. (He was using them for adrenal studies at the time and decided that the cats were becoming sickly on the diet of cooked meat he was providing.) After experimenting with different kinds of diets, he eventually discovered that the ideal diet for his cats was one-third raw milk, two-thirds raw meat, and a supplement of cod liver oil. (This finding should not frighten those who feed a commercial diet, which now supplies all the necessary vitamins that are destroyed by cooking.)

A raw-food diet differs from a home-cooked diet in that the food is given to the cat raw. Advocates of a raw diet believe that cooked or processed food isn't natural for cats (after all, what they eat in nature isn't cooked), and that the cooking process destroys necessary enzymes and vitamins in the food.

Because cats have stronger stomach acids than humans do, they are better able to digest raw (or natural) foods. Most cats usually live well on a raw diet. If you are feeding your feline a raw diet, use caution when handling raw meat to avoid exposing yourself to *Escherichia coli* (*E. coli*) and other bacteria that may be present in raw foods. Consult your veterinarian for advice and recipes before offering this diet.

If you feed your cat a home-cooked or raw diet and go away on vacation, you'll have to leave prepared food for her and show the person who's taking care of your pet exactly how to prepare the meals.

Technically, you could feed your cat just mice or birds, but that is both aesthetically and ethically unappealing, at least to me. I am sure the cat wouldn't care.

Your cat will rely on you for a regular feeding time; once you set a schedule, you must stick to it.

Free Choice Versus Scheduled Feeding

You can free-feed your feline safely because cats have enough self-control to regulate what they eat. You can't do this with dogs, who will eat whatever is in front of them until they are sick; they have no self-control. Of course there is a reason for this. Cats, being by tradition loners, are used to having their food to themselves to eat whenever they wish. Dogs, who are pack animals, know from their history that if they don't eat it now, someone else will. It makes little difference if the dog is a long-time pet or the cat shares her home with others. It's in the genes. Of course, there are some exceptions in both species. It is perfectly safe, therefore, to free-feed your cat, as long as you take note of how much she is eating (and this is harder to do if you own more than one cat). Free feedings are definitely more convenient, too.

If you feed canned food, however, you'll have to set up a regular feeding schedule so that the food doesn't spoil. You can feed your cat according to your own schedule, for example before you go to work or when you come home in the evening. Keep in mind that once you set this schedule, you must stick to it because your pet will rely on you for a regular feeding time.

Some owners offer a combination of free feeding and scheduled feeding. Before they leave for work, they put out a small portion of dry food for daytime consumption, and when they return home at the end of the day, they offer another scheduled portion. If you practice scheduled feedings and go away for any length of time, you'll need to have someone come to your house to continue feeding your cat at the scheduled feeding times. A cat who free-feeds on dry food may be left enough food for an overnight trip or a weekend.

If you have a cat on a special diet, make sure you feed her separately (behind closed doors) so that the other pets don't get to her food and so she won't be able to nibble on their food either. In these cases, it's an advantage to have set mealtimes rather than free-choice feedings.

How Much to Feed

While commercial brands include recommendations for amounts to feed, you can take them with a grain of salt. Like people, cats vary widely in caloric needs. Begin by observing the manufacturer's guidelines, but if you notice your cat gaining or losing weight, simply adjust the amount you feed.

In general, the amount of food that a cat or kitten requires depends on her size, weight, age, and activity level. Cats who are allowed to go outside or who exercise a lot will burn more calories and eat more than will a sedentary animal. Feeding amounts will also vary because all cats and kittens have different appetites. Basically, an adult female requires approximately 200 to 300 calories a day. An average male needs between 250 and 300 calories daily. Adult-formula dry cat food contains approximately 400 calories per cup, and canned food contains about 150 calories per cup. The actual calorie count varies depending on the brand of food. The average cat needs approximately 8 ounces (227 g) of food a day.

Because kittens are still maturing, they need about two to three times as much nourishment as an adult, and they require small meals given several times throughout the day. They should be fed food (wet or dry) specifically designed for kittens until they reach one year of age, because they need more proteins, fats, and calories than do adults. These formulas are designed to promote healthy growth and development. If a kitten is not given the right amount of nutrients or is otherwise poorly fed, she can develop muscle problems, immune disorders, vision problems, and have retarded growth. An adolescent cat (from six months to one year) may look like an adult, but she's still growing and requires extra calories and nutrients as well.

Seniors are generally less active than adults and should be given several small meals throughout the day. Some older cats will not have much of an appetite, so you should offer an appropriate food three to four times a day and adjust the feeding schedules and amounts according to what your pet will eat.

Cats will stop eating when they are full, so the basic premise is to adjust the

Feeding Behavior in the Wild

In nature, wild and feral cats may eat as many as ten small meals within a 24-hour period. Part of this feeding behavior, which is wrapped into the genes, is the so-called *appetitive phase*, in which the cat stalks, captures, and kills prey. Then she eats it. A cat will catch a bird or a mouse and consume almost all of it—including the bones, feathers or fur, internal organs, and muscle meat. The meat and internal organs provide essential proteins, vitamins, and minerals, while the bones and/or feathers are a source of fiber. The prey's stomach contents provide the small amount of vegetable matter the cat needs.

The modern domestic cat is not very different in behavior from her wild counterparts. Cats are obligate carnivores. That means that they must eat meat; they must have animal-derived protein to survive.

The amount you should feed your cat depends on her size, weight, age, and activity level. For example, kittens and cats have different feeding requirements.

portions you offer according to your individual feline's size and activity level. You are the best judge of her appetite, so use the portion and feeding schedule that best suits her needs. Do some experimentation. For example, offer the amount of food recommended on the labeling and see how long it takes your cat to finish it. If she eats everything right away, consider increasing the portion. Pet food manufacturers usually recommend feeding an adult cat approximately 1/2 to 1 cup (227 to 454 g) of dry food a day.

Switching Foods

Although research shows that cats like variety, for both physical and temperamental reasons, cats don't like switching food too fast—unless the animal is used to a wide variety of food from kittenhood, as mine are. Sudden changes in diet can alter the number of normal bacteria in the intestine and make it harder for the food to be digested, leading to digestive

If you overfeed your cat tuna meant for people, she will not receive sufficient vitamins and minerals to keep her healthy.

upset. Switch slowly, over a period of 7 to 10 days, by gradually mixing some new food with the old until the changeover is complete.

 ## Force-Feeding

When cats become ill, specifically with kidney failure, they lose their appetites. Some will weaken almost to the point of death. In some cases, your veterinarian may instruct to you to begin force-feeding.

To do the job right, you'll need plenty of paper towels, a bowl of lukewarm water, and a small syringe. You will need to feed three or four times a day, usually giving about four syringes at each feeding.

Mix up some highly palatable, delicious cooked food (easier to digest and safer) in a blender. If you wish to add a supplement, throw in some digestive enzymes and liquid amino acids in the amount recommended by your vet.

Fill the syringe first. It's hard to fill a syringe and hold a squirming cat at the same time. Cats don't like to be force-fed. That's why it's called force-feeding. Hold the cat so that she is facing away from you. If she backs up, she'll back up into you. Press on each corner of the jaw to get her to open her mouth; insert the syringe, and bingo!

Cats who cannot be force-fed may have to be tube-fed, a more dangerous process that should be supervised by your vet.

 ## The Right Treats

Treats can be rewards for good behavior, a little pick-me-up in the middle of the day, or just a way to bond with your cat. The best treats, like the best foods, are made of high-quality materials, tasty, and not too fattening. Lean chicken and turkey are excellent choices, but even better are treats specially formulated for cats. Fatty foods are a definite no-no, and cats can't taste sugar anyway. However, remember that if you give your cat treats from the table, you will make a lifelong beggar of her.

If you decide to get a commercial treat, look for the AAFCO label. Treats without this label might be superior, but unfortunately you don't have any real way of knowing. However, this criterion isn't so important if the treat in question is a very special one that is given only occasionally. Only when treats make up a substantial

Special Dietary Needs

Cats with medical conditions or those at different stages of life, such as seniors, often benefit from specific dietary changes. Foods are available that are designed to help cats with a wide variety of health challenges, and your vet may recommend these types of food at some point in your feline's life. Throughout your cat's life, a good-quality food is essential to her health and well-being. Your cat is, at least in part, what she eats.

If your cat has problems eating, try warming the food, adding some tuna juice to it, or feeding smaller amounts more often. Cats who are particularly stressed need nutrient-dense, high-calorie meals. They should also eat in a stress-free environment.

portion of the cat's daily caloric and nutritive intake do you need to pay much attention to this.

If your cat is on a slimming diet, consider a low-calorie treat, or else break up the treat into even smaller portions.

Feeding the Older Cat

Older cats tend to get even more finicky than they were in their prime, so you may have to entice them to eat and drink more. Adding some juice from canned tuna is one way to increase the palatability of both food and water. And, if you have been using dry food, switch to the tastier canned stuff. Special high-calorie foods are also available for your cat to nibble on and still maintain weight. It also helps to feed smaller amounts more often.

Interestingly enough, and in contrast to dogs, older cats need about the same amount of calories as they did when they were kittens. In other words, their metabolism does not slow down! However, they will get fat if they don't get enough exercise, and older cats do tend to exercise less than young cats. Older cats also may have a problem digesting fats as well as they used to, so you may have to switch to a more digestible kind of food if you notice a problem. Do not restrict the protein intake of your cat unless she has a kidney problem.

You may consider supplementing you older cat's diet with vitamins A, C, and E. Some evidence suggests that, because they tend to eat less, older cats may not be getting their full complement of these vitamins.

The Fat Cat

About 40 percent of the cats in this country are obese. And that's really too bad. Fat cats are four times as likely to develop diabetes and five times as likely to develop lameness. Obese cats are more likely to require veterinary care for lameness caused by joint diseases such as arthritis or muscle injuries. They are three times more likely to be presented to veterinarians for nonallergic skin conditions, probably caused by the cats' inability to clean themselves as effectively due to their size. They have higher rates of cardiovascular disease, respiratory disease, and even neurological problems. And they are twice as likely to die in middle age.

You know your cat is too fat if you can't feel her ribs and if the tuck in front of the hindquarters has disappeared. Fat cats have a noticeable paunch as well. By the way, here is the latest profile of an overweight cat: altered, apartment-dwelling, mixed breed, and eating prescription cat food. (Prescription diets tend to be calorie dense.)

However—and please listen—be careful about putting your overweight cat on a diet. While humans and dogs can take some crash dieting (although it's not good for either of them)—it can be fatal to cats, inducing a deadly condition called fatty liver disease (see Chapter 7 for details). Some vets are so worried about this disease that they don't recommend dieting for any cat unless she weighs over 14 pounds (6.3 kg). If you do decide to put your fat cat on a diet, go very slowly. Divide her food into three or more meals if you don't free-feed. If you do free-feed, be careful about the amount you put down—and this gets tricky if you have more than one cat. You're better off sticking to a plan with served portions.

And keep your cat busy. Exercise is fun and weight-reducing without the dangers of crash dieting. Find the most entertaining toys you can, and help your cat work off those extra pounds (kg).

Obesity can lead to many health problems. If your cat is overweight, switch to scheduled feedings so you can control what she eats.

Chapter Seven

Good Grooming

"No amount of time can erase
the memory of a good cat, and no
amount of masking tape can ever
totally remove her fur
from your couch."
— Leo Dworken

Cats are pretty self-sufficient, especially in their own eyes. They bill themselves as elegant, self-cleaning creatures who need no help from their human slaves in the grooming department. In fact, it's been estimated that cats spend about 10 percent of their waking hours grooming themselves. However, their methods of self-cleaning are, well, a little primitive. Their cleaning material is cat spit, known formally as saliva. They simply lick their fur and gnaw at anything that doesn't belong there, including fleas, ticks, mats, and scabs.

This method works fine (most of the time) for young, healthy, shorthaired cats, but does not always prevent the formation of hairballs. While hairballs are the subject of innumerable cat jokes, they can be very un-funny—especially if surgery is required to remove them. Older cats have less energy for self-grooming, and many longer-haired seniors develop large mats and consequent hotspots and sores.

Besides, left to their own devices, cats will not brush their teeth or wash the inside of their ears. You can bet on it. But up-to-date cat owners are not above giving their cats a little boost in this area, whether their feline companions appreciate human help or not. Cats are notably unappreciative of this help in any circumstances, but you'll have to overlook their disdain, and do it anyway.

It's important to groom your pet regularly, and here's why. First (and most obviously), it keeps your cat clean, cleaner than she can manage on her own. Second, it gives you an opportunity to check for ominous lumps, ear mites, broken teeth, and skin problems. The hands-on treatment your cat gets during a thorough grooming doubles as a home health exam! Third (believe it or not), proper grooming, especially brushing, helps create a loving bond between the two of you. Your cat will not tell you that she appreciates your attentions, but she does. I could mention a fourth consideration as well—it keeps more cat hair off the carpets and furniture and so makes your life easier. But that would be a selfish motive, wouldn't it?

Beauty From the Inside Out

With cats, beauty is less than skin deep. Thick, soft, clean fur is the sign of a healthy cat, and healthy cats are beautiful by definition. A great coat starts from the inside, however, with good nutrition. Brush and comb all you want, but a lustrous and full coat thrives on a healthy diet. The vitamins, proteins, and fatty acids inside your cat have a wonderful way of turning into silky hair outside your cat.

Coat Care

All cats, but especially longhaired cats, benefit from regular brushing. Although cats groom themselves, long hair is not "natural" in cats, and longhaired cats should have a through brushing several times a week to keep their hair from matting and their skin in top condition. This is especially true of older cats, who lose the will and

All cats benefit from regular brushing. It helps to prevent their fur from matting and keeps their skin in top condition.

ability to keep themselves as clean as formerly.

While you don't need an arsenal to groom your cat, a few simple implements are essential. Which ones you choose may depend on the kind of fur your cat has. Each type of coat thrives best under slightly different treatment. Everybody knows that cats come in longhaired and shorthaired varieties, but that's not the end of the tale. Not all shorthairs are equal! Some, like the beautiful Bengal, have silky hair that lies quite flat. Others, like the Manx, have thicker fur, with a dense undercoat. And while some longhairs like the Norwegian Forest Cat have sleek, easy-to-groom fur, the Persian has a coarse coat that knots up with infuriating regularity. And then there are those curly-coated breed such as the Selkirk Rex. If you have a Selkirk Rex, be forewarned that too-frequent brushing will diminish the desired curl in the coat. And don't try to straighten out the whiskers—they're supposed to curl like that. Regardless of hair length, though, most cats have a double coat, with a soft, woolly undercoat and an outer coat composed of longer guard hairs.

MATS, KNOTS, AND SNARLS

Before you begin brushing your cat, examine the coat for tangles, knots, and matted fur. Most mats develop in the undercoat. Each outer guard hair develops in its own follicle, but the undercoat grows in clumps. That's where the matting comes in. As the cat starts to shed out, those clumps get matted.

If you come across a knot, don't pull it out. Instead, work out the tangled hair with your fingers or try to brush or comb it out. This is effective for many small knots. If that doesn't work, and you have clippers, use those. If you don't have clippers, try using (believe it or not) a seam ripper (used in sewing). Slide your finger between the knot and skin to isolate the knot. Then gently loosen the hair with the seam ripper, starting at the outside of the knot. Be very careful not to cut the skin. If you do, your cat will never (and I mean *never*) forgive you. The snarl in the coat will be nothing compared to the snarl you'll get from your precious pet. If you don't have a seam ripper, you'll have to make do with scissors. Isolate the mat and use basically the same procedure. You can slowly slide one blade of the scissors through the bottom of the mat and cut upward (not horizontal to the skin). Be very careful! Cats have extremely sensitive and fragile skin that cuts or tears easily. And remember that mantra: Cats do not forgive... Cats do not forgive...

If you have allowed your cat's fur to get matted right down to the skin, you may have to see a professional groomer to have the coat shaved. In extreme cases, you may have to take your cat to the vet to be sedated or even anesthetized for this procedure. Afterward, assuming you have learned your lesson, groom out the new coat as it grows in, promising yourself and your cat not to let this happen again.

COMBS

When grooming a cat, a good comb is your first line of defense, especially for longhaired felines. Use combs and rakes to help detangle snags and remove mats. The best comb for most cats is a 7.5 inch (91.1 cm) steel comb with about 1-inch (2.5 cm) long teeth. Get one that has both coarse and fine teeth instead of two separate combs; you don't need yet another comb to lose track of.

For the face, a flea comb (a metal comb with fine, closely spaced teeth) is perfect. A flea comb, as the name suggests, is also handy to check for fleas, although your cat should be on a flea preventive. If your comb does trap a flea, drown it in some flea shampoo (or, if you're feeling really brutal, crush it in a tissue). If you have a longhaired cat, clip away any stray hairs that may lie against the eye and cause irritation or damage to the cornea. Use only rounded-edge scissors, of course.

If you want, use a pin brush instead of a comb. Pin brushes are quite gentle on the skin and good for separating the individual hairs, releasing incipient snarls. They work almost as well as combs, and some cats prefer them. (To make cleanup easier, you can slip a torn knee-high nylon over the pin brush. The pins will poke through, and cleanup is as easy as throwing away the nylon!)

A neat sort of combination tool is the slicker brush, which has fine wire pins bent at a right angle. This baby is excellent for removing dead hair and is equally useful on longhaired and shorthaired cats. Some slicker brushes are flat; others are curved. The curved ones work best on longhaired cats and the flat ones seem to work better for shorthaired cats. Follow by a brushing, which is especially useful for felines with medium-length hair.

Shedding Cycles

All cats shed. Some shed more than others, but there's no such thing as a shed-free cat. Every hair has its own little life cycle: the *anagen phase*, in which it is actively growing; the *catagen phase*, in which it is just lying there waiting to be petted; and the *telogen phase*, in which it is ready to fall out. It is not true that longhaired cats are worse shedders than their shorthaired cousins, although their shed hair is often more noticeable because it may come out in tufts rather than in individual hairs, as is typical of with shorthairs. During the hair growing season, your cat's hair will grow about a third of an inch (7 mm) a month.

Normal shedding is a seasonal event that corresponds in a vague sort of way with day length. Cats who spend time outdoors seem more attuned to this process than do indoor cats and, while they don't shed any more than do indoor cats, they tend to concentrate their shedding in the spring and fall. Indoor cats, exposed only to artificial light, shed moderate amounts of hair all year long. Siamese seem very fond of shedding all year round also, just as a matter of principle, I suppose. Shedding can also be caused by stress and illness, so if your cat suddenly begins shedding more than she normally does, a trip to the vet may be warranted.

Because shedding is a natural process, it's not possible to eliminate it. However, faithful combing and brushing will remove the telegen-phase hair before it actually lands on your sofa. Proper amounts of fatty acids in the diet also help to keep the skin and coat in tip top shape. Some products on the market claim to reduce shedding, but their effectiveness has not been proved.

BRUSHES

Brushing removes hair and dander, and it also distributes the natural oils throughout the fur. However, especially in low humidity, brushing can produce a lot of static electricity, which cats truly hate. Be careful.

Brushes come with bristles that vary in stiffness. If your cat has a tendency to get a knotted coat, choose a stiffer brush. A soft brush works best on sleek, more trouble-free coats; it's also a good choice for first-time brushing sessions because it is the most comfortable for your cat.

For breeds with an undercoat (most cats), choose a brush with boar's hair bristles. These are very effective at removing dead hair without irritating the skin. Breeds without much undercoat, like Siamese, do better with a rubber brush.

After you get any knots removed, brush your cat from head to tail in the direction of the hair growth, using long, gentle strokes. The belly area is sensitive and will be the trickiest to groom.

If you have a cat that panics at the sight of a brush, use stealth. You can buy a grooming mitt (which has small rubber nubs all over it) or a small rubber brush than fits snugly in your palm. The grooming glove is also excellent for cats with very close, dense coats like the Burmese, Siamese, and Cornish Rex. (The Rex is also the only breed of cat entirely without an undercoat, which explains why the breed sheds so little.) With any luck, your cat may have no clue she's being "groomed" until it's all over.

The more you brush your cat's coat, the nicer she will look, and the healthier she will be. You have nothing to lose.

🐈 Dental Care

Good oral hygiene is an important part of maintaining your cat's overall health, so brush your cat's teeth every day. It only takes a minute, and it will prevent tooth decay and gum disease. Regular brushing is also a good way to monitor mouth and head health. While you are dealing with your cat's teeth, take a few moments to check her head for any signs of abnormalities. Swelling, discharge from the eyes or nose, or a face that suddenly seems crooked or asymmetrical are all signs of trouble.

Most cats don't care for the whole tooth brushing thing, but they will tolerate it. And it is never too later to start! It usually works best if you brush your cat's teeth first thing in the morning before you feed her. That way, she will know a reward is coming.

Another benefit from daily brushing is that it also removes plaque before it has had time to mineralize and do real damage to teeth. Plaque forms every 6 to 8 hours in your cat's mouth; the only way to get rid of it is to brush your cat's teeth regularly. Studies show that 70 percent of cats show signs of gum disease by the time they are three years old. Unfortunately, the most common dental disease of cats, feline dental resorption lesions, which leads to tooth loss, often begins below the gum line, so it may develop without your noticing. This is another reason why you and your vet must be partners in dental care.

HOW TO BRUSH YOUR CAT'S TEETH

Sometimes you'll read articles that give you nifty advice on how to make tooth brushing fun for your pet. With cats, this is not usually possible for a cat, fun is tearing a mouse into shreds, not getting her teeth brushed. But that's no excuse not to do it.

Brushing your kitty's teeth is not complicated. Use toothpaste (or a gel or rinse) designed for pets, preferably one containing chlorhexidine and hexametaphosphate. It's also a good idea to get a little cat toothbrush (they're really cute). They are very soft and are designed to fit more easily into your cat's mouth. If she won't tolerate any kind of toothpaste,

Good oral hygiene is an important part of maintaining your cat's overall health, so brush your cat's teeth regularly.

just dry brush, which will remove a great deal of plaque all by itself.

The first step is to get your cat to allow you to insert something into her mouth. For best results, brush early in the morning, before your cat has had breakfast and may be a bit hungry. Start with your finger dipped in some broth, and let her lick it. Keep trying this and eventually she will let you actually rub your broth-soaked digit along her gum line. Then wrap some very thin gauze (dipped in broth) around your finger and use that. Next, do the same using a toothbrush but, before inserting it into her mouth, let her lick it so she gets used to the feeling of the bristles.

The first few times you brush, you may have to content yourself with just doing the fangs. You can slowly you work your way to the back teeth. Don't worry about brushing the inside of the teeth—most of the bad stuff accumulates on the outside.

Ear Care

Cleaning your cat's ears properly is an important way to keep her healthy. To do the best job, you have to restrain your feline in a thick towel, leaving only the head exposed. Clean the parts of the inner ear you can see with a cotton tip applicator moistened with a commercial ear cleaner designed for cats.

Don't put the applicator deep down into the ear canal (which in cats is very long). Doing so might injure the delicate structure of the ear or stimulate the cat to shake her head violently, causing trauma. You should always be able to see the tip of the applicator.

Nail Care

The hardest part about grooming a cat is trimming the claws. With outdoor and some indoor cats this is not always necessary, but if it is, you should know how to do it. And so should your cat.

Cats are usually able to keep their own nails in excellent condition by ripping your furniture to shreds. (You should see my new leather couch.) To solve the problem, you can always have your cat declawed; however, this is a practice opposed by the American Animal Hospital Association, the Cat Fanciers Association, and nearly all humane groups. Declawed cats are also more likely to *bite* you as a replacement for not being able to scratch you. There's always something.

As mentioned earlier, one humane alternative is to use vinyl nail caps that can be glued onto your cat's claws. These effectively cover the claws so there is no damage to the furniture, even when your cat does scratch.

Another possibility is to trim your cat's nails yourself every couple of weeks. To do this, you'll have to get your cat accustomed to having her paws held for several minutes at a time without freaking her out. Practice while she's relaxed and quiet. You can gently massage them to get her used to this.

NAIL CLIPPING

Part of the preparation for nail trimming is knowing the cat's nail anatomy. In the center of the nail is the pinkish quick, or blood and nerve supply. Don't cut that or you will precipitate a bleeding episode. Just clip the sharp tip of the claw before the quick (which is the pink part inside). One of the truly great things about cats is that almost all of them, even black cats, have white nails, so it's easy to see the quick. If you do cut the quick by mistake, you can stop the bleeding by touching the end of the nail with a styptic pencil. If you cut into the quick by accident, and you have used a styptic pencil or cornstarch to stop the bleeding but it docs not stop, call your vet. Of course, the cat will never forgive you, but by this time she no doubt has an entire list of grudges against you anyway, so another one won't matter. You probably won't have to do the rear claws because they are not what cause most of the damage.

Use small clippers, either those designed for people or special ones designed for cats, some of which include a nail guard to prevent overcutting. Cat nail trimmers look like small scissors; each blade has a half-circle indentation.

For best results, hold the cat in your lap, and press her

Trimming your cat's nails isn't absolutely necessary. If she is using a scratching post, she's taking care of her nails the natural way—and she won't scratch at your furniture!

157

Grooming Rules

The main rule about grooming cats is this: Be as expeditious as possible. Do not trade on your cat's good will for one moment longer than necessary, especially if water is involved. Some people attempt to appease their cats by storing the grooming materials in a plastic bag along with some catnip. The theory is that the cat will be so allured by the catnip that she'll accept the grooming. You can try this, but don't hold your breath.

toe pad to extend the claw. Clip the nail just a bit below the quick. This is also a great opportunity to inspect for split and damaged claws.

It's best to begin nail trimming when your cat is young and more accepting of new things. If you have a young cat, get her used to having her feet held and handled. That way, it will be easier for you to clip her nails should the necessity arise. If you aren't comfortable doing this, take your cat to the vet, who will show you how to do this properly, or seek the services of a professional groomer.

Eye Care

A cat's eyes require very little attention during grooming. If your cat has runny eyes, gently wipe away any discharge using a cotton ball dampened with warm water. Be careful not to touch the eye with the cotton ball. A cat's eyes are extremely sensitive, and you may scratch the eyelid or cornea. If something gets in the eye (dust, dirt, or hair), flush it out with saline solution and wipe around the outer edges with a cotton ball or gauze. If your cat has a serious eye ailment, don't try to treat it yourself; take your pet to the vet for treatment as soon as possible.

Bathing Your Cat

Most of the time, you do not need to bathe a cat, especially a shorthaired one. Cats are excellent self-groomers. (That barbed tongue is a wonderful tool for removing dirt.) This is a good thing, because they really do hate getting wet. You know this if you have ever opened a door to let your cat go out when it was raining. Mine just sit there and then turn a withering glance on me, as if to say, "Unless you turn the rain off, I am not going out." They also strongly object to the sound of running water, especially if it is running over their backs.

At any rate, there are times when bathing is necessary due to some sort of accident, or if the cat neglects her grooming. The coats of some longhaired cats can get too oily. When the time comes for an unavoidable bath, be sure to collect all the necessary implements before bathtime. These include a good feline shampoo and towels. If you suspect a fight, wear gloves.

One truly necessary implement is a second person. While a

professional groomer or a vet tech can handle bathing a cat alone, most of us will have a much easier time if we can bribe someone to help us.

Here's the usual scenario:

- Person A secures the cat.

- Person B puts a rubber bath mat in the bottom of the sink to help the cat stay upright.

- Person B starts running the water in the sink, checking the temperature. (The water level should only reach the cat's belly.) If necessary, hold the cat by the scruff of the neck.

- Person B begins washing the cat (not too much shampoo, please) while Person A maintains a firm grip. The cat will pretend she is being killed. She will screech and yowl and hiss and growl. Pay no attention. Do not comfort the cat. Speak in a low, but cheerful and matter-of-fact voice.

- Don't pour water on the head. Wipe the cat's face with a moist towelette instead. That should be sufficient.

- Rinse with warm water.

- Keep rinsing.

- Rinse some more.

- Pat the cat down with a towel. If you have a quiet blow dryer you can use it set on low or medium, but most cats will furiously object. Simply put the wet cat in a warm room.

- Beg the cat's pardon. (It will not be given.)

After the bath, your cat will begin to lick herself all over. This is completely normal.

If all your friends suddenly declare family emergencies that won't allow them to help, much as they'd *love* to of course, then you're on your own.

Cats are excellent self-groomers, so they don't usually need to be bathed—unless they get into a dirty mess.

Special Grooming Problems

Cats are curious, and they can get into many unpleasant substances that will need to be removed from their coat.

SKUNKED

If your cat is unfortunate enough to be sprayed by a skunk, pray you have some commercial de-skunking spray around. If not, you can make up your own by mixing 1 quart (0.95 l) of hydrogen peroxide, 1/4 cup (240 ml) baking soda, and 1 teaspoon (5 ml) liquid soap. Rub this mixture into the coat. Rinse your cat, then bathe with a mild shampoo. Throw the de-skunking mixture away afterwards; the mixture may be volatile.

The tough part about all this is that cats tend to get hit directly in the face. You'll have to use cotton balls and dab them carefully around several times. It will probably only happen once. Cats are much smarter than dogs and remember things like this.

REMOVING SUBSTANCES FROM FELINE FUR

It is important to stress that cat owners should never use gasoline, turpentine, kerosene, paint remover, or similar substances to remove tar, paint, or oil from a cat's coat. Small amounts of sticky substances such as gum, tar, or paint can carefully be cut out of the coat. Large amounts of tar can be removed by soaking the affected fur in vegetable oil or mineral oil for 24 hours, then using pet shampoo to wash off the substance.

Cornstarch can be sprinkled on smaller patches of oil and then brushed off. As a last resort in cases where the entire animal is covered in oil, shampoo your cat with a gentle dishwashing detergent, and follow up with a cat shampoo. If your cat has gotten into something really sticky or oily, you may need to have her professionally groomed.

Detanglers and Degreasers

When bathing longhaired cats, it helps to use a detangler or conditioner after shampooing. You can also use about half a cup of vinegar to 2 quarts of warm water to remove the last soapy residue if you like. Soap left in the fur will dry your cat's skin.

If your cat has gotten into something awful that precipitated a bath, you may want to use a degreaser on her body before shampooing. Usually it's not necessary, but some cases may require the additional attention. You can buy nontoxic degreasers at a supermarket or pet store.

Grooming the Older Cat

As cats age, they lose flexibility in their muscles and joints and may not be able to bend, stretch, and reach to wash themselves like they used to. They also may lose interest in their appearance and won't wash as often as they once did. This is why they often look a little scraggly.

If you have a senior cat, you may have to help groom her. You can keep your older cat looking good by gently brushing (or combing) her each day. Brushing helps to spread natural oils on the fur and prevents it from becoming dry and brittle. It also increases blood circulation and stimulates the nervous system, which makes your cat feel better.

The Professional Groomer

If you don't feel confident about grooming your pet or just don't have as much time for it as you'd like, you can always use the services of a professional pet groomer to tend to your feline's grooming needs. Ask your vet, trusted cat mentor, or breeder to recommend someone who knows how to deal with cats. Many groomers are dog-savvy only; check to make sure the groomer knows how to hold and restrain a cat in the least stressful way.

Good grooming facilities are clean, well-lighted, well-ventilated, and staffed with friendly, knowledgeable people who take the time and trouble to listen to you and respond to your needs. Dogs and cats should be housed in separate areas, and all pets should be monitored. The groomer should keep complete records of every pet client.

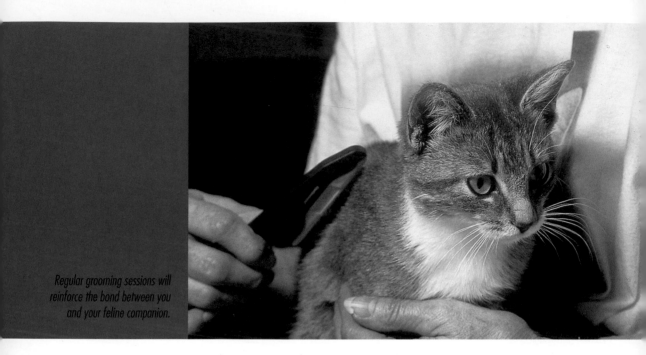

Regular grooming sessions will reinforce the bond between you and your feline companion.

There are a few things you'll need to do before making your cat's first appointment. First, if your cat tends to be a bit, well, irritable when groomed, it's only ethical to clue the groomer in on this necessary bit of information. Also, your cat should be up-to-date on vaccinations and in good health before being left at a grooming facility. Some states require that groomers be licensed in flea and tick applications. If this is true in your state, check to make sure that the groomer is so certified.

Grooming as a Health Check

A grooming session can double as a health check. Good grooming will uncover all sorts of lumps and bumps, chipped teeth, dirty ears, poor gum color, brittle or sparse hair, and other marks of impending illness.

Before you begin the grooming session, take a minute to inspect your cat's body. Part the fur and spot-check a few areas for signs of fleas or ticks, which is especially important if you allow your cat to go outdoors. Also take a look at the coat. It should be shiny, with no missing patches of fur. The skin shouldn't be very dry or flaky, and the fur shouldn't be brittle. Check the paws and look for cracked footpads or overgrown or ingrown claws.

Next, check inside the ears and look for ear wax buildup or signs of ear mites. Open your cat's mouth and examine the teeth and gums. The gums should be pink and healthy, and no teeth should be missing or broken. If your cat has very bad breath, it could be a sign of gum disease or another ailment. The eyes and nose should be clean and clear, not runny.

Taking a few extra minutes to examine your cat before you groom her keeps her healthy and alerts you to any physical changes that may indicate a health problem.

Grooming as Bonding Time

One of the least appreciated aspects of grooming is that it can be an excellent bonding time for you and your cat—as long as it is confined to gentle brushing. However, let us be frank. Sugarcoat it any way your like, no cat enjoys getting a bath or having her teeth brushed. Some cats will learn to endure it, but none of them will think the better of you for plunging them in soapy water and scrubbing.

Be patient with your cat when you groom her. Offer her a treat after every session as a reward for allowing you to put her through the ordeal. Also, cats love attention, and fussing over your cat will certainly build the bond of trust between you. The more often you groom your feline, the more she will come to expect it—and the better she'll look and feel.

All in a Tangle

If your cat is so seriously matted that the groomer cannot remove the mats and tangles in 30 minutes (the top time a cat should have to submit to grooming), give him your permission to shave your pet and promise to do better next time.

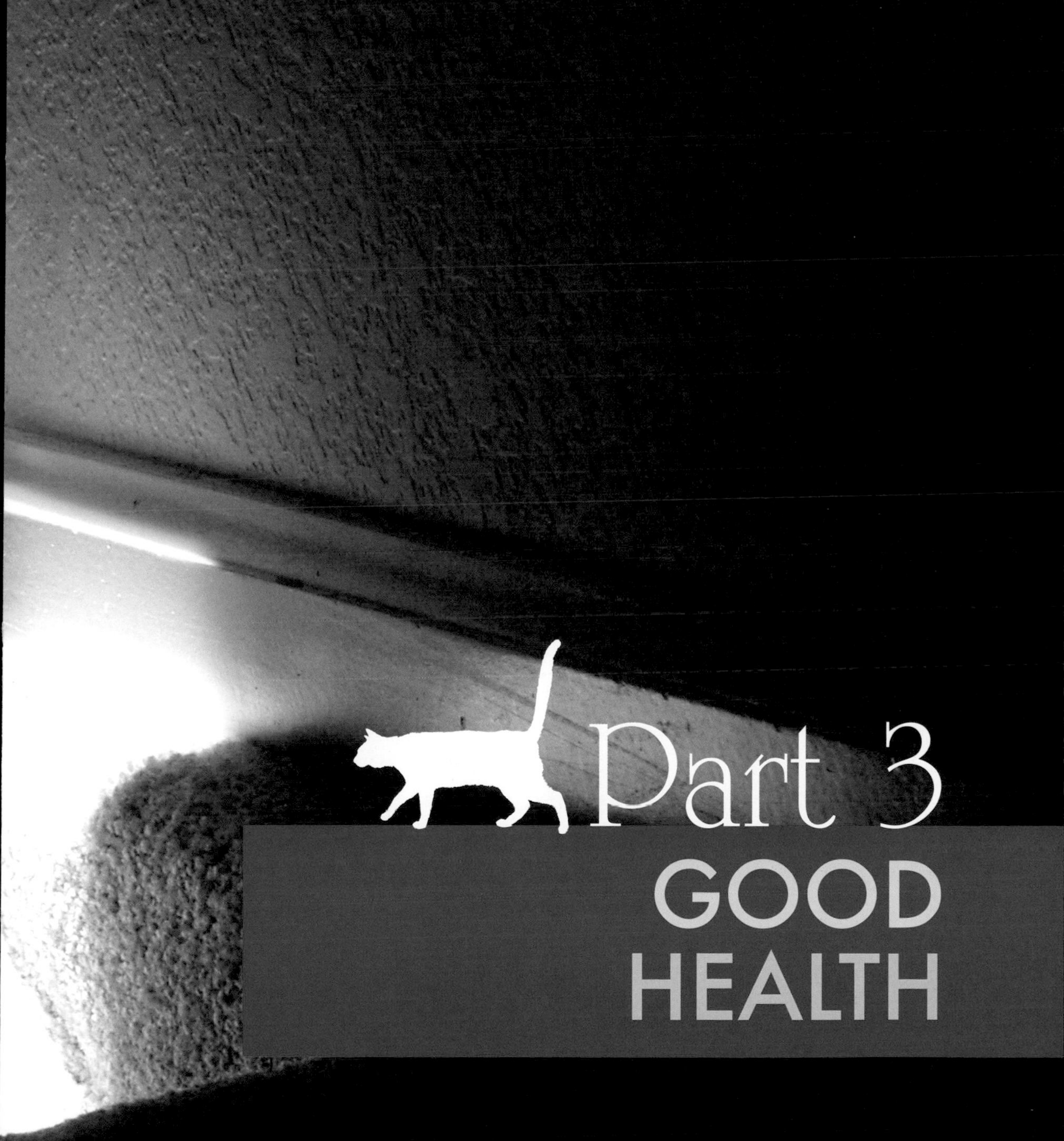

Part 3
GOOD HEALTH

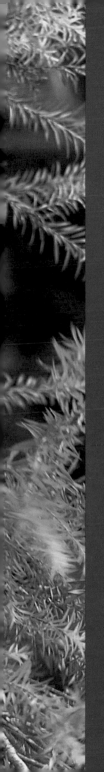

Chapter Eight

Your Healthy Cat: and This Is What Cats Are Made of...

"The smallest feline is a

masterpiece."

—Leonardo da Vinci

So far, we've talked about the importance of exercise, grooming, companionship, toys, and nutrition. All these are important, not just in themselves, but as aids in developing good health for your feline. Without basic good health, however, almost nothing else matters.

Keeping your cat in good shape is comparatively easy. With due diligence on your part, and with the help of your vet, your cat will be around to comfort, annoy, love, and charm you for all of her nine healthy lives.

To offer the best care possible, it helps to know something about feline anatomy. While I talk about various systems in the cat's body, it's important to realize that many organs or parts of the body involve more than one system, just as one system makes use of multiple body parts.

Special Sense Organs

Nature designed the cat's body, sense organs, and natural instincts perfectly for survival in the wild. Cats can hear sounds that we can't hear, see things that we can't see, and smell and sense the world around them in ways that we can't begin to grasp. These remarkable abilities were part of their evolutionary

Nature designed the cat's body, sense organs, and natural instincts perfectly for survival in the wild. Although they are much smaller than their ancestors, domestic cats have retained the same extraordinary physical characteristics and instincts.

adaptation to being solitary nocturnal hunters. Although domestic cats are much smaller than their ancestors, they have basically retained the same physical characteristics and instincts. If we know how their unusual and rather extraordinary senses work, we may be able to understand our cats better.

THE EAR

Of course you know where your cat's ears are but, as with people, only part of the ear is visible. The external, upright part of the ear is called the *pinna* or *auricle*. This funnel-shaped structure directs sound into the external ear canal.

The middle ear includes the eardrum and tympanic cavity (*osseus bulla*), which is right behind it. Inside it are three tiny bones (the hammer, stirrup, and anvil) that form a "chain"; these parts of the ear vibrate when struck by sound. The middle ear is connected to the pharynx (in the throat) by the Eustachian tube. The Eustachian tube permits air from the pharynx to pass in and out of the middle ear and helps keep pressure normal. The inner ear is actually inside the skull and consists of an osseous or bony labyrinth containing fluid-filled membranes. It also contains a spiral tube called the cochlea (which contains nerves), a vestibule, and three semicircular canals. The canals and vestibule help maintain balance, something pretty important to a cat.

So, the ear not only lets cats hear, it also helps them maintain balance. The body is very clever doubling up this function in this way. That's nature for you. Wonderful thing.

CAT'S-EYE

Cats, of course, are famous for being able to see well at night. While they can't see in total darkness, they can see clearly in about one-sixth the light that people need. One thing that helps is the tapetum, a reflective layer of cells behind the cat's retina. This reflects the light and bounces it back off the cones. Although cats are good at spotting far-off movement, they don't see well up close. Cats also have an inner, third eyelid. Called a *nictitating membrane*, it protects the eye from dryness and damage, especially as cats stalk prey through the underbrush. If the eyes are inflamed or irritated, you may see this membrane protrude. That is a signal to take your cat to the vet.

TASTE AND SMELL

The sense of smell is a cat's primary resource for identifying things in her environment. As a complement to that, her sense of taste helps her to

Due to the placement of their eyes, cats cannot see directly beneath their noses.

determine what is safe to eat. Cats have about twice the number of smell receptors in their nasal passages as do people. Part of their olfactory organs are at the base of the mouth so, in a sense, cats also have a sense of smell in their mouths. In cats, smell is associated with taste in that both senses carry out similar tasks: analyzing chemical substances at a distance (smell) or on direct contact (taste). However, a cat's most powerful response to food is through her sense of smell, not taste. Interestingly, being strict carnivores, their response to sweet is much weaker than ours, but they can detect sour, bitter, and salty. It appears they can even "taste" water.

Kittens are born deaf and blind, but their sense of smell is already working well. Day-old kittens can distinguish between their own home and another. They also prefer to use one of their mama's nipples exclusively, which they locate by smell. If your indoor cat escapes the house in a panic and does not take time to scent-mark her territory, it is possible

The sense of smell is a cat's primary resource for identifying things in her environment.

for her to end up as a stray because she will not "recognize" your property as her own. Keep tags on your cat at all times, even if she is an indoor cat.

TOUCH

Cats, of course, have special implements of touch—those whiskers, which are very sensitive to air flow pressure. Using them, they can detect an object's presence (including prey) from a distance, sort of like radar. Cats usually have 24 whiskers, 12 (2 rows of 6) on each side of the face. Whiskers are thicker than ordinary hairs, and they are attached to a tightly packed cluster of nerve endings that can detect the slightest movement. Never clip a cat's whiskers—she needs them.

Sensors

In addition to those on their muzzles, cats have whisker-like hairs above their eyes and on the backs of their front legs. These act as touch sensors that enable them to navigate around objects in low light and to feel changes in air currents around objects.

The Cardiovascular (Circulatory) System: Transport

The cardiovascular system consists of the heart and blood vessels. Its job is a simple one: Get the goods moving around the body so all parts get some oxygen, nutrients, hormones, chemicals, antibodies, and the like. It also carries away the leftovers, regulates body temperature, and maintains the electrolyte balance.

THE HEART

Located in the chest between the lungs and between the third and fourth rib, the cat heart is a muscular pump contained inside a thin membrane (the pericardial sac). The cat heart, like our own, has four chambers: the right and left atrium and the right and left ventricle. The blood basically goes from right to left. The right atrium collects the blood from the outer reaches of the body, contracts, and squeezes the blood through the tricuspid valve into the next chamber, the right ventricle. As this ventricle contracts, it squeezes the blood into the pulmonary artery and then into the lungs. Here it picks up oxygen and divests itself of carbon dioxide. The oxygen-rich blood enters and collects in the left atrium, which sends it through the mitral valve into the left ventricle, the main pump house for the body. It uses the aortic valve to send the blood out through the aortic artery and then throughout the body. It's easy to remember this. An "atrium" is a waiting room (the blood "waits" there and the "ventricle" "vents" the blood out).

The right and left halves of the heart are separated by a muscle wall called the septum. The septum "separates."

BLOOD

Blood. It's the symbol of life. It transports oxygen, carries away waste, and protects against disease. Blood (both cat blood and human blood) consists of red blood cells, white blood cells, platelets, and plasma. Red blood cells are most populous (explaining why blood is indeed red). They contain hemoglobin, the protein that transports oxygen. They circulate in the blood for about 120 days in cats before they wear out and are destroyed in the spleen and liver.

White blood cells come in different forms: neutrophils to fight bacteria, lymphocytes to make antibodies, eosinophils to control allergic and inflammatory reactions and to fight parasites, and basophils, which function much like eosinophils. Platelets are not really cells, but pieces of material that plug up leaks and keep your cat from bleeding to death. Plasma is the fluid part of the blood. (If your cat gets an abscess, the collected pus is largely made up of white blood cells.)

THE BLOOD VESSELS

The biggest blood vessels are the arteries, which emerge from the heart and carry the blood out to the rest of the body. Veins carry blood back *into* the heart. The tiny blood vessels between the arteries and veins are called capillaries. Capillaries have membranous walls that allow oxygen and other substance to flow directly between the blood and the tissues. Think of them as a kind of "changing station."

The Digestive System: The Fuel Supply

The digestive system includes the mouth, teeth, salivary glands, esophagus, stomach, intestine, pancreas, liver, and gall bladder. Its job is to absorb and digest food and eliminate solid wastes from the body. Ah, nothing is more romantic than a trip down the alimentary canal, also called the gastrointestinal tract.

MEALY MOUTH

Food is first grasped by the teeth and tongue and enters the mouth. During her lifetime, a cat has two sets of teeth: a deciduous set and a permanent set. Kittens have 26 temporary teeth that begin to erupt at about two to three weeks of age. Adults have 30 permanent teeth that emerge at about three to four months: 12 incisors, 4 canines (sorry), 10 premolars, and four molars. (You would think that the fangs on a cat might be called the felines, and that all of a dog's teeth are called "canine" teeth. But that's the way of things.)

Most cats don't chew food (especially kibble, which they swallow whole; you may have noticed this yourself if you've ever seen your cat vomit soon after a meal). In fact, cats cannot chew; they have no flat-crowned, crushing teeth. Except for the canines and molars, most cat teeth are essentially nonfunctional!

As the food is swallowed, it passes into the back of the mouth or pharynx. (Air goes through there as well.)

EASY ON THE ESOPHAGUS
Much like ours, the feline esophagus is basically a hose that connects the mouth to the stomach. The esophagus walls are composed of muscles that move in wave-like contractions to push food through the cardiac sphincter into the tummy.

STOMACH: THE MIXING ROOM
The cat's stomach is basically a sac-like structure designed to hold food (it can hold more than you think) and begin the digestive process. The interior surface is made up of folds that help grind and digest the food. The stomach lining secretes enzymes and acids to break it down. The partially digested food then leaves the stomach through the pyloric sphincter and enters the duodenum, which is the first part of the small intestine. This occurs several hours after ingestion.

INTESTINAL FORTITUDE
The small intestine stretches from the stomach to the large intestine. If stretched out, it would be about two and a half times the animal's total body length. It's called small not because of its length, but because its diameter is narrower than that of the colon.

The feline small intestine has three parts. The first part (connecting to the stomach) is the duodenum. The gallbladder and pancreas connect to the duodenum by the bile and pancreatic ducts, respectively. The liver also sends enzymes important for digestion through these ducts to mix with the food in the duodenum. The middle part is the jejunum, which has small, finger-like protrusions called villi. These provide a large surface area to absorb nutrients.

Electrolytes
Fluid (water) balance and electrolyte balance are inseparable. Electrolytes have many functions, in both cat and human physiology, including maintaining the fluid balance within and between cells, helping enzymes to work, and allowing the transmission of nerve impulses.

If the balance of electrolytes is disturbed, disorders can develop. Loss of electrolytes can have serious consequences for the body. In severe dehydration, the loss of electrolytes can result in circulatory problems, such as tachycardia (rapid heart beat), and problems with the nervous system, such as loss of consciousness and shock.

173

Like their wild cousins, cat's are designed to gorge on a meal, and then not eat again for many hours or sometimes days, which allows for proper digestion and the elimination of toxins associated with a meat-based diet.

Everything left then goes into the ileum, which connects to the large intestine.

The large intestine connects the small intestine to the anus. Its primary function is to absorb water from stool, so the body doesn't dehydrate. It also, of course, stores the stool until it can be conveniently eliminated. Like the small intestine, the large intestine has several parts. The cecum is a small, finger-like projection near the junction with the small intestine. No one is sure of its exact function, but it's a dead end. The longest portion of the large intestine is called the colon, and it ends at the rectum, just inside the anus.

OOH, THE GALL OF IT!

The gallbladder is a balloon-like organ nestled between lobes of the liver. The liver produces bile (whose function is to digest fat) and drains it into the gallbladder, which stores it. The gall bladder then releases bile when needed into the small intestine through the bile duct.

LOVING THAT LIVER

On the surface, the liver doesn't look like much. Just a big old reddish-brown mass of lobed meat, so to speak. Ah, that view totally belies how important this organ is. The liver is the largest internal organ of the body. It metabolizes protein, fats, and carbohydrates; stores vitamins and minerals; produces blood-clotting factors; helps digest food; and detoxifies wastes. Altogether, it is estimated that the liver performs 1,000 bodily functions! Amazingly, every part of the liver is capable of performing all this work; it's the only organ in the body that can do this. So while I am categorizing it with the digestive system for now, it really does so much more!

The liver does its good work through blood vessels that travel through and practically saturate it. Every blood vessel leaving the gastrointestinal tract passes through the liver, for one thing. In fact, about 15 percent of the animals' blood is in the liver at any one time. If you squeezed your cat's liver, lots of blood would coming pouring out of it like a sponge. Although I am sure you have no interest in squeezing your cat's liver.

The liver actually produces some important proteins like albumin (important in regulating blood functions) and some globulins. It monitors many of the others, taking careful note of protein availability elsewhere in the body. It also stores and releases carbohydrates and fats that the body needs. It also stores and metabolizes fatty acids and triglycerides, and all the vitamins except for vitamin C. The liver also stores iron, copper, and zinc. Liver products form bile, which goes from the gallbladder into the bile duct and then into the small intestine to help in the breakdown of food.

Just as important, the liver plays an important role in detoxification. It processes ingested toxic chemicals, wastes from protein metabolism, old hemoglobin from red blood cells, and much more.

The Endocrine System: The Special Interest Group

The endocrine system includes hormone-producing glands, such as the thyroid gland, parathyroid glands, adrenal glands, and part of the pancreas. Hormones are special substances that travel through the bloodstream and affect or regulate other organs.

THE PANCREAS

The cat's pancreas is a small v-shaped structure located near the stomach and attached to the wall

The Liver's "Nine Lives"

One of the tricky things about the liver is that it is such a hard worker that it has to be almost shot before you know anything is wrong with it. That applies to people as well. The fact that the liver acts like one unified "glob" accounts for its success; if one part goes bad, the rest of the liver tries to make up for it. In feline medicine, it sometimes happens that, by the time the tests show something might be wrong with the liver, it has already worked itself out of the diseased condition and is on the way back to normalcy. Cats have been known to regrow a liver that has been largely excised in surgery.

175

of the small intestine. It produces hormones (insulin and glucagon) to regulate blood sugar levels, and it produces enzymes to help the intestine digest food.

THE THYROID GLAND

The feline thyroid gland, located in the front of the neck, produces hormones that regulate many metabolic processes. It consists of two lobes, one on each side of the windpipe, deeply buried in the soft tissues of the neck. The thyroid secretes T_4 and T_3 hormones that stimulate body tissues to produce hormones and increase the amount of oxygen used by cells. It also produces the calcitonin hormone that works with the tiny parathyroid glands to regulate calcium levels.

The Immune System

The world is a dangerous place, filled with vicious viruses, brutal bacteria, foul fungi, and ferocious foreign proteins. The immune system has a double duty: to identify and then destroy foreign invaders. It first works to discriminate between proteins that are naturally part of the body and those that aren't.

When a strange foreign agent enters the body, the immune system wakes up and begins to marshal its forces. If it's a brand new visitor, the immune system may take a little time to recognize it, and your cat may get sick before the invader is destroyed. In all probability, however, it will eventually destroy the foreign agent, although some invaders (like anthrax) are so terrible that it is very unlikely the unfortified immune system will be able to cope with it at all.

When the interloper has been killed off, the immune system cleverly tucks away in its cellular memory banks all the particulars of the encounter. If the enemy shows up again, the immune system will be ready to mobilize instantly and destroy the evil agent *before* it can cause sickness. This is the secret of vaccines.

The Integumentary System

The integumentary system is comprised of the skin and fur. The skin is the largest organ of the body. It protects the underlying organs; its thin sheath basically keeps your cat together. The fur helps insulate against heat loss, water loss, parasites, and other dangerous things.

The skin itself is made up of several cell layers containing sebaceous (oil-producing) glands. It also contains blood vessels, hair follicles, and nerve endings. The tough outer layer of skin is the *epidermis* and the inner layer is the *dermis*. A cat's skin is also much more loosely attached than is the case in people, giving felines additional flexibility.

HAIR

Cats have four types of hair: the short fluffy undercoat, the primary or guard hairs, the awn hairs (thinner than primary hairs), and whiskers.

The ratio of one kind of hair to another differs from breed to breed and largely accounts for the differences in the quality and type of coats.

Every hair grows from a hair follicle in the skin, hangs around for a while, and then sheds. Each hair follows its own rhythm. This is a good thing, or else all the hair would fall out at the same time. All cats shed to some extent, but outdoor cats tend to shed more heavily in the spring and fall as they replace their winter and summer coats.

The Musculoskeletal System: Structure and Movement

Every cat is a miracle of movement, and that miracle rests on a solid foundation of bones, ligaments, tendons, and muscles.

Although there are between 30 and 40 breeds of cat, they all share the same basic body structure.

BONES

The average cat-with-a-tail measures roughly 30 inches (76.2 cm) and has 244 bones. This is about the same number that people have, but cat bones are arranged differently and are adapted to the cat's specific predatory needs. Their spines, for example, are extremely flexible, which gives them the jumping ability, balance, and ability to move quickly that they need. The bones are also light, which helps movement.

Unlike in people, cats don't have a fully developed collar bone, and this allows for much more complete movement in the shoulder (and also lets cat's creep into tiny places). The hipbone is also connected to the spine in a way that allows free movement.

Bones are tough—everybody knows that. They need to be because they

In comparing the anatomy of a cat to that of a human, the internal organs are very similar, but the bone structure is very different. The cat's spine consists of 30 spinal vertebrae versus 25 in humans. Cats' shoulder blades are attached to the body with muscles, not bony joints, thus allowing them to move in directions impossible for humans. Their spines are extremely flexible, which gives them the jumping ability, balance, and ability to move quickly that they need. Cats have such amazing flexibility that they can roll into a ball, sleep curled up, squeeze into narrow spaces, stretch out like a wire, flex their spines 180 degrees sideways, and arch their backs to the point where the hind and front paws touch.

provide the framework for the whole body, and they also protect the delicate internal organs. They are made mostly of calcium and phosphorus.

Inside the central cavity of the bones is the spongy bone marrow. This stuff is pretty important because it contains cells that produce red blood cells, white blood cells, and platelets. Cats need all three types of cells (as do we). Red blood cells carry oxygen, white blood cells fight infection, and platelets help form clots. Where would we be without them?

MUSCLES

The muscular system is one of the largest and most important in the cat's body. In fact, your cat has more than 500 of them! (However, in the tail, the only powerful muscles are near the root.)

Muscles contract to allow for movement, and they come in two varieties—smooth and striated. The smooth muscles are found mostly in organs, such as the stomach, and these work automatically. The striated muscles are attached to the skeleton and are under the control of the cat, at least most of the time. The voluntary muscles are most often attached to the joint-forming bones.

The cat's most amazing muscles, however, are found in the paws. Voluntary muscles are attached to the claws in such a way that they enable her to extend or retract them at will. The forelimb is very flexible indeed and can move not only forward and backward as when running, but also across the chest or even up above the head for climbing. The hind limbs are considerably less flexible. Although a cat's legs appear rather short in comparison with the rest of the body, this is deceptive.

TENDONS

Tendons are made of tough connective tissue and attach muscle to bone.

LIGAMENTS

Ligaments connect bone to bone; they are made of tough, fibrous material. Most of them span across joints.

JOINTS

Joints are pretty interesting in themselves. A joint is defined as the place where two bones are connected and held in place by supporting tissues. Some joints have a great range of motion; others have almost none (like the joints between the bones in the skull).

Joints come in three types: synovial, fibrous, and cartilaginous. Synovial joints include movable joints, such those found in the legs. In these joints, the ends of bone are covered with cartilage; the joints themselves are full of synovial fluid that acts as a lubricant. The area outside the capsule is called the joint cavity. These joints have the greatest range of motion. Fibrous joints, on the other hand are pretty rigid—like those that hold the skull bones together (did you know the skull has 40 bones?) Cartilaginous joints are formed when two or more bones are joined by cartilage—good examples are the joints of the spine. They allow some movement. The intervertebral discs are actually cartilage that join vertebrae together.

PAWS, PADS, AND CLAWS

Nothing is softer and sweeter than a cat's paw or nastier than the extended, sickle-shaped claws.

Each cat toe has a claw attached. These retractable claws are designed to grasp and hold onto prey. They grow throughout the cat's life. Growing from within, the old outer layers are shed as the cat ages. Using them frequently usually keeps them short enough for practical use.

Fatty footpads are located beneath each toe. They act like shock absorbers and contain sweat glands. It's a mistake to think cats are sharpening their claws on furniture and the like; they are actually spreading their scent around.

It's rather common, by the way, for cats to be polydactyl—to have extra toes. Some people call this a "double-pawed" cat, but it's only the toes that are extra, not the whole paw. Normally, cats have five toes on each of the front paws and four on each of the hind paws, but some cats are blessed with extra toes, especially on the front feet. There's a genetic component to polydactylism, and breeding two polydactyl cats will increase the chance of polydactyl kittens. This is actually a genetic defect and, as far as I know, there are no plans to produce an entire breed of polydactyl cats.

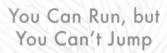

The Lymphatic System

Just as in humans, the cat's lymphatic system includes the lymph nodes and lymph vessels. It is part of the immune system, and it also works with the cardiovascular system to return fluids that escape from the blood vessels back into the bloodstream. The immune system helps the body fight off disease, protecting it from many kinds of disease-causing agents including bacteria, viruses, toxins, and parasites. It reacts to unique molecules called antigens, and uses antibodies and cell-mediated immunity to rid the body of foreign substances.

The Nervous System

The feline nervous system is very similar to the human nervous system. The nervous system coordinates the activity of the muscles, monitors the organs, constructs and also stops input from the senses, and initiates actions. Cats have the same array of receptors on their skin and in their bodies, and these all report on the cat's state of being.

You Can Run, but You Can't Jump

The breed of cat called the Munchkin, which is short-legged (like a Dachshund dog) as the result of a natural mutation, is the only cat who lacks significant jumping prowess—it can run, climb, and jump, although not as high as its long-legged cousins. And, by all accounts, this breed is a freak of nature.

BRAIN AND SPINAL CORD

If you've got a brain in your head, you've probably figured out that the brain is the headquarters for interpreting all the information that pours in from the body and then figuring out what to do about it. The spinal cord is the main lane along this information highway. The brain itself has three major parts: the brainstem, the cerebrum, and the cerebellum.

NERVES

Nerves are special cells bundled into fibers. The most important part of a nerve is called the neuron, which is capable of responding to stimuli and then conducting that information electrically to the brain.

Some nerves act as messengers to relay information, some activate muscle, and some do both. Cranial nerves emerge from openings in the skull and lead to the face, eyes, and tongue. The other nerves, called peripheral nerves, come from the spinal cord and go out to the rest of the body.

🐾 The Respiratory System

The respiratory system includes the mouth, nose, trachea, lungs, and the smaller airways (bronchi and bronchioles). The respiratory system is responsible for taking in oxygen and eliminating waste gases like carbon dioxide. Because cats do not sweat through the skin (except through the paw pads), the respiratory system is also critical in regulating temperature.

As the cat inhales, air enters the nose, pharynx, and larynx into the trachea. The trachea carries the air into the bronchi, which supply the lungs. Cats have right and left lungs, just like us.

🐾 The Urogenital System

The urogenital system includes the kidneys, ureter, urinary bladder, urethra, and the genital organs. This is true for all organisms, not just cats. The urinary system is responsible for removing waste products from blood and eliminating them as urine.

The most important part of the renal system is the kidneys. The kidneys are filters that clean toxins, especially urea, a by-product of protein from the blood. They do more than that, though! They maintain the right amount of water in the body, keep blood pressure in check, maintain the electrolyte balance, keep blood at the correct pH, and help the body absorb calcium, too.

The genital organs are involved in reproduction, of course, and are sometimes considered separately as the reproductive system.

THE ANAL GLANDS

Anal glands are so fascinating that they deserve their own section. Located on either side of the cat's anus, these oval glands secrete a really—er—pungent, pasty fluid that's released when the cat defecates. Both male and female cats have anal glands, as do dogs and some other animals. The fluid's most important job, however, is its use as a territorial marker, a practice similar to leaving a calling card for subsequent visitors to read. Cats will also spontaneously express their anal glands when alarmed, much in the same way as skunks do. Otherwise, they seem to have no additional function other than to get clogged up, impacted, or infected.

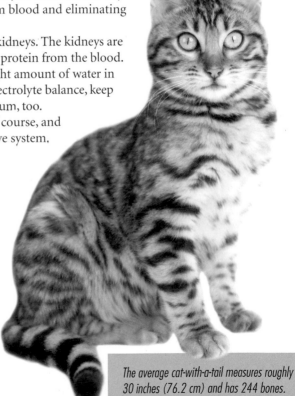

The average cat-with-a-tail measures roughly 30 inches (76.2 cm) and has 244 bones.

🐈 Your Cat and Your Vet

Your cat will never enjoy going to the vet, but it's necessary for her health, so she (and you) will just have to put up with it. Unfortunately, simply because many cats dislike going to the vet and riding in cars, owners often put off taking their pets until they are really sick. But by the time your cat is really sick, it may be too late. Cats often hide their illnesses (any sign of weakness in the wild can be deadly), and so it's up to you to notice subtle changes in appearance or behavior that may signal something is wrong. Examples include:

- change in activity level
- change in eating or drinking habits
- change in elimination patterns, quantity, or appearance
- change in temperament

It is imperative to take your cat for a checkup at least once a year. Twice

Cats often hide their illnesses, so it's up to you to notice subtle changes in appearance or behavior that may signal something is wrong.

a year is even better, especially for senior cats. Don't be afraid to ask questions about anything you do not understand. Your vet is your cat's best friend (after you, of course).

✎ Finding a Veterinarian

One way to find a good veterinarian is to inquire among local friends who themselves are committed cat owners and who have the same dedicated attitude toward their pet's health care that you do. If you don't know another cat owner, you can investigate online many veterinary membership organizations (like the American Veterinary Medical Association [AVMA]) that may be able to refer you to a qualified vet in your area.

Once you have a recommendation that you would like to consider, pay the clinic a visit. Obviously, it should be clean, friendly, and well-organized. It should also be close to where you live, if possible. While it is not necessary to pick one right next door (although that could be handy), time is always a factor in a veterinary emergency. An extra ten-minute drive could mean death for your pet in more serious cases. In the same way, make sure the hours are convenient for you. When the clinic is closed, you should know the location of the nearest emergency clinic as another alternative.

While you are screening possibilities, check on the vet's special areas of interest and expertise, and learn how diagnostic procedures and other specialty care is handled. Not all vets do ultrasound, CT scan, endoscopies, and other procedures—if the vet you like doesn't offer these options, ask where your cat might be referred if these services become necessary.

Ideally, you want to choose a vet who is committed to cat care; some vets actually have cat-only practices. They are more up-to-date with feline medical issues and are more likely to have "cat-sized" equipment. If your vet treats both cats and dogs, it's best if there are separate entrances or at least separate waiting rooms, which makes the visit much less stressful for your feline.

Will You Still Love Me If I'm Polydactyl?

It's rather common for cats to be polydactyl—to have extra toes. Some people call this a "double-pawed" cat, but it's only the toes that are extra, not the whole paw. Other nicknames include "boxers" or "boxing cats," "mitten cats," "thumb cats," or "six-finger cats." Normally, cats have five toes on each of the front paws and four on each of the hind paws, but some cats are blessed with extra toes, especially on the front feet. Some owners feel that these cats, due to their extra digits, may demonstrate a higher degree of manual dexterity, which will allow them to open latches and drawers and in general be able to access more places than can cats with normal paws.

Ernest Hemingway and Teddy Roosevelt both had polydactyl cats named Prince Six Toes and Slippers, respectively.

 The Annual Vet Visit

The annual visit will include a nose-to-tail checkup, which generally includes:

- weighing in
- temperature check
- inspection of teeth and gums
- check of eyes, nose, and ears for abnormal discharges and other problems
- checking the skin for abscesses and parasites
- fecal exam for worms and other internal parasites
- palpating the cat's internal organs

Any necessary vaccinations or booster shots will also be given. If something sparks your vet's concern, he may ask for a blood test, chemistry panel, urinalysis, or urine culture.

LAB TESTS

Your vet may require lab tests from time to time to get a proper diagnosis. Here are some normal values for cats:

- temperature: 101.5°F (36.8°C)
- heart rate: 120–140 beats per minute
- resting respiratory rate: 16–40 breaths per minute

URINALYSIS

Your vet may do a urinalysis, usually to evaluate kidney function. It can evaluate for pyuria (white blood cells in the urine); hematuria (blood in the urine); crystalluria (crystals in the urine); the presence of abnormal amounts of glucose, ketones, and protein; and urine concentration.

Your cat's mileage may vary. Talk to your vet about what it may mean if your cat shows abnormal values.

FECAL EXAM

An annual fecal exam is recommended to screen for intestinal parasites. Kittens are examined twice, once at about nine weeks of age and then again a month later. Cats, especially those who spend time outdoors, should have a yearly test. Fecal exams are also a routine step in diagnosing the cause of diarrhea or vomiting. Treatment will depend on the specific type of parasite and the age and condition of the cat.

BLOOD PANELS

The blood chemistry panel is a vital tool in the diagnosis of many cat diseases. Most vets also recommend routine blood testing for kittens or newly acquired adults to screen for feline leukemia virus infection as well as feline immunodeficiency virus.

 Vaccinations

This is a topic fraught with contention. Ideas about when to vaccinate, what to vaccinate for, and which cats to vaccinate are changing constantly. Guidelines for the vaccination of cats have been strongly influenced by the appearance of vaccine-associated sarcomas (cancers), especially with feline leukemia virus vaccines and killed rabies virus vaccines.

Your vet is your best friend with regard to this issue. However, the AVMA places all vaccines into one of two categories: core (recommended for all cats) or noncore (recommended only for some cats).

Core vaccines are those that protect against rabies, panleukopenia (feline distemper), and the respiratory viruses, which are the herpes virus (which causes rhinotracheitis) and calicivirus. These vaccines are in the core category because they are safe, effective, and the diseases they protect against are severe (rabies and panleukopenia) or easily transmitted (the respiratory viruses). The core vaccines, minus rabies, are often combined into one vaccine referred to as FVRCP.

The panel recommends noncore vaccines only for those cats with a significant risk of exposure to the particular infectious disease the vaccine protects against. The AVMA panel on vaccination recommends the following protocols.

FELINE CORE VACCINES

These are vaccines recommended for all or most cats: feline herpes virus 1 (FHV1), feline calicivirus (FCV), feline panleukopenia virus (FPV), and rabies.

For the initial kitten vaccination series (under 16 weeks): one dose of vaccine containing modified live virus (MLV) FHV1, FCV, and FPV is recommended at 6 to 8 weeks, 9 to 11 weeks, and 12 to 16 weeks of age.

For cats older than 16 weeks of age, one dose of vaccine containing FHV1, FCV, and FPV is recommended. After a booster at one year, revaccination is suggested every three years thereafter for cats at low risk of exposure.

Interview the Veterinary Staff, Too

Remember that few vets are loners these days. Most of them work with partners, veterinary technicians, nurses, or other assistants. So it's important to evaluate the entire staff, including the people at the front desk, whose attitude and competence really make a difference.

Signs of a Healthy Cat

- normal activity and exercise
- normal, elastic gait
- normal appetite and thirst
- able to swallow without difficulty
- regular weight (no unexplained weight loss or gain)
- normal bowel movements
- healthy pink gums
- clean smell
- clear, bright eyes
- clean, odor-free ears
- flea and tick free
- clean, soft coat
- normal breathing (no sneezing, coughing, or labored breathing)
- uses litter box regularly
- does not vomit or regurgitate food
- does not have seizures

According to recommendations of the vaccine-associated sarcoma task force, these vaccines are administered over the right shoulder.

FELINE RABIES VIRUS VACCINES

Kittens should receive a single dose of killed or recombinant rabies vaccine at 12 to16 weeks of age. Adult cats with unknown vaccination history should also receive a single dose of killed or recombinant rabies vaccine. For the recombinant vaccines, boosters are recommended at yearly intervals. The recombinant rabies vaccine is theoretically less likely to be associated with sarcomas. For the killed rabies vaccines, a booster is required at one year, and thereafter, rabies vaccination should be performed every three years using a vaccine approved for three-year administration. According to recommendations of the vaccine-associated sarcoma task force, rabies vaccines are administered subcutaneously as distally (low down) as possible in the right rear limb.

FELINE NONCORE VACCINES

Optional or noncore vaccines for cats include: feline leukemia virus, feline immunodeficiency virus, feline infectious peritonitis, and vaccines for *Chlamydophila felis*, *Bordetella bronchiseptica*, and Giardia. The AVMA panel considers the feline infectious peritonitis (FIP) vaccine noncore because only cats who come into close contact with other cats have a significant risk of exposure. Most of the panelists recommend the FIP vaccine only for cats living in a specific high-risk situation such as cats in a multi-cat household, cattery, or shelter.

The feline leukemia virus (FeLV) vaccine is noncore because only outdoor cats and cats living with a FeLV-positive cat are exposed to the virus. However, some panel members recommend vaccinating all kittens against the leukemia virus. Most vets also recommend that all multiple-cat households and cats going outdoors be vaccinated. They also recommend that all cats be tested for leukemia virus.

FELINE LEUKEMIA VIRUS (FeLV) VACCINE

A number of FeLV vaccines are available on the market, and many have reasonable efficacy. It is generally suggested that outdoor cats be vaccinated against FeLV. Vaccination is most likely to be useful in kittens and young adult cats; acquired resistance to infection develops beyond 16 weeks of age. Vaccination is not recommended for FeLV-positive cats and indoor cats with no likelihood of exposure to FeLV, especially for cats older than 16 weeks of age. Initially, two doses of vaccine are given at two- to four-week intervals, after which annual boosters are recommended. According to recommendations of the vaccine-associated sarcoma task force, FeLV vaccines are administered subcutaneously as distally as possible in the left rear limb.

FELINE IMMUNODEFICIENCY VIRUS (FIV) VACCINE

The FIV vaccine is an inactivated vaccine that was released in July 2002. Questions remain regarding the vaccine's ability to protect against all FIV subtypes and strains to which cats might be exposed. Therefore, the decision regarding whether to use this vaccine is not straightforward, and the risks and benefits of its use should be carefully discussed with your vet. Its routine use in indoor cats is not recommended.

FELINE INFECTIOUS PERITONITIS (FIP) VACCINE

The FIP vaccine is an intranasal modified live virus product. The efficacy of this vaccine is controversial, and duration of immunity is short. Although exposure to feline coronaviruses in the cat population is high, the incidence of FIP is very low, especially in single-cat households (1 in 5,000). Most cats in situations where FIP is a problem become infected with coronaviruses before 16 weeks of age, which is the age at which vaccination is first recommended. It is not generally recommended to routinely vaccinate household cats with the FIP vaccine.

FELINE CHLAMYDOPHILA FELIS VACCINE

Chlamydophila felis causes conjunctivitis in cats; however, this disease responds readily to antimicrobial treatment. Immunity induced by vaccination is probably of short duration, and the vaccine provides only incomplete protection.

FELINE BORDETELLA BRONCHISEPTICA VACCINE

This is a modified live intranasal vaccine. *Bordetella bronchiseptica* is primarily a problem of very young kittens, in whom it can cause severe lower respiratory tract disease. It appears to be uncommon in adult cats and pet cats in general and should respond readily to antibiotics in older cats. The vaccine could be considered for young

Annual veterinary checkups and up-to-date vaccinations are essential if you want your cat to stay healthy.

cats at high risk of exposure in large, multiple-cat environments.

FELINE GIARDIA VACCINE

A killed giardia vaccine has been marketed for use in cats, but it has limited use and may induce vaccine-associated sarcomas. Not recommended.

Spaying and Neutering

Responsible pet owners spay and neuter their cats. There are simply too many cats in the world and not enough good homes for them all. While there are many responsible cat breeders in the world, it's by far the best idea for nearly everyone to get their pets altered. Pregnancy is a risky business at any time—I love my girls much too much to risk their lives. If I want a cute kitten, I know where I can get a dozen of them: at my local shelter.

Unneutered male cats will spray in the house and, if you let them out, they will get into fights and come home (if they come home at all) with torn ears and abscesses. Who needs that? Neutered males are at a low to zero risk for testicular cancer, prostate disease, certain hernias, and some skin diseases.

In addition, breeding cats is expensive and time consuming. There is a risk the mother may abort or miscarry, or that the kittens will be born deformed. The mother may also reject the kittens, and you will have to bottle-feed them around the clock. If all the kittens live, you must find homes for them, but what happens if you can't? Or what if you do, and the owners decide to give them back to you a few years later? Or you discover that they are being badly treated? Having your cat altered will save you all that emotional stress.

Female cats should be altered before their first heat. You'll not only avoid the chance of an accidental pregnancy, but you will practically eliminate the chances of your cat developing mammary cancer. Unspayed cats may develop a severe uterine disease called pyometra, in which the uterus becomes full of pus. It's best to avoid all these unnecessary medical problems whenever possible.

The Aging Cat

It's always fun to compare a cat's age to a human's, but you'd have to use a sliding scale. It used to be said that one "cat year" equals seven human years, but that doesn't make sense at all. A one-year-old cat is almost full grown; a seven-year-old human is still a small child. A 1-year-old cat actually corresponds to a 15-year-old human, a 2-year old to a 25-year-old. After that, each cat year corresponds to approximately four human years.

Like people, cats age differently. Some cats are "old" at 8 or 9 (that's about 55 for us). Others are quite active well into their teen years. Part of the difference depends on their genetic heritage and part upon the care you give them. This includes plenty of clean fresh water, proper nutrition, attention, and exercise.

PHYSICAL CHANGES

Some significant differences are apparent between older cats and their younger counterparts. In general, older cats:

- have a weaker immune system
- are prone to hyperthyroidism
- may have high blood pressure
- can dehydrate more easily
- are prone to dental problems
- have thinner, less elastic, more easily infected skin
- have impaired kidney function
- are more prone to inflammatory bowel disease

Older cats are usually less active than ther younger counter parts.

- groom themselves less often and less efficiently
- are more prone to diabetes
- are more prone to cancer
- have some degenerative joint disease
- have thicker, more brittle claws
- may be less alert and more easily confused

To help your older cat, try to brush her fur daily, especially in cats with long or thick hair. This will remove loose hair and mats than can injure her sensitive skin. Be sure to check the claws too, as they tend to thicken in older cats. They may need trimming.

Dental disease is also more common in older cats. Studies also show that 70 percent of all cats show signs of gum disease by age three. Signs include yellow and brown buildup of tartar along the gum line, red inflamed gums, and persistent bad breath. Dental disease can cause such pain that your cat may even exhibit behavior changes due to her sore mouth, such as reluctance to eat or dropping food. Keep on brushing your cat's teeth and take her to a regular dental appointment at least once every six months.

BEHAVIORAL CHANGES

Many older cats exhibit behavioral changes. But the good news is that 80 percent of behavior changes in geriatric cats have an underlying medical condition that can be effectively treated.

Older cats are usually less active than their younger counterparts. Their immune system is weaker, and their skin is less elastic, making them more prone to infections and skin problems. Some seniors may experience partial or total hearing loss. While many older cats develop a haziness around the iris, their vision is not necessarily impaired. However, cats with high blood pressure commonly do suffer some vision loss. All of these impairments may cause changes in your cat's normal routine.

Senior cats may also develop arthritis and, while they don't show the lameness characteristic of dogs and people, they do get stiff and may have trouble accessing their litter boxes. Your fussy older cat needs (and may insist upon) a clean litter box. Clean it thoroughly once or twice a day. As cats age, they often have more difficulty with small, dry stools. If you notice this in your cat's litter box, encourage the cat to drink more water (even if you have to flavor it with broth).

Because older cats are less likely to groom themselves than younger ones, it becomes much more important that you groom your feline and inspect her coat regularly. The claws of older cats often become thicker and even brittle; be sure to examine them regularly and trim them when necessary.

Like older people, aging cats may experience memory loss and show signs of senility, including:

- excessive vocalization
- mewing
- disorientation
- wandering
- avoidance of contact

SPECIAL DIETARY NEEDS

Good nutrition is more important than ever as your cat ages. Select a senior cat food with balanced nutrients. Older cats especially benefit from canned food and its higher water content. (Older cats tend to drink less.) Weight

The oldest cat on record lived to the ripe old age of 36. That's almost scary.

control is critical and highly individual. Some older cats need lower calorie, high-fiber diets to prevent obesity. Others need higher calorie diets to maintain or increase their body weight. If your cat seems disinclined to eat, try warming her food in the microwave. (You may have to leave the kitchen, though.) You may also need to use, at least for the short term, an appetite stimulant.

Potassium is of special importance for the older cat. This critical electrolyte is important for muscle strength. It has been found that a mild form of hypokalemia (low blood potassium) has been identified in many older cats resulting in poor appetite and weakness. All this used to be attributed to the aging process. Now, low potassium is suspected. It's actually rather hard to identify if cats are low in potassium because, while potassium in the blood can be normal, it can still be lacking in the body. Not only that, but we know that a lot of potassium is lost in cats with poor kidney health (a common problem in older felines). In a chicken-and-egg kind of scenario, the low potassium also has an adverse effect on the kidneys. The good news is that you can add potassium to your older cat's diet via a tablet or powder. Talk to your veterinarian.

Cancer, followed by kidney disease, is the most common ailment of older cats.

Like people, cats age differently, but they are generally considered seniors at around age eight or so.

EXTRA VETERINARY CHECKUPS

To keep your older cat healthy as long as possible, make sure she gets frequent medical checkups. If something is starting to go wrong, it may be treatable if spotted early enough. A thorough geriatric physical exam will include:

- exam and medical history
- complete blood count
- chemical panel
- fecal exam
- urinalysis
- thyroid level test
- testing for feline immunodeficiency virus (FIV) and feline leukemia virus (FELV)

These tests may point out the common problems of geriatric pets, which include:

- obesity or other nutritional disorders
- dental disease
- hyperthyroidism
- kidney disease
- diabetes
- heart disease
- inflammatory bowel disease
- tumors and cancer

Genetics, life history, and environment will all play a part in determining how your cat will age.

🐈 Life Insurance

You are your cat's best friend, and you owe it to her to provide her with the best care possible for her entire life. Providing her with appropriate daily care, regular veterinary checkups, vaccinations, and lots of love will ensure that your feline companion will be a healthy and happy member of the family for years to come.

Chapter Nine

Feline Illnesses & Diseases

"A cat is a cat is a cat."

— e.e. cummings

"And a sick cat is no fun at all."

—Diane Morgan

Unbelievable as it seems, cats are mortal beings. And the chief price of mortality is sickness. Every organ of a cat can be affected by some failure, injury, or virus. We don't have the room to talk about every ailment your cat can suffer, but we'll target the major problem areas.

🐈 Signs of Illness

Every disease is different. Some cause obvious and alarming signs of illness, while others present themselves more subtly. Some actually have no visible signs at all until the condition is far advanced, while some very scary looking signs may actually represent only a mild disease. Some subtle signs may signal something quite serious. This is a very convincing reason why regular vets checks are important—and why it is important for you to talk to your veterinarian whenever you notice something is "not quite right" about your cat.

Here are some typical signs of illness or disease in cats:

- abnormal bowel movements
- abnormal distension of the abdomen
- abnormal vocalizing
- bad odor from mouth
- bleeding
- blood in stool or urine
- bloodshot eyes
- bloody nose
- change in color of mucous membranes
- change in temperament
- diarrhea
- difficulty or abnormality in movement
- difficulty or straining to urinate or defecate
- eye twitching
- lameness
- loss of appetite
- loss of balance
- lumps and bumps
- poor coat or skin

Signs vs. Symptoms

While we often use the words "signs" and "symptoms" interchangeably, technically, only people have symptoms because the word properly refers to the subjective feeling that accompanies a "sign." If cats could talk, they'd have symptoms too.

- rapid breathing
- seizures
- swollen face, neck, rectum, or mammary glands
- unexplained weight loss
- vaginal discharge
- vomiting

Common Health Concerns

While cats are generally healthy creatures, they, like the rest of creation, can fall prey to various structural defects, bugs, bacteria, viruses, accidents, and other ills. As a careful and caring owner, it's part of your responsibility to be aware of what's "out there."

Ear wax (cerumen) in cats is dark brown. In some diseases, such as infection, the cat produces an over-abundance of ear wax.

EAR AILMENTS

Cats are some of the best "hearers" in the business. Like all night hunters, they must be alert to every rustle in the bushes. Ears are also delicate structures, and when something is the matter with them, they can be extremely painful or itchy. Luckily, most ear ailments in cats present obvious signs that any good cat owner will notice.

The inside of normal feline ear should have very few hairs and be faintly pink or parchment in color. They should not be particularly moist. There should be no large accumulation of dirt or wax.

EAR INFECTION

An ear infection means than some fungus, mite, or bacteria has taken up its abode in your cat's ear. While infections of the outer ear (*otitis externa*) are very common in dogs, they are fairly rare in cats. Persians seem more prone to them than other breeds. Because the average healthy cat seems quite resistant to ear infections, an infection may indicate a problem with the immune system.

Cause: Several kinds of bacteria and

As a responsible pet owner, you need to be alert for any signs of illness and act quickly if you think your cat is sick.

at least one type of fungus might cause an ear infection. It may also be caused by a foreign body, tumor in the ear canal, or ear mites.

Signs: Signs of ear infection include head shaking, red or inflamed ears, foul odor, or a black or yellow discharge. Chronic infection could lead to a closed ear canal.

Treatment: Don't try to medicate your cat yourself. Take your cat to a vet who can examine her with an otoscope and get a sample of the discharge. Your vet can prescribe the proper medication after an examination and perhaps an ear culture.

EAR MITES (OTODECTES CYNOTIS)

Ear mites are tiny organisms that resemble ticks. They are extremely common in cats, especially in kittens and outdoor cats. In fact, ear mites are the most common cause of outer ear inflammation in felines. Some cats are extremely sensitive to just a few mites; others seem unbothered by large numbers. But few or many, they are not doing your cat any good, so get rid of them.

The mites themselves are too tiny to be easily seen by the naked eye, although people with good eyes can see tiny white dots.

Most ear ailments in cats present obvious signs that any good cat owner will notice, such as scratching at the ears and head shaking.

They typically inhabit the surface of the ear canal, munching away on ear wax and other secretions. They can also be found on other areas of the body or in the environment. (They do not burrow into the skin, however.) If the mites are not treated, they can facilitate problems such as yeast and bacterial secondary infections over the long term, or they may even puncture the eardrum.

Causes: Ear mites are transmitted from host to host by physical contact. These things are very contagious, by the way, even between species. It is possible, but not very likely, for you to get ear mites from your cat.

Signs: You can usually tell if your cat has ear mites. Your cat may start shaking her head a lot and scratching at her ears, which are filled with debris that looks like coffee grounds (that's waste product from the mites). The insides of the ears will look dirty, usually with these dark brown or reddish-brown granules. Sometimes a black crust forms, as well. This crust can clog the ear canal over time.

Cats can shake their heads so violently from ear mites that they can develop a hematoma or large blood blister, owing to rupture of a small blood vessel. This usually occurs on the inner, concave, side of the ear. If this occurs, take your cat to the vet. Sometimes the tissue can be reabsorbed (although there is usually scarring), but surgery may be needed.

Treatment: Because mites are so easily transmissible by physical contact, treatment for mites often must include all household pets. Treatment of the home, however, is not necessary.

Your vet can give you a good prescription product to treat the mites. Some over-the-counter products are also available, but most of these must be used for 21 days, over the entire life of the ear mite. Treatment includes flushing out the ears and treating the cat with medication. Other animals in the household should be treated, even if they show no overt signs of infestation.

DEAFNESS

Partial or total hearing impairment is not uncommon in cats. The cause is often congenital, but certain disease conditions can also produce it.

Causes: Hearing loss in cats falls into three general categories, each with a different cause.

- *Aging:* Hearing loss often exists in older cats, resulting from a combination of nerve damage and the fusing together of the bones of the inner ear.
- *Conduction Deafness:* This type of deafness is caused by tumors and/or infection (otitis). Conduction deafness may be reversible by treating the root cause.
- *Nerve Deafness:* This type of deafness can be congenital, as in the case of blue-eyed white cats, or acquired, through drugs toxic to cats' ears, or neoplasias (tumor-like growths).

Signs: Because cats can compensate for early degrees of hearing loss, their human companions may be unaware of the problem until complete deafness occurs. By being attentive, you may spot the following symptoms: failure to respond when spoken to or called, easily startled, very loud meowing, signs of dizziness or disorientation, shaking the head or clawing at the ear (may also be indicative of ear infection or mites), pus or other drainage from the ear, unpleasant odor about ears, or pink or scaly areas at the tips of the ears (in white cats or cats with light colored ears).

Treatment: There is no treatment for deaf cats, but most of the time, your cat will manage perfectly well.

199

EAR WOUNDS

Cats who go outside may frequently be bitten by other cats and receive a wound or tear in the ear. These frequently become infected and can be treated with ordinary antibiotics.

EYE AILMENTS

While the eye of the cat is a beautiful and mysterious object, it can also fall victim to various disease conditions, just as our own can.

ANTERIOR UVEITIS

Anterior uveitis, a common condition in cats, is an inflammation of the fluid chamber in the front part of the eye. It also involves the iris and the tissues surrounding it.

Causes: Anterior uveitis may be caused by trauma or generalized disease like high blood pressure, infection, cancer, or blood coagulation disorders.

Signs: Signs include eye color change, bloodshot appearance, tears, or a partially or fully closed eye. In some cases, the eye may be bloody or even blind.

Treatment: Because this condition can be confused with conjunctivitis, the veterinarian will want to differentiate it from other causes. Treatment depends on the underlying disease. Therapy is with medications by eye drop, mouth, or injection. They include steroids, nonsteroidal anti-inflammatory drugs (NSAIDs), or antibiotics. The cat may also need treatment for glaucoma. The prognosis depends on the cause and severity of the disease.

BLINDNESS

Blindness refers to a total lack of vision. Most blind cats can adjust perfectly well to a state of "lights-out." After all, they are nocturnal! In the first place, there are degrees of blindness, and many blind cats are not totally blind. In addition, the loss of sight is usually gradual, giving the animal time to adjust to her altered state. Sudden blindness poses more of a challenge, with cats losing their litter box training or being reluctant to leave their beds. Blind cats may also be more skittish and aggressive, with a tendency to lash out now and ask questions later. You can hardly blame them.

Once a blind cat becomes accustomed to her new world, she can maneuver around the house, often memorizing distances between objects in the home environment and jumping from one to another. That's why it is critical not to rearrange the furniture. And of course you should not let your blind cat wander outside, even if she was formerly an indoor-outdoor cat. You can

An established link exists between white coat color, blue eyes, and deafness in cats. However, not all blue-eyed white cats are deaf; several different genes causing the same physical attributes are in play here. Still, congenital deafness is extremely rare in non-white cats. A blue-eyed white cat is not the same as an albino cat with washed-out blue eyes, although it's hard to tell the difference by looking.

Deafness can result from effects of the dominant white (W) gene. Dominant white masks all other eye colors, and cats may have blue or orange eyes, or one of each. Those with blue eyes are much more likely to be deaf than those with, say, orange eyes. If a white cat has one blue eye, she is likely to be deaf on that side. Cats carrying the W gene are not always solid white; many have colored spots on their heads that may disappear with age.

A dominant piebald or white-spotting gene (S) is also found in various cat breeds, but apparently deafness is not associated with this gene. Longhaired cats have a higher prevalence of blue eyes and deafness than do shorthaired cats. White cats carrying the underlying CS Siamese dilution pigment gene can have blue eyes without deafness, and it is thought that the presence of this gene explains why purebred white cats are less often deaf than mixed-breed white cats.

Purebred cats carrying the white (W) coat pigment gene include:

- White
- White Scottish Fold
- European White
- Norwegian Forest Cats
- White Turkish Angora
- Foreign White
- White American Wirehair
- White Cornish Rex
- White American Shorthair
- White Devon Rex
- White British Shorthair
- White Manx
- White Exotic Shorthair
- White Persian
- White Oriental Shorthair

enrich your blind cat's life with belled toys and plenty of catnip. If you have other cats, they will soon figure out that Susie is blind and amazingly become quite tolerant of her.

Signs: The actual onset of blindness may be difficult to pinpoint because a cat's senses of hearing and smell can often compensate for a decrease in vision. Cats will learn to accommodate their disability by relying on hearing, scent, and memory. Whiskers also come in especially handy! (The whiskers on blind cats can actually wear down with overuse.)

Causes: Some cats are born disabled and others have suffered accidents or the degenerative effects of old age. Some kinds of blindness are caused by untreated feline hypertension. A disabled cat can still lead a full and enjoyable life, given a chance and an understanding owner. Other common causes of blindness are chlamydia and mycoplasma. More than one causative agent may be present.

Signs: In cases of sudden blindness, the cat will start bumping into things. (Sudden blindness is an emergency.) Gradual onset of blindness is harder to spot because, being quite intelligent, your cat will learn the layout of furniture and adjust to it.

Treatment: Treatment will depend on the cause and may include various medications. Feline herpes virus (FHV-1) and chlamydia infection, however, can be chronic conditions. (FHV-1 cannot be transmitted to people; it is a species-specific virus.)

Cataracts

Cataracts are an opacity or cloudiness of the lens of the eye.

Causes: They can result from inheritance (primarily seen in younger cats), following an injury to the eye, or as a degenerative condition in older cats.

Treatment: Surgical removal is the only known treatment for cataracts. When left untreated, they can lead to glaucoma.

Conjunctivitis

Conjunctivitis is swelling and inflammation of the tissues around the eyeball, the lining of the eyelids, and the third eyelid. It may occur in one or both eyes. The problem may come and go. Conjunctivitis is the most common ailment affecting the eye of the cat. Young kittens are most commonly affected. In most cases, an infected kitten also has a respiratory infection. Cats with Persian-type faces are also more prone to conjunctivitis.

Causes: The eye can become irritated due to allergies induced by pollens or grasses, or from infections caused by viruses, bacteria, or fungi. If the white portion of the eyeball (sclera) is also inflamed, this condition is occasionally referred to as "pink eye."

Infection can also be caused by FHV-1. About 80 percent of infected cats eventually become long-term (chronic) carriers of the virus.

Signs: The major signs are redness, watery eyes, mucoid discharge, and squinting. The cat may show signs of upper respiratory discharge.

Treatment: Treatment of conjunctivitis can be difficult, and the disease may resurface. Your veterinarian must examine the cat, search for causes, and prescribe the correct medication. FHV-1 conjunctivitis cannot be cured, although some treatment options are available. Talk to your vet.

CORNEAL ULCERS

The cornea is a layered, clear membrane that makes up the surface of the eyeball. An ulcer is an erosion that goes through it.

Signs: Most affected cats keep their eyes squeezed shut. There may be a discharge. Corneal ulcers are very painful, and cats may try to rub the eye with their paw.

Causes: Trauma, possibly obtained from a cat rubbing her eye on the carpet, can cause ulceration. It may also be caused by a chemical burn, such as from a harsh shampoo. The FHV-1 or other pathogens may also cause it.

The onset of blindness may be difficult to pinpoint because a cat's senses of hearing and smell can often compensate for a decrease in vision.

Treatment: Treatment depends on the cause. Abrasion may heal in a few days, but your cat needs medication like atropine for pain and to prevent infection. Sometimes the vet will stitch the eye shut for a few days to promote healing.

If a virus is the cause, cats are immediately put on antiviral medications; antibiotics are also often added along with pain relievers.

GLAUCOMA

Glaucoma is a condition characterized by abnormally high pressure within the eye. It is really a disorder of the outflow of fluid (aqueous humor) from the eye, not initial overproduction of the fluid. In other words, the fluid is not

A cat's eyes should be clean, clear, and free of any discharge or tearing.

able to drain away properly. The high pressure causes damage to the optic nerve, which eventually causes blindness. It may be the most common cause of blindness in cats.

Causes: Sometimes (rarely) glaucoma arises spontaneously, that is, with no discernible cause. This is called primary glaucoma (common in dogs). Cats are more likely to be victim of secondary glaucoma; it can be caused by inflammation, lens luxation, (dislocations), or even a tumor (in which case only one eye is usually affected). Lens luxations usually only occur in the cat with chronic anterior uveitis

Signs: Signs include red or cloudy, painful eyes, squinting, tearing, dilated pupils, vision loss, and an enlarged eye.

Treatment: In early stages, glaucoma can be treated with medication to decrease the production of fluids inside the eye and to control inflammation. Later cases require surgery, sometimes using laser therapy or cryotherapy (freezing). This will not restore vision, but will reduce or eliminate pain. If the glaucoma is caused by a luxated lens, the lens can be removed. A calcium channel blocker has recently been developed that may help prevent damage to the retina and optic nerve. If medications are given, it is important that they be administered precisely as prescribed.

PROGRESSIVE RETINAL ATROPHY

Progressive retinal atrophy (PRA) is a term for a collection of untreatable eye diseases that will slowly lead to total blindness.

Cause: PRA has a genetic component, and kittens whose parents have no history of the disease are at less risk of developing it.

Signs: PRA is not painful; the eye will have a normal appearance, especially in the early stages. The cat may show a reluctance to navigate stairs, especially at night. As the disease progresses, you may notice a dilation of the pupils and the reflection of light from the back of the eye. The lens of some cats may become opaque or cloudy.

Treatment: There is no way to treat this condition, or even to slow its progress.

TUMORS OF THE EYE

Tumors in the eye can include melanoma and eyelid tumors. While eyelid tumors are less common in cats than in dogs, when they do appear, they are more likely to be malignant. Squamous cell carcinoma (SCC) is the most frequent type of eyelid tumor in the cat. Lymphosarcoma and mast cell tumors may also appear.

Causes: The causes are not known.

Signs: The signs include swelling and mass formation on the eyelid surface or eyelid margin, ulcerated or red area on eyelid margin, tearing, discharge from the eye, conjunctivitis, cloudy eye, rubbing of the eye, bleeding from the area, and squinting.

Treatment: The recommended treatment is surgical removal. In some cases, the whole eye must be removed. Certain types may respond to medical therapy or cryotherapy (freezing).

ORAL/DENTAL DISEASES

Dental disease of all sorts is common in cats, especially as they age. Good dental care can help reduce its incidence. Almost nothing hurts more than a toothache, which is why it is essential to make sure your cat gets regular dental checkups. You certainly don't want to commit her to a lifetime of pain.

MALOCCLUSION

Malocclusion describes teeth that are not correctly positioned in the mouth. This can traumatize the soft tissue in the mouth.

Cause: Malocclusion occurs in young cats whose teeth do not erupt properly; it can also occur from trauma.

Signs: Two of the same kind of teeth should never try to occupy the same position in the mouth. If there are, the cat has malocclusion. If it is caused by developing teeth, it will appear in cats between the ages of 14 and 24 weeks of age.

PERIODONTAL DISEASE

In this condition, bacteria combine with saliva and food particles to form plaque, which combines with calcium salts and turns into rock-hard tartar. Eventually, the bacteria work their way into the gums and even the jawbone. This periodontal disease is both severe and irreversible. If the bacteria get into the bloodstream, they can infect the heart, liver, and kidneys. Studies show that 70 percent of cats show signs of gum disease by age three. Oral disease is common in cats infected with feline leukemia virus (FeLV), feline immunodeficiency virus (FIV), and feline calicivirus (FCV).

Causes: Poor dental care and the accumulation of food particles and bacteria are the main causes.

Signs: Signs of periodontal disease include red, swollen, bleeding, or receding gums, mouth pain, and bad breath (not fishy bad breath, but rotting-meat bad breath).

Treatment: Periodontal disease may be irreversible; you must take the cat to the vet for tooth cleaning and treatment.

FELINE DENTAL RESORPTION

Also called cervical line lesions, this is the most common dental disease of domestic cats, even though it largely went unrecognized until the 1970s. In this disease, lesions often begin below the gumline and develop undetected. The lesions are graded from I to V in order of severity.

Causes: The cause is unknown.

Signs: The first observable sign to the pet owner is a severely inflamed gum. This will eventually result in tooth loss. Take the cat to the vet if you notice something like this.

Treatment: In mild cases, the tooth may sometimes be restored with sealants that contain fluoride to strengthen the enamel. More serious cases are beyond treatment. Cats with a history of this problem should have a dental checkup every six months.

STOMATITIS AND GINGIVITIS

Stomatitis is an inflammation of the mucous membranes in the mouth, while gingivitis is an inflammation of the gums. Otherwise they are very similar. Siamese and domestic shorthairs may be more susceptible than other breeds, but this is debatable. When the disease occurs in cats of three to five months of age, it is called juvenile-onset stomatitis.

Causes: Multiple causes may be involved, including hypersensitivity or allergic reaction to bacterial plaque, immunosuppression, or possibly even

Cats can fracture a tooth—oddly enough, the first sign of a fractured tooth is sneezing. If left untreated, broken teeth will cause painful abscesses.

a food allergy. About 15 percent of cats with chronic oral inflammation are infected with FeLV, FIV, or both, so that is a connection worth exploring.

Signs: This disease can cause a great deal of pain. Affected cats have ulcers in the damaged area. The cat may become aggressive, irritable, or may show reluctance to eat.

Treatment: If regular dental care does not keep the problem under control, tooth extraction of all teeth behind the canines may be necessary.

EXTERNAL PARASITES

At one time, almost all cats and dogs in this country were flea and tick ridden. (So were people.) Nowadays, however, it is a simple matter to keep your cat parasite free. It is practically criminal not to.

FLEAS

Fleas are parasites of most mammals and are most abundant during warm, humid weather. In fact, flea larvae are killed by drying. The life span of each individual flea is about 6 to 12 months, but that hardly matters because they reproduce so fast. There are 250 species in the US, but only a few afflict dogs and cats. The most common is the well-named cat flea, *Ctenocephalides felis*. Rather oddly, this is also the most common flea found on dogs. And they can pass them between each other.

The adult flea lives most of its life on its host, and it lives by sucking blood. They are irritating because of their frequent bites. They also cause allergies and, in young kittens, can actually cause anemia if a large infestation is present. The cat flea also carries the larval stage of the tapeworm *Dipylidium caninum*, and they can carry disease as well. So get rid of them. (The female fleas are responsible for taking the most blood.)

Even if you don't actually see the fleas, the appearance of black "flea dirt" on your pet is a sure sign they are there. Because cats groom themselves so carefully, they eat all the fleas they can find. The adults live permanently on the cat, but the eggs drop off onto the carpet or wherever.

At any particular time, only about 1 to 5 percent of the flea population in the area consists of adults. The rest are eggs, larvae, and pupae hanging around the house and yard, so it helps to vacuum frequently. If your house is infested, you'll need to resort to foggers and sprays to eliminate them. Outside, they tend to hang around in shady places—sunlight kills them.

Prevention and Treatment: For effective control, the adult fleas must be killed and reinfestation from the environment must be prevented. Many products are available including collars, shampoos, sprays, liquids, foams,

Oral Hygiene and Infection

High glucose levels in the blood and urine create ideal environments for infection in several body tissues. Because dirty teeth are a common source of infection, and prevent insulin from working properly, your vet may want to clean your cat's teeth before any treatment begins.

powders, pills, and spot-ons. Talk to your vet about finding a product that is safe and effective for your cat.

Older flea preparations contain organophosphate, carbamate, pyrethroid, or pyrethrum insecticides. These are potentially toxic and are *not* safe for cats. However, some great modern topical repellents like Frontline and Advantage work sort of like a total-body flea collar. Frontline (Merial) kills adult fleas and is available both as a pump spray or spot-on. Advantage (Bayer) kills adult fleas and is available as a spot-on. These new products are safe because they act at receptors that are present only in insects not mammals. (Old-fashioned flea collars are not very effective and may cause unpleasant side effects in cats.)

Look for a long-acting treatment to kill adults on all the animals in the home, and also eliminate them from the environment. To keep your home flea-free, vacuum frequently. Sodium polyborate applied to rugs kills immature fleas by desiccation. If you have an infestation, use an insect development inhibitor to destroy the immature fleas. If your animals live completely indoors, no further treatment may be required.

There is absolutely no reason for the modern feline to be pestered by this outdated enemy.

TICKS

Ticks are bloodsucking arthropods (not insects), closely related to scorpions, spiders, and mites. If you see a tick on your cat, remove it as soon as possible to reduce the possibility of disease transmission. There are hundreds of species worldwide, but only two families live in the United States: the Ixodidae (hard tick) family and the Argasidae (soft tick) family. They are all nasty, and some carry Lyme disease, Ehrlichia, and Rocky Mountain spotted fever. One of the most serious tick-borne diseases is Cytauxzoonosis, a protozoal disease first reported in Missouri in 1976. It is carried by the American dog tick. It is about 95 percent fatal. The affected animal has no signs for about 20 days, then massive organ failure and bleeding occur. It is not really possible at present to treat this disease effectively, and you certainly don't want your cat coming down with it!

Signs: Ticks may appear on your cat's skin as a small, dark speck or, if swollen with blood, like a small growth

Treatment: The best way to get rid of ticks is to prevent their attaching to your cat in the first place. Several different options are available for tick control; Frontline Top Spot and ECTO-Foam are two of them. Talk to your vet and always be sure the product is labeled for cats. You may also want to treat the environment.

MANGE MITES

Mange is the common name for skin diseases caused by parasitic mites. Although uncommon in cats, several kinds can cause problems; the most common being the ear mite (*Otodectes cynotis*) discussed earlier. Other types of mange that can affect cats are feline scabies, demodectic mange, and walking dandruff (cheyletiellosis), to name a few.

Feline Scabies (Notoedric Mange): Feline scabies, *Notoedres cati*, acts much like its canine counterpart. These pests burrow deep into the skin, forming tunnels where they deposit their eggs. It affects cats of any age, breed, or color.

Cause: This mite is transmitted directly from cat to cat, and so is more common in outdoor cats.

Signs: Signs include severe itching or hair loss, starting on the head and neck and then spreading to the body. The mite lives its whole life on your cat, burrowing into the skin and laying her eggs as she goes. However, diagnosis of this condition cannot be made just by looking at it. Your vet will need to test the cat by performing a skin scraping.

Treatment: It is very important to use a feline-safe product to kill this mite. Don't use the same thing you did on the family dog. It will kill the mites all right, but might kill the cat too. The safest thing is to clip all long hair and bathe your cat with a gentle shampoo. Then apply a 2 to 3 percent lime sulfur dip (Lymdip). It smells nasty, but it works. Repeat once a week for six to eight weeks. Products that have been used safely on cats include amitraz, ivermectin, and Revolution.

All cats in the household should be treated because they may be harboring mites as well. You can get this kind of mange from your cat, but it will only itch for a little while. The mites don't really like you.

Demodectic Mange: All cats probably have small numbers of the Demodex mites that cause this allergic condition living in their skin, just like all pets (and humans) have small numbers of skin bacteria. In normal cats, the mange mites live quietly in the hair follicles without bothering anybody. But, in a few cases, they get out of control, with the numbers of mites multiplying to the point where they start to cause trouble, immune reactions, inflammation, irritation, and stimulation of the sebaceous glands. Mange can infect cats of all ages or breeds, although Burmese and Siamese seem most vulnerable. Even in them, however, it's not very common.

Causes: *Demodex cati* (which is long and graceful) and *Demodex gatoi* (which is fat and stubby) are the two Demodex mites of cats.

Signs: The disease can take two forms: localized and generalized. The

Fleas don't like high altitudes. So, if you live in Denver, you and your cat are most likely flea free.

localized form is the more common, with hair loss and scaly skin on the eyelids, head, ears, and neck. Itchy lesions may be present. The generalized form may also affect the body and legs and may be the result of a disease that is suppressing the immune system. It is diagnosed by skin scrapings.

Treatment: Treatment choices for the localized form include a topical antiparasitic medication. Oral medication is also available. If a cat develops the generalized form, your vet will probably try to determine the underlying condition. Lime sulphur dips are also available. You cannot get Demodex from your cat. (People have their own species of mange.)

Walking Dandruff (*Cheyletiella blakei*): *Cheyletiella* mites live right under the scales of the skin. And indeed, they look like dandruff, although you might need a magnifying glass to spot them. *Cheyletiella* mites are present all over the United States, so there's a chance your feline could become infested. Kittens are more susceptible than are older animals.

Causes/Transmission: The mite is transmitted by close contact with affected animals.

Signs: Because cats groom themselves so carefully, they may not show any overt signs of this parasite. Some can be detected by a fecal exam. Some cats have an itchy, flaky coat as a result of the mites.

Treatment: If you notice them, you can kill *Cheyletiella* mites with an insecticide, such as ivermectin, obtainable from your vet. You will also have to treat the bedding because this disease is very infectious. These mites can be transmitted to people and temporarily cause an itchy rash.

How to Remove Ticks Safely

To remove a tick, wear gloves to protect yourself. Then grasp the tick as close to the head as possible with tweezers (or a tick removal tool available from any pet supply store). Use steady pressure, and pull the tick straight out without twisting it. Drop the tick into alcohol or flush it down the toilet. Clean the wound with a disinfectant. Wash your hands thoroughly with soap and water, even if you did wear gloves.

Some cats are allergic to tick bites and develop a "hot spot" or inflammation that causes the cat to chew or lick the affected area until it becomes ulcerated. It is common for the spot where the tick was embedded to become irritated afterward (and no, the head did not get stuck in there). Touch it up with a little hydrocortisone spray to reduce the inflammation.

INTERNAL PARASITES

Not all parasites live visibly on the outside of the body. Those you can't see can be even more dangerous because the damage they do is invisible to you.

ROUNDWORMS (ASCARIDS)

Roundworms are the most common internal parasites of both cats and dogs. Cats are susceptible to two different varieties: *Toxascaris leonina* and *Toxocara*

Cats that come into contact with the outdoors, strays, or yard dwelling prey are at risk of developing internal parasites such as roundworms, heartworms, or intestinal protozoa.

cati. They are most likely to be spread during spring and summer. Females can produce 200,000 eggs in a day; these can exist in the soil for years. Roundworms can also cause disease in humans.

Cause/Transmission: Your cat may ingest infective roundworm eggs from the area in which she lives, or she may contract them by eating mice or other small animal hosts carrying worm larvae in their digestive tracts. Infection in kittens may occur through the mother's milk.

Signs: Roundworms cause a pot-bellied look and poor growth in kittens because they absorb food meant for the infested animal. They can also damage the lining of the intestine. In severe cases, the cat vomits, has scanty stools, and becomes weak. These worms are much more serious in kittens than adults.

The worms may be detected in the stool. They are big and white, and look sort of like spaghetti.

Treatment: Many dewormers kill roundworms (deworming can begin in kittens as young as three weeks). But most affect only the adult worms, leaving the migrating or encysted larvae untouched. That's why most deworming must be done again a few weeks later.

HOOKWORMS

Hookworms (*Ancylostoma braziliense, Uncinaria. stenocephala, Ancylostoma tubaeforme)* are found throughout North America. They are more common and more dangerous in dogs than in cats, but both species can acquire them. *A. braziliense* infects both dogs and cats. *A. tubaeforme* specializes in cats. The adult worms are small and live in the small intestine, where they attach themselves, feed on the host's blood, and lay eggs. (They possess large mouths with hook-like teeth, hence the name.) Hookworms feed at several places in the intestine each day, injecting an anti-clotting chemical. They can cause severe disease, and are most common in warm humid environment. The greatest danger is anemia. A diagnosis of hookworm is made by finding the eggs in feces. Feline hookworms do not infect people directly.

Cause/Transmission: The eggs are passed in the cat's feces into the soil where they can persist for months; the next cat can swallow the larvae when washing up after digging in the soil.

Signs: If anemia from hookworms is present, the gums will look pale, and the animal will become weak. Sometimes black, tarry stools can be seen. Growth in young animals is stunted, and the coat may appear dull and dry. Animals may become emaciated.

Treatment: Most dewormers that kill roundworms will also kill hookworms. The treatment is both safe and simple.

WHIPWORMS

Whipworm (*Trichuris serrata*) infections are rare in cats. If they do occur, the worms are usually present in small numbers, and signs of the infection are rarely present. There have been several cases of more serious infections, in which the cat had small amounts of blood in the stool and was anemic.

Cause/Transmission: A cat becomes infected by ingesting food or water contaminated with whipworm eggs. An infection is diagnosed by finding the eggs in the feces.

Signs: Almost none. In extremely rare cases, the cat may become anemic and have blood in the stool.

Treatment/Prevention: Currently, no US Food and Drug Administration (FDA)-approved medications are available for treating whipworm infections in cats. A cat with a confirmed diagnosis must be treated with medications other than traditional dewormers. To prevent exposure, litter boxes should be cleaned thoroughly and, if possible, allowed to dry in direct sunlight. Also, any feces in the yard should be picked up on a daily basis. Routine fecal examinations and deworming can help control this parasite in other areas where it may be a problem.

TAPEWORMS

Tapeworms (several species, including *Dipylidium caninum*) are flat, segmented worms that are transmitted to dogs and cats who ingest fleas or who hunt and eat rodents infested with tapeworms or fleas.

The adult form of *D. caninum* lives in cats, dogs, foxes, and sometimes people. The adult worm lives in the small intestine, where it hooks itself onto the intestinal wall and can grow to be 20 inches (51 cm) long. Tapeworms can be seen as chains of segments or single segments in the feces of infected animals; these segments resemble grains of rice.

Signs: Oddly enough, most common tapeworms do little damage to the cat. But they are disgusting. Who needs them?

Signs of an internal parasitic infection may include unexplained weight loss, diarrhea, vomiting, small white segments in the feces, and poor coat. Your vet can confirm infection and provide appropriate treatment.

Causes/Transmission: The lifecycle is rather complicated because it requires two hosts: the flea and the cat. But we don't need to go into all that.

Treatment: The most common treatment is a medication called praziquantel. The best way to prevent tapeworms is to have good flea control for your cat.

HEARTWORMS

Heartworms (*Dirofilaria immitis*) are long, slender parasites than can attain a length of 12 inches (30.5 cm). Normally they live floating in the right ventricle of the heart and nearby blood vessels. Because the cat's blood vessels are smaller than those of dogs, heartworms can do them even more damage. Cats with heartworm disease live in the same places that dogs with heartworm do, which is over the entire continent of North America. However, cats are more resistant to the disease and require more exposure to it to actually come down with it. According to some authorities, in contradistinction to dogs, mosquitoes that feed on cats don't infect other cats with heartworms, although there is disagreement on this point. However, most infected cats have only a half dozen worms or so. Yet, even a small number of worms can cause serious, even fatal disease. Heartworms generally live for only a couple of years in cats, and cure without any treatment is often common.

Causes/Transmission: Transmitted only by mosquito bites, heartworm is less common in cats than in dogs, and the cat is not considered a normal host for the parasite. However, it does occur, and it may be more common than previously realized. Male cats seem to be more susceptible to becoming infected than female cats.

Signs: Signs of heartworm vary. They may include coughing, difficulties in breathing (like asthma), vomiting, lack of appetite, and lethargy. In some cases, sudden death occurs, and no one ever knew anything was wrong.

The disease can be hard to diagnose in cats because the heartworms rarely release larvae into the circulatory system (blood analysis is the main test for heartworms in dogs).

Treatment/Prevention: Medications are available to prevent heartworm infection in cats. Cats given these prevention drugs have not shown signs of toxicity. However, no drug is approved for treating heartworms in cats. The drug used to treat heartworms in dogs is toxic to most cats. The worms are often left to die on their own, and owners keep their fingers crossed.

COCCIDIA

Coccidia, which are one-celled organisms (protozoa), come from fecal-contaminated soil. Most coccidia in cats are of the genus *Isospora*. This species is not infective of people (although some other strains of coccidia may be, as in toxoplasmosis). They multiply in the intestinal tract, most often in cats and kittens younger than six months of age. They can also occur in adults whose immune system is suppressed or in animals who are stressed. The coccidia lifecycle is very complicated and has many stages of development. However, prompt removal of feces helps prevent environmental contamination.

Causes/Transmission: Oocysts, or immature coccidian, are passed in the stool, therefore any infected kitten is infectious to others. In some cases, oocysts are swallowed by mice, and the host becomes infected.

Signs: The major sign of the disease is diarrhea, sometimes with blood and mucus in it. However, most infected cats have no signs at all. In serious cases, there may be vomiting, abdominal pain, and dehydration. Death is possible, especially in a young kitten.

The diagnosis of coccidia is made by identifying the tiny eggs in a fecal sample. This isn't easy—these eggs are much smaller than those of the average intestinal worm.

Treatment: No specific medicine will kill coccidia, although sulfa drugs or antibiotics used for 10-14 days inhibit their reproduction. Therefore, elimination of coccidia from the intestine is not rapid. Small kittens may need hospitalization.

GIARDIASIS

Have you heard of "traveler's diarrhea?" Well, that's *giardiasis*, and you don't have to travel to get it. Giardiasis is one of the most frequently occurring waterborne diseases in the US. The culprit is the one-celled parasite *Giardia lamblia*. It comes in two forms: the trophozoite and the cyst. Cats under three years of age are more often infected than are older cats.

Causes/Transmission: Most cats (and people too, because we can acquire the parasite) and other animals contract giardiasis by ingesting the parasitic cysts in feces-contaminated drinking water. Once they enter the animal, they

It is possible, although by no means certain, that cats and dogs can pass *Giardia* to humans.

Toxoplasmosis

One type of coccidia, a single-celled parasite called *Toxoplasma gondii*, causes a disease known as toxoplasmosis, which is of particular danger to pregnant women because it can cause disease in the fetus.

The most common source of infection for pregnant women is consuming improperly cooked meat (especially pork, lamb, and venison), not necessarily from contact with the feces of cats, despite the bad press cats have gotten. However, the clever pregnant woman will require her husband to clean out the cat litter box anyway. Always.

According to the Centers for Disease Control, more than 60 million people in the United States are infected with the toxoplasmosis parasite right now, but most have no symptoms. That's because of our great immune system.

live in the small intestine.

Signs: The major sign of giardiasis is acute diarrhea and pale, foul-smelling feces. (Not that cat feces smell good under the best of conditions.) However, most infections with *Giardia* are asymptomatic, meaning that the cat doesn't show signs of the disease. Approximately 4 percent of pet cats in North America are expected to have *Giardia* at any one time. Otherwise healthy animals seldom experience diarrhea or indeed any other symptoms unless they are exposed to a very high number of *Giardia*.

A very accurate test is used to diagnose this disease; it is done on the stool sample using enzyme-linked immunosorbent assay (ELISA) technology.

Treatment: Several antiparasitic drugs are available from your vet to treat *Giardia*. In general, the prognosis for giardiasis is good to excellent.

SKIN AILMENTS

ABSCESSES

The abscess is one of the most common afflictions of the outdoor cat. Most abscesses start out as cellulitis, an infection of the tissues under the skin. Soon however, the area fills with pus (accumulated white blood cells drawn to the area to fight the infection). Voila! You have an abscess. The organisms most often involved are *Pasteurella multocida* and *Streptococcus*, bacteria that need little or no oxygen.

Causes: Abscesses usually occur as the result of a quarrel with another cat. Cats are territorial animals, and such arguments over property lines are rather frequent. Males are the most likely victims (and perpetrators). Because cats' teeth are needle-sharp and tiny, they can make an infective puncture wound that heals over very quickly and does not drain. (When dogs fight, they tend to shake their heads while biting down, thus creating a laceration that will bleed out more cleanly. Cats just sink in their teeth.) Neutered animals, especially neutered males, are less apt to fight and, hence, to develop abscesses.

Signs: The abscess will be contained in a fibrous capsule in an attempt to keep the infection from reaching other tissues. There may be a loss of hair and dead skin over the spot. The first sign of an abscess may be swelling and pain in the area. The skin will feel hot. Eventually the abscess will rupture, and the pus will drain out.

Treatment: In some cases, abscesses heal quite nicely on their own, if you keep them open and clean and let them drain. You may wish to use a disinfectant like iodine or chlorhexidine to flush it out. A follow-up of antibiotics is also recommended, usually an inexpensive antibiotic like ampicillin or amoxicillin. (Your vet may be willing to prescribe them over the phone.) Antibiotics given within 24 hours will generally stop the spread of the infection. Warm compresses for 15 minutes three times a day are also a good idea.

For serious cases, you should consult a veterinarian, especially if the abscess continues to grow and does not rupture. The vet may wish to remove it surgically and insert a tube to help it drain. Aftercare is the same for an abscess that has ruptured at home.

Some abscesses do not respond well to standard therapy; in these cases, underlying or complicating factors such as FeLV infection may be present. Sometimes the abscess may be caused by some unusual organism that requires a different course of antibiotics.

ACNE

Just like a teenager, cats can get acne, although older and even senior cats seem most vulnerable. It is relatively common, but most cases are mild, localized, and actually pass unnoticed.

Signs: Acne usually looks like blackheads, sometimes progressing to pimples on the chin and lower lips.

Causes: Acne is caused by excessive production of sebum from the skin glands in the area. No one is sure why this happens. It might result from poor grooming habits, food allergies, dirty food bowls, immune system problems (eosinophilic granuloma complex), a condition secondary to ringworm or mange, or even an abnormality in the keratinization of the skin.

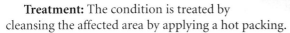

Treatment: The condition is treated by cleansing the affected area by applying a hot packing.

Use 2 tablespoonfuls (29.6 ml) of Epsom salt per quart (0.9 l) of water and apply a very moist warm compress for 5 to 10 minutes. Your vet may also prescribe oral antibiotics for three weeks or so.

Topical medications may also be prescribed and benzoyl peroxide shampoos (2.5 percent) recommended. Don't use the benzoyl peroxide gels made for people; the concentrations are usually 5 percent, which can be irritating to cats.

The condition usually clears up in a week or two with treatment. Remember to keep all food bowls scrupulously clean. There may be a recurrence of the problem; sometimes the only treatment is to control the excessive sebum production by daily cleansing with warm water, an antibacterial soap, and a washcloth. Don't try to pick at the pimples yourself because that will just spread the infection.

EOSINOPHILIC GRANULOMA COMPLEX

It's a mouthful, isn't it? Here's what it means. Eosinophils are a special type of white blood cell that the immune system uses to fight pathogens at the site of infection. Reacting to the presence of a foreign body, eosinophils will be sent to a particular spot of skin, and inflammation will occur. If all goes well, they

will conquer the invaders and fade away into the night. Sometimes, however, they hang around for a long time and the resultant inflammation can give rise to a lump that may then develop into a granuloma, a type of skin lesion that looks like a raised sore.

Cause: The actual cause is unknown—allergies, spider bites, self-licking, bacterial or viral infections are all suspect, but the mystery remains. It should be, because it refers to a whole collection of skin problems in cats. It can occur in different forms: eosinophilic ulcer, eosinophilic plaque, and eosinophilic granuloma. (A push is under way to discard some of this terminology as not being helpful or even accurate, despite being widely used.)

Signs: The eosinophilic ulcer usually occurs on the upper lip near the canine tooth. This doesn't become itchy, but it looks horrible. Often, it's impossible to tell where or how it originated. Eosinophilic plaque usually shows up as a raised, ulcerated, tough and scaly lesion on the abdomen or inner thigh. It is often seen in younger cats and may be an allergic reaction.

Treatment: Treatment depends on the cause (which is hard to figure) and may include antibiotics, corticosteroids, or surgery. The problem tends to recur in some cats.

Feline Miliary Dermatitis (Scabby Cat Disease, Feline Eczema, Blotch)

This syndrome is not actually a specific disease but a catch-all term for a whole set of symptoms.

Causes: Causes might include allergies (the most common cause by far); bacterial, yeast, or fungal infections; parasites; autoimmune diseases; nutritional disease; or hormonal abnormalities.

Signs: Small crusty bumps appear on the cat's skin. They may be confined to the head or the area where the tail meets the body, or they may cover a large area. They are usually itchy. The word "miliary" actually refers to millet seeds, to which the lesions bear a remarkable resemblance.

Treatment: While easy to diagnose, the treatment depends on finding the cause, which can be tricky. Obvious suspects like fleas, lice, and mites should be ruled out first. Ringworm is also possible, but it may take weeks to make sure (it takes a while to grow the culture in a lab). A fecal exam will test for internal parasites. The next step may be to test for a food allergy, in which case the cat will be put on a special diet to see if the scabs disappear.

In addition, the vet may want to try the cat on a course of antibiotic, antifungal, or steroid treatment. In some cases, he may even request a biopsy. In any case, adding a fatty acid and extra biotin to the cat's diet will help the skin heal.

Hair Loss (Alopecia)

Hair loss in cats occurs for a number of reasons.

Causes: Among the more common causes are psychogenic problems (stress), allergies, chemotherapy, demodectic mange, folliculitis, endocrine and hormonal problems, and as a secondary response to other diseases such as FIP, FeLV, ringworm, or fleas. Some pregnant animals lose hair as well.

Signs: Some cats scratch at the spot; others do not. Other signs may be present, depending on the cause of the hair loss.

Treatment: Treatment will obviously depend on the cause of the hair loss. Some hair loss doesn't need any treatment at all.

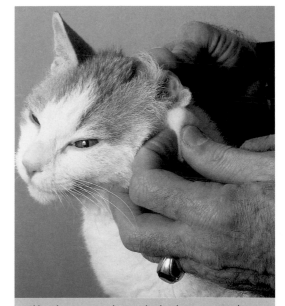

Although cats are sturdy animals, they have sensitive skin and are prone to a wide variety of skin conditions and ailments due to allergies, infections, or injuries. Examine your cat's body regularly.

RINGWORM

Ringworm (*Microsporum canis, Microsporum gypseum*, or *Trichophyton mentagrophytes*) is the most common infectious skin disease of cats. The name is confusing, however, because ringworm is not a worm at all but rather a fungus that favors high humidity and feeds on dead skin cells.

Cause/Transmission: It is transmitted through direct contact with infected spores (the skin comes into contact with the spore). Very young and old animals are most at risk.

Signs: While some cats show no signs of infection, others present broken or brittle hair, patchy hair loss, scales or crusts (mostly on the head and feet), areas of self-mutilation, or pruritus (itching).

Treatment: Treatment includes a combination of topical and systemic therapies, plus extensive hygiene measures and decontamination of the environment (don't forget the heating and cooling vents). All affected animals should be treated by administration of both oral medication (systemic therapy) and by treatment applied directly to the coat and skin (topical therapy). The most popular topical treatment is a lime sulfur dip (which smells unpleasant). Talk to your vet about your options.

An injectable ringworm vaccine is available for cats. It has been used successfully in some ringworm eradication and control programs but, because of the resistant nature of the ringworm fungus, there are cases where the vaccine fails to control or completely cure a ringworm infection.

SQUAMOUS CELL CARCINOMA (SCC)

This kind of cancer often attacks nonpigmented, thinly, or noncoated areas like the ears, noses, and eyelids.

Signs: The first signs may be a pink area with some scaling or hair loss. Then the skin starts to crust. If this is not treated, squamous cell carcinoma can develop.

Causes: Squamous cell carcinoma in cats can originate when your cat spends too long soaking herself outdoors in the sunlight.

Treatment: Squamous cell carcinoma requires surgery. Prognosis depends on how early the treatment is performed and where the cancer is. If it appears on the ears, the affected portion can easily be removed. It's wise to keep your cat out of the sun during the peak hours (11 AM to 3 PM) or to provide a powerful sunblock.

ALLERGIES

Allergies are common in cats, although perhaps not so common as in dogs and people.

Causes: Animals with allergies have an immune system that is hypersensitive to foreign substances (allergens) and treats them as if they were deadly invaders.

Signs: In cats, allergies are most commonly expressed by itchy skin either on one spot or all over the body. Less often, an allergy can affect the respiratory system, in which case sneezing, coughing, or discharge from the eyes or nose will occur. A third path an allergy might take is through the digestive system, manifesting itself in vomiting or diarrhea. Stress and anxiety are also factors that can make allergies flare up.

Cat allergies can further be divided into four broad groups: flea allergy (so common it gets its own group), contact allergy, food allergy, and inhalant allergy.

If your cat has tested negative for the more common causes of her skin ailment, the next step may be to test her for a food allergy, in which case she will be put on a special hypoallergenic diet to see if the condition disappears.

FLEA-BITE ALLERGY

While most cats can handle a flea bite without much trouble, some animals suffer severe itching—so severe that the cat may begin chewing ferociously at her own skin (usually at the base of the tail) in an effort to get relief. This results in open sores that can in turn develop into a bacterial infection. (See feline miliary disease.)

Treatment: The obvious solution to this situation is to get your cat on a good monthly flea preventative. If this is not possible, your vet may want to put the cat on steroid injections. Don't panic. For some reason, cats have fewer side effects from steroids than do other species. Another mark of their superiority, I suppose.

CONTACT DERMATITIS

Contact allergies are the least common and result from an overreaction to a substance to which the skin is exposed, such as a flea collar, certain plants, medications, or wool. They come in two types: allergic (which take some time to develop) or irritant (which occur the first time the substance makes contact with the skin and is not a true allergy). This type of dermatitis is more painful than the itchy type. The skin may form blisters.

Signs: Typical signs include itching (which may be severe) or the appearance of red bumps (papules). Other signs include secondary bacterial infection, crusting, and thickening of the skin.

Treatment: If you can determine the culprit substance, its removal will also get rid of the allergy.

FOOD ALLERGY

Some cats are allergic to certain foods, and it usually happens after the animal has been eating the same food for several months. It is estimated that between 10 and 20 percent of feline allergies are food-related, and most victims are under the age of two years.

Causes: The usual culprits are beef, dairy products, or fish. Together they account for almost 90 percent of the reported cases of food allergy.

Signs: Food allergies can produce a variety of clinical signs including itching, wheezing, and digestive problems (the most common).

Treatment: Your vet may wish to test for food allergies using a specially prescribed hypoallergenic diet (composed of substances to which your cat has not been previously exposed, such as duck, for example), which the cat must consume for a rather lengthy period. If the signs are gastrointestinal, a two- to four-week trial is usually long enough. However, if the pet has dermatological signs, a trial of twelve weeks or more is common.

The ideal hypoallergenic food has a limited number of highly digestible protein sources (which should be novel to the cat), no additives, and is free of excessive amounts of vasoactive amines (amino acids that affect the dilation of blood vessels). The digestibility of the protein is a very important factor. An incompletely digested protein can incite an allergic response because of residual antigens.

During this allergy-testing period, the cat cannot eat any other foods, including treats or even vitamin tablets.

In cats, allergies are most commonly expressed by itchy skin either on one spot or all over the body.

INHALANT ALLERGY (ATOPY)

Inhalant allergy is the most common of all kinds of cat allergies.

Causes: Suspect allergens include tree, weed, grass pollens (an allergy to Bermuda grass is common), molds, mildew, and dust mites. Many of these allergies occur seasonally, such as those related to ragweed, cedar, and grass pollens.

Signs: Most cats react to these pollens not by sneezing like we do, but by intensely scratching themselves. Unfortunately, many cats are allergic to several allergens, and suffer from itching year-round, even if any individual allergy is seasonal.

TESTING FOR ALLERGIES

Although tests for food allergy are available, they are not yet very reliable. For other allergies, your vet has two choices: intradermal skin testing and serum-based tests. Intradermal skin testing (injecting bits of the suspect allergen under the skin and examining the site the next day) is the most accurate, and it delivers the fewest false positives (except the test for dust mite allergy). However, it's a rather difficult test to interpret, and your vet may suggest that your cat see a specialist to have it done. Several weeks prior to the test, other allergy treatments must be stopped.

The serum or blood test is easier to do because it simply measures IgE (antibody) levels in the blood. However, it results in many false positives.

TREATMENT OF ALLERGIES

If any allergy is discovered, and the source of the allergy cannot be easily eliminated, your vet has several treatment options.

Cats appear to respond fairly well to the antihistamine chlorpheniramine (Chlor-Trimeton), and perhaps even better to the newer antihistamine fexofenadine (Allegra).

He may wish to use steroids to block the reaction. He may prescribe a hypoallergenic shampoo and frequent bathing to remove surface allergens. In some cases, this means a lower dose of steroids is needed, because the cat is exposed to fewer allergens.

Another route is desensitization (allergy shots), which works very well for about 75 percent of cats. Small amounts of the identified antigen are injected weekly in an attempt to redirect the cat's immune system. Don't expect a response for two to five months, though. If

Food Intolerance

It's easy to confuse food allergy with food intolerance. Food intolerance is not based on a problem with the immune system. For example, one common type of food intolerance is to lactose (milk sugar). This occurs because the body has a deficiency of lactase, the enzyme that breaks lactose down. The lactose stays in the intestine and causes diarrhea and gas. To make things worse, cats can also be truly allergic to dairy products. Other kinds of intolerances are reactions to additives or an overreaction to vasoactive amines in the food.

desensitization appears to help, injections will continue for several years. A realistic goal is to significantly reduce the severity of the itching; in some cats, itching may stop completely. Steroids are not used with this treatment protocol, except on an intermittent basis. (This approach is not used with food allergy.)

Cyclosporine (Atopica) is somewhat new to veterinary practice; however, it's about as effective as steroids, without the side effects. It's also effective and safe for cats and good for granulomas. But it will cost you a bundle.

In almost every case of allergies, it is also helpful to add fatty acids and biotin to the diet to help the skin stay elastic and repair itself. This alone may cause a dramatic improvement in about 25 percent of cases and is helpful in about 75 percent of cases. And there are no side effects.

Illnesses and Ailments

Like human beings, cats can acquire a number of diseases. Some are genetically inherited, some are "caught" from other animals; some just seem to appear out of nowhere. While it is beyond the scope of this book to provide detailed information on every disease to which cats are susceptible, we'll cover the major ones.

MULTISYSTEM DISORDERS

While some diseases attack one organ or system, others affect multiple systems and have multiple signs. We'll start with these.

CANCER

Cancer is a group of more than 100 different diseases. Cancer occurs when cells become abnormal and keep dividing and forming more cells without control or order. It can occur in almost any organ or system. Cancer spreads throughout the body by a process called metastasis, in which the cancerous cells break off and travel through the bloodstream or lymphatic system. Then they lodge and grow in other parts of the body, usually the lymph nodes, liver, spleen, kidneys, and lungs.

We will look at the few more common ones.

Causes: Causes are variable, depending on the type of cancer. Often, the cause is simply not known.

Signs: According to the Veterinary Cancer Society, here are the most common signs of cancer in cats and dogs:

- abnormal swellings that persist or continue to grow
- bleeding or discharge from any body opening

- difficulty breathing, urinating, or defecating
- difficulty eating or swallowing
- hesitation to exercise or loss of stamina
- loss of appetite
- offensive odor
- persistent lameness or stiffness
- sores that do not heal
- weight loss

Of course, many of these signs can also appear in other diseases, so don't jump to the conclusion that your cat has cancer. Cancer is classified into two types: sarcomas and carcinomas. Sarcomas are derived from structural tissues, like bone, muscle, or connective tissue. Carcinomas are cancers derived from nonstructural tissues such as skin cells, blood, and glandular tissue. Both are bad.

Treatment: The only way to definitively diagnose cancer is by looking at its cells under a microscope. The cells can be obtained with a fine-needle aspirate (FNA) or a biopsy.

Conventional treatment options are surgery, radiation therapy, or chemotherapy.

If you notice any unusual growth on your cat, it's important to have your cat seen by the vet right away. Cats with cancer may refuse to eat, and it's important to encourage them to do so. A starving cat will not get well. Avoid giving carbohydrates to cats with cancer—tumor cells love carbohydrates and thrive on them. They don't like fat at all and high-quality protein only slightly more. Adding omega-3 fatty acids to the diet of cats with cancer is very helpful for starving tumors.

MUSCULOSKELETAL DISORDERS

The muscles and skeleton provide the framework and power potential for everything your cat does. When the musculoskeletal system becomes diseased, your cat can be seriously affected.

ARTHRITIS

Like dogs and people, cats can get arthritis, although luckily, because of their lighter weight and build, it doesn't seem as serious. In cats, arthritis seems to strike most frequently in the hips, elbows, and spine. Arthritis is a progressive disease. This means it will not get better on its own, but will worsen over time.

Causes: Arthritis doesn't have just one cause (like old age). Contributing

Pain Meds for Cancer

For any kind of cancer, don't forget to give your cat appropriate pain medication. One option is fentanyl patches, which are applied to the skin and slowly release the active ingredient.

factors might include certain congenital disorders; developmental disorders, such as hip or elbow dysplasia; disc disease; fractures involving the joint; inflammatory disease (from conditions like polyarthritis); or ligament, tendon, or muscle disease.

Signs: Signs of arthritis include difficulty in getting up, favoring a limb, limping, reluctance to climb or jump, and stiffness.

Treatment and Prevention: Arthritis can be treated both medically and surgically to help slow its course. Sometimes, an actual joint replacement can be done. In some cases, the noninflammatory kinds of arthritis are called degenerative joint disease (DJD).

The best way to prevent arthritis or make it less serious is to keep your cat's weight within normal limits. The more weight those poor old joints have to support, the tougher it is on them. Overweight cats also tend to be less active, which results in even more weight gain—it's a vicious cycle. Everything you do to relieve your cat's arthritis will be more effective if your cat is at her proper weight.

The aim of treatment is to minimize further damage and to relieve pain and inflammation. Helpful substances for preventing and treating arthritis are glucosamine (an amino derivative of glucose) and chondroitin, naturally occurring substances found in the cartilage of living animals.

Cats with arthritis also benefit from a warm place to sleep. It makes them feel better and actually seems to help the arthritis as well. A comfortable orthopedic bed is an added plus. Some cats (not all) may enjoy a massage. Put kitty litter boxes and food and water bowls where your cat can reach them easily. In some cases, it helps to lower the sides of the litter box.

Medications used to treat arthritis include Butorphanol, a pain reliever that comes in both injectable and tablet form, and is available through your veterinarian. It can cause sedation in cats, which in most cases is undesirable because you want the cat to move about. Corticosteroids are effective, but have undesirable side effects. Low doses of aspirin 80 mg (one-quarter of an adult aspirin) once a week may be therapeutic. (The stuff stays a long time in the cat's system.) However, it is very easy to overdose a cat with aspirin. Follow your veterinarian's guidelines. Methylsulfonylmethane (MSM), a natural anti-inflammatory, and omega-3 fatty acids help the immune system and may also be helpful. Because of their small size, surgical treatment or joint replacement is seldom done on cats. Medicinal patches have also been used with some success. Consult your vet regarding these options.

For people who favor homeopathy, *Rhus Tox* is the most commonly used remedy. Arnica may also be used with older cats. Herbalists often try using nettles or alfalfa.

Some practitioners use the term "degenerative joint disease" as a synonym for arthritis. Others believe it is a slightly different condition. If you hear this phrase from your vet, ask him to clarify the condition.

Feline Polyarthritis: One particular type of arthritis, feline polyarthritis, attacks multiple joints over time. In one form of the disease, the cartilage erodes from the ends of the feet, wrist, and hock of the bone that makes up a joint. In another form, erosion is so severe that the actual bone beneath the cartilage is painfully exposed. (This is like rheumatoid arthritis in humans.)

Typically, younger or middle-aged male cats (both neutered and intact) are affected.

Treatment: There is no cure, and even powerful pain relievers and anti-inflammatory drugs may not help. Some cats appear to be in so much pain that they must be euthanized.

Arthritis and Calicivirus Infection: Calicivirus is most famous for causing respiratory infection, but it can also affect the joints. (Some cats can actually come down with it from the distemper-rhinotracheitis-chlamydia vaccine given to kittens). Luckily, most will recover from it on their own.

Osteomyelitis: A bacterial form of arthritis also exists, which may occur as result of bite wounds. If the infection spreads into the bone itself, it is called osteomyelitis. This disease can be very serious.

Treatment: Treatment involves flushing out the joint and putting the cat on antibiotics.

Steroids and desensitization treatment for allergies cannot be used at the same time because they interfere with one another.

DISKOSPONDYLITIS

Diskospondylytis is a bacterial or fungal infection of the vertebrae.

Cause: Oddly enough, you can blame grass awns and foxtails for this problem. The awn pierces the skin and brings the bacteria with it. (This is somewhat of a guess.)

Signs: It can produce swelling, fever, pain, and bone deformities, which put pressure on the spinal cord. Diagnosis can be difficult, and treatment depends on identifying the causative agent.

Treatment: A bacterial infection is treated differently from a fungal one, requiring different medications. If the disease is caught before the bone is deformed, the prognosis is excellent.

HIP DYSPLASIA

While most people have heard of hip dysplasia in dogs, many don't realize it has also begun to appear in cats. Big breeds like Persians, Maine Coons, and Himalayans are most commonly affected.

Cause: This is a hereditary defect caused by a combination of "bad genes."

Cats, like humans, are prone to osteoporosis as they age. The best way to prevent arthritis or make it less serious is to keep your cat's weight within normal limits.

Hip dysplasia is a defect of the hip joint in which the head of the femur does not correctly fit into the hip socket. This hip joint laxity results in abnormal weight bearing. Also, the two surfaces rub painfully against each other, and eventually arthritis develops.

Sign: Limping is the major sign.

Treatment: If you suspect hip dysplasia in your cat, talk to your vet. Surgical treatments are available. In mild cases, you can try glucosamine, but be careful to get a high-quality brand. Your best bet is to get it through your vet. Good breeding is eliminating this disease in dogs; the same can be done for cats.

PATELLAR LUXATION

Although this disease is better known in small dogs, cats can have it as well. Abyssinian and Devon Rex may be the most vulnerable breeds. It is very common for the condition to affect both legs.

Signs: If your cat has it, you can hear the knee (which is of course on the back leg) pop in and out; this eventually causes lameness. However, since it does not always cause lameness, more cats may be victims of the condition than commonly suspected.

Treatment: Talk to your vet about your options. In some cases, rest may help. In other cases, surgery is recommended.

CARDIOVASCULAR DISEASES

Your cat's circulatory system is her lifeline, and most diseases that strike it can be serious, even life-threatening.

ANEMIA

Anemia is a condition in which there is an abnormally low number of red blood cells (the cells that move oxygen around the body) or a deficiency in hemoglobin (a pigment inside red blood cells to which oxygen binds) in the blood. It is not a specific disease, but rather the result of a disease process.

Because the heart has to work harder to provide oxygen to the cells in anemic cats, these animals have an increased heart rate and may also breathe harder.

Causes: Anemia can be caused by an immune-mediated disease, in which the body attacks its own red blood cells; blood-loss from trauma or a blood clotting disorder; cancer (tumors of the intestinal tract); chronic disease; infectious agents such as FIV, FIA, or FeLV; parasites (fleas, ticks, or hookworms); and reactions to certain drugs or toxins (including onions).

Signs: Signs of anemia include pale gums and listlessness. The most common screening for anemia is the packed cell volume (PCV) test, also called the hematocrit. A complete blood count (CBC) should be performed on all cats suspected of having anemia, regardless of the cause.

Treatment: Treatment will depend on the underlying cause. In many cases, an important part of the treatment involves giving IV fluids or a blood transfusion. If internal bleeding is suspected, an exploratory operation may be necessary.

Feline Infectious Anemia (FIA): FIA is a specific disease caused by the bacterial parasite *Haemobartonella felis* (*H. felis*), which attaches to the red blood cells.

Causes: It has recently been discovered that actually two distinct species of *Haemobartonella* organisms infect cats. Together they are called feline hemoplasmas, and the new names given to the two species are *Mycoplasma hemofelis* and *Candidatus mycoplasma haemominutum*. Aha! The culprit is a mycoplasma, not a rickettsia, as formerly thought. It is important to be aware of the differences between these species, because they have different effects in cats.

When the immune system detects the invader, it destroys the blood cells, causing anemia. The route of transmission is not clear, although fleas, ticks, mosquitoes, and other cats have all been implicated.

Signs: Signs include fever, pale or yellow-tinged mucous membranes, rapid breathing, tenderness throughout the body, weakness, and weight loss. Many cats have *H. felis* present in their blood without showing any signs of the disease. *M. haemofelis* (sometimes called the large strain) often results in anemia in cats, while *Candidatus m. haemominutum* (sometimes called the small strain) often causes no clinical signs at all, or disease may appear only when the cat is stressed with another disease or health problem.

About 20 percent of cats with this disease are also infected with the FeLV (FeOral antibio LV). These cats are more likely to have severe symptoms.

Treatment: Antibiotics like doxycycline or tetracycline given for three to four weeks are usually successful in treating the disease, although it may recur during times of stress. Corticosteroids are sometimes used as well. Cats may remain carriers of the organism for long periods. There is no vaccine against the disease. This disease is not transmissible to people.

FELINE CARDIOMYOPATHY

Cardiomyopathy is fancy name for any disease of the heart muscle. In this condition, the muscle thickens and enlarges. When the heart walls are thick, the heart chambers get smaller. All types of cardiomyopathy can cause congestive heart failure (fluid in the lungs). Older cats may have a thickened heart muscle because of some underlying disease like high blood pressure, kidney disease, or hyperthyroidism. In this case, the underlying disease must be addressed first. Males seem to be slightly more affected than females.

If you have a multiple-cat household, illness and disease can easily be passed from one cat to another. Always check with your vet to see if it is necessary to quarantine sick individuals.

Signs: No matter what the underlying cause and specific type of heart failure, the signs are the same, although the cat may have been sick for a very long time. Unlike dogs, coughing is not a major sign of heart failure in cats. They may seem breathless and lethargic. Unfortunately, cats who are seemingly healthy can get sick and die very quickly before their owner is even aware that something is wrong. A cat diagnosed with hypertrophic cardiomyopathy (HCM) and heart failure will usually live only from several months to three years with therapy.

Treatment: Multiple medications are typically needed; these include diuretics, medications to dilate the arterial walls, blood thinners, or heart stimulants. Affected cats must sometimes be tube-fed or force-fed. Treatment has been traditionally directed toward resolving the clinical signs of the disease.

COMMON FORMS OF HEART FAILURE

The most common form of heart failure in cats is HCM, a thickening of the primary heart muscle called the left ventricle. The term is reserved for cases in which the cause is unknown. The problem can occur either in the flowing-in or flowing-out stage.

Causes: The disease is connected to a recessive trait, and the most common breeds affected are Maine Coon Cats, American Shorthairs, Ragdolls, and Persians. Males are affected more commonly than females. Cats who develop the disease when younger (one to four years) tend to have a more serious form of the disease. It may take weeks or months to progress to a serious stage. The vet can tell where the problem is with an echocardiogram and other tests.

Treatment: Medications.

Another kind of cardiomyopathy leads to enlargement of the left atrium, which can result in blood clots.

Treatment: Cats with this condition are sometimes prescribed aspirin two times a week, one of the few times when aspirin is an appropriate therapy for cats.

Another type of heart muscle disease is *restrictive cardiomyopathy*. This can sometimes be a late stage of hypertrophic disease, or it may appear as a primary disease. Restrictive cardiomyopathy is much more difficult to treat than hypertrophic cardiomyopathy. The restrictive form is often associated with an unidentified inflammatory process within the heart muscle.

Treatment: Medications.

Another condition, *dilated cardiomyopathy*, results from a combination of enlarged heart chambers and weakened muscle. The heart cannot pump blood efficiently.

Causes: It is known that a deficiency of taurine, an essential amino acid, will cause dilated cardiomyopathy.

HYPERTENSION (HIGH BLOOD PRESSURE)

Hypertension is common in older cats. It can result in damage to blood vessels, especially those in the retina of the eye. There may even be retinal detachment and sudden onset blindness. Retinal detachment is an emergency situation that can lead to permanent blindness unless the retina reattaches within a few days.

Causes: Causes include stress, as well as kidney, thyroid, or heart disease.

Signs: Look at the eyes. The pupils may be large and not constrict in the presence of light. Blindness may develop. Some cats may be depressed or withdrawn.

Nutraceuticals

A nutraceutical is defined as a food or naturally occurring food supplement thought to have a beneficial effect on health. Nutraceuticals are not classed as drugs, so you can get them without a prescription.

For example, two of the most popular nutraceuticals are glucosamine and chondroitin. Glucosamine provides the "building blocks" for making new cartilage, while chondroitin stops the destructive enzymes that break down cartilage in the joint. Chondroitin also enhances cartilage growth.

As animals age, they can't seem to produce enough of these substances to keep the joints in good shape, so a supplement is useful. Crustaceans are an excellent, inexpensive source of glucosamine; it's in the shell. Supplemental chondroitin is usually derived from the cartilage of cattle and shark. It is possible that shark cartilage is the most effective source, but for the sake of our endangered species, please select the stuff from cows. There are no side effects from these supplements, except possibly in cats with diabetes.

The only caution is that the nutraceutical market is not well regulated, and not all products are what they claim to be. Your best bet is to purchase a pharmaceutical-quality supplement from your veterinarian.

When the nervous system goes awry, your cat may develop seizure disorders. Although no cures are possible, most cats can live happy lives with appropriate diagnosis and medication.

Treatment: Drugs that lower blood pressure in humans can be used to treat high blood pressure in cats. Amlodipine and benazepril are commonly prescribed. If no underlying conditions are present, the disease can be managed rather easily. If other conditions are present, these must be treated first.

NERVOUS SYSTEM DISORDERS

The nervous system controls the movement of the muscle and joints. In fact, it is the command system for everything the cat does. When the nervous system goes awry, a lot of other things go wrong too.

CEREBELLAR HYPOPLASIA

Sometimes a kitten is born with an underdeveloped cerebellum, the portion of the brain responsible for the control of motion.

Cause: Usually the cause is a panleukopenia infection, feline infectious enteritis, or feline distemper prior to birth, but trauma or poisoning in the uterus could also be the cause.

Signs: Affected kittens have tremors and jerky movements; they may fall down. These kittens may not grow as large as unaffected kittens or they may have slower development. However, the signs don't get worse as the animal ages. In fact, kittens will often be able to compensate for the condition.

Treatment: Although no cure is possible, they can live very happy lives and make great pets; however, these animals should remain indoor pets.

COGNITIVE DYSFUNCTION

Cognitive dysfunction is similar to Alzheimer's disease in human beings.

Signs: Signs include loss of bowel or bladder control, reduced level of activity, increased sleeping, irritability or aggression, excessive vocalization, and lack of grooming. The cat may no longer wish to interact with the family.

The condition may be diagnosed by default after brain tumors, trauma, hyperthyroidism, and other disease are ruled out.

Treatment: Drug treatment is the only option (deprenyl or selegiline). Typically, a low dose is given once a day for three weeks or so to see if any

positive behavioral changes have occurred. A majority of cats respond
positively, at least to some degree, and seem much happier than before.

EPILEPSY

True epilepsy is a seizure disorder of unknown origin. Most affected cats show
the first signs between the ages of two and three years.

If your cat has a seizure, pay close attention. Everything you notice will
be of help to the vet since he is unlikely to observe it for himself. Length of
seizure, characteristic movements, twitching, and salivation are all important
clues. In a full seizure, the cat may foam at the mouth, twitch, urinate, defecate,
or vocalize. Some cats even propel themselves into the air! Do not panic; a
seizure probably bothers you more than it does the cat.

Sometimes the seizure may not be complete. A cat may seem to enter an
altered consciousness state and simply behave in bizarre ways, which can
include lack of coordination and running into things. Some cats just develop
a blank stare for a few seconds, although if that is the only symptom, I doubt
you'll notice. My cats have a blank stare pretty much all the time. The rest of
the time, they're glaring at me. Or they're asleep.

Cause: Regardless of the terms used, the primary goal when treating a
cat with seizures is to identify the disease causing the seizures, assuming it is
epilepsy only if no other cause can be found. In an attempt to find the cause
of epilepsy, your vet will perform a complete physical along with blood tests
to look for FeLV, toxoplasmosis, FIV, and FIP. A urinalysis and chemistry panel
may also be in order. He may recommend a trip to a veterinary neurologist
(now we're talking expensive) for a neurological examination if he can't find
anything.

Treatment: Epilepsy is chronic and incurable, but it can be treated.
Treatment for epilepsy is usually not started until a pet has had several seizures
(and the cause remains undetermined). Often, anticonvulsant drugs are
not given unless the cat has more than one seizure a month or the seizures
last more than half an hour. Phenobarbital is the initial drug of choice.
Phenobarbital is a sedative that calms nerves within the brain. Diazepam
(Valium) may also be effective but is more likely to cause liver problems. The
goal of therapy is to stabilize the nerves inside brain, without giving so much
medication that the cat remains sedated. This is a fine line, and it may take a
while to figure out the correct dosage.

If your cat has a single prolonged seizure or continuous seizures without
recovery between them, the condition is called status epilepticus and is
extremely serious. You must seek veterinary attention (usually an intravenous

233

dosage of diazepam) for your cat immediately or she can die. With proper medication, the prognosis for this disease is good.

FELINE HYPERESTHESIA (ROLLING SKIN SYNDROME)

Feline hyperesthesia is a term that refers to a condition in which cats seem abnormally sensitive to stimuli. In many cases, they actually seem possessed, a state of affairs possibly accounting for the cat's bad reputation in some quarters. This disease is similar to a seizure disorder. It appears to be most common in Siamese and Siamese crosses, usually appearing between the ages of one and four years. It tends to show up in adult cats rather than in kittens.

Causes: Suggested causes have included aberrant electrical activity (partial seizure) in areas of the brain that control emotions, grooming, or predatory behavior; overvaccination; genetics; and muscular lesions along the spine with concomitant irritation.

Signs: Signs of the disease include aimless running or wandering, dilated pupils and staring, excessive grooming, extremely sensitive skin, apparent hallucinations, hiding, persistent vocalization, tail twitching or general annoyance with the tail.

The behavior usually occurs in the evening or mornings, and an episode may last anywhere from a few seconds to several minutes. They may occur every few days, or be an almost constant presence. Following an episode, the animal seems extremely confused.

Treatment: In some cases, medications may be appropriate. Either clomipramine (Clomicalm) or fluoxetine (Prozac) are most commonly prescribed. Anticonvulsants are sometimes helpful in the treatment of feline hyperesthesia, possibly because of its partial seizure component. It is not advisable to stroke your cat along the back (if there are lesions along the spine).

RABIES

Rabies is a well-known and deeply feared disease; all warm-blooded animals are vulnerable.

Causes: Rabies is caused by a virus found in the saliva of infected animals. It is transmitted to pets and people through bites or by contamination of an open

Rabies is 100 percent fatal in cats, so have your cat vaccinated against the deadly disease, especially if she goes outdoors.

cut. A cat can give rabies to people. The incubation period is between two and four weeks in cats.

Signs: Rabies affects the brain, but also pushes the animal into respiratory failure. Many will lick at the site of the bite. Some animals become extremely aggressive when they contract the disease (this is the so-called "furious" form); others get very lethargic. Some become disoriented, and some have seizures. But all die.

Prevention: Rabies is 100 percent fatal in cats, although there have been one or two cases in which humans have survived, although it cannot be said that they were well afterward. It's more reasonable to assume that if you get rabies you will die. And there are *more* cases of cats with rabies than of dogs with the disease. This makes sad sense when you think about the increasing number of feral cats. Have your cat vaccinated against rabies. The vaccination is extremely effective, and even if bitten, it's unlikely your cat will contract the disease. It's the law anyway. Because of the aggressive stance we have taken against this disease, we have practically eliminated its occurrence in human beings in the US, although parts of the rest of the world are not so lucky.

If your cat is bitten by a wild animal or appears with bites wounds, call your local health department or animal control officer to report it. You must do the same if your cat bites someone.

There has never been a case of rabies in the British Isles or Australia. Or Antarctica, of course.

GASTROINTESTINAL DISORDERS
The gastrointestinal system controls digestion.

COLITIS
Colitis is an inflammation of the large intestine; it can be acute or chronic.

Causes: Colitis can be caused by infection, colon cancer, food allergy, dietary indiscretion, or parasites, but a specific cause is often not found.

Signs: Signs include painful straining to eliminate and the production of small amounts of soft feces. There may also be lack of appetite and vomiting, as well as weight loss. However, many cats with the disease appear (and apparently feel) normal. The disease becomes serious only if ulceration of the colon develops.

Treatment: Treatment depends on the cause of the disease, which must be addressed first. Sometimes a special bland diet is helpful. If the cause is bacterial, an antibiotic may be prescribed. Chronic colitis

Seizures

Seizures that have a known cause, such as poisoning, drug overdose, tumors, or infection, are not properly called epilepsy. When the cause is none of these and is in fact unknown, it's called idiopathic epilepsy or just plain epilepsy.
Idiopathic epilepsy is rarer in cats than in dogs. When the cause of seizures in cats can be determined, the three most common culprits are viral non-FIP encephalitis, feline cerebral ischemic encephalopathy, or a tumor (meningioma).

can be controlled with sulfa drugs. Anti-inflammatory and anti-motility drugs may also be prescribed.

CONSTIPATION

Constipation is not a disease in and of itself, but a sign of disease. It is fairly common in cats, especially older ones.

Cause: The most common cause of constipation is dehydration. Other reasons include intestinal obstruction, megacolon, or tumor.

Signs: Constipation is characterized by infrequent or absent defecation, and the passage of hard, dry feces. Increased straining may also be present. A cat with constipation should be seen by a veterinarian to determine the underlying cause.

Treatment: In mild cases, you can try supplementing the cat's diet with bran or a similar bulk-forming material. Groom the cat regularly to reduce hairball formation. Big hairballs don't do anything good for the colon.

DIARRHEA

Like constipation, diarrhea is not a disease in and of itself, but a sign of another problem, often damage to the digestive system. Episodes of diarrhea are usually self-limiting and nothing to worry about. However, it can be so devastating, especially to young kittens, as to actually be worse than the disease that prompted it.

Causes: Causes are many and include dietary indiscretion (garbage, grass, milk), a change in diet, toxins, stress, parasites, viruses (feline panleukopenia [FPV], FeLV, FIV, FCV), bacteria (including *Campylobacter*), and hyperthyroidism.

Signs: *Acute diarrhea* originating in the small intestine usually lasts less than 48 hours. The stools seldom contain mucus, although blood may be present. The stools are brown or reddish-brown. The animal exhibits a sense of urgency to defecate; she may continue to strain after defecation. The cat usually loses her appetite. *Chronic diarrhea* originating in the small intestine lasts 7-10 days or even longer. The cat passes a large volume of watery stool. She may have movements two or three times as often as her normal frequency. The feces are brown unless there is blood in the stool, in which case it will have a black, tarry appearance. Little or no mucus is present.

In *large bowel diarrhea*, on the other hand, cats will pass small amounts of soft feces, occasionally containing some fresh blood or mucus.

Treatment: If your cat has diarrhea, stop feeding her for 24 hours, although she may be given water. If the diarrhea clears up, you can start feeding her

If your cat has diarrhea, stop feeding her for 24 hours, although she may be given water. If the diarrhea does not stop, take her to the vet.

boiled chicken. If the diarrhea does not stop, take her to the vet. Treatment will ultimately depend on what is causing the disease.

Herbal remedies include slippery elm or carob mixed with honey or water. Both are very soothing and quite effective given three times a day for three days.

For those who like to use homeopathic remedies, the following, given three times daily, are commonly used for specific types of diarrhea:

- *Arsenicum Alb.*: diarrhea with frequent vomiting
- *Belis Per.*: yellow, smelly diarrhea
- *Colchicum*: ineffectual urging, soft stools
- *Colocynthis*; diarrhea with colic and pain
- *Croton tig*:for frequent watery diarrhea
- *Merc cor.*: frequent diarrhea with straining and blood, forceful spurts
- *Natrum Sulph*: diarrhea with gas, large quantities, yellow and liquid
- phosphorus; copious debilitating diarrhea

Typical flower essences include crab apple, vine, and cedar.

HAIRBALLS

Odd that something so lovely and important as hair can cause such a mess in the gastrointestinal tract. But it does. Most of it gets expelled through the digestive system, but sometimes the ingested hair balls up and cannot be passed. Most of the time, the cat will vomit it up. However, hairballs can become more serious. They can block the intestines; in fact there are cases on record of a cat having a hairball the size of a baseball! That is not something I would want to see.

Causes: Cats spend a great deal of time in self-grooming and, during the process, they swallow lots of their own hair. Longhaired cats like Persians and Himalayans, of course, are most likely to develop this problem.

Signs: Serious signs of hairball impaction include dry hacking, retching, inability to defecate (or its opposite, diarrhea), and a swollen belly. If you notice any of these signs, call your vet immediately.

Treatment: Products are available that will help "pass" a hairball by lubricating the digestive tract. Most are petroleum-based laxative gels that coat the hair and the stool and allow it to pass through the digestive system. Cats usually like the taste of these things and eat them readily. Hairball treatment initially is given every day for a week or so, and every couple of days thereafter for maintenance. Use these products only under the guidance of your veterinarian. Frequent, long-term use may result in vitamin deficiencies.

Some high-fiber (3.5 to 10 percent) foods and treats also claim to be helpful in lubricating hairballs, although these products usually cause the hairball to be vomited up, not passed. Do not add butter or vegetable oils to your cat's food for this purpose, however. They will probably be absorbed by the digestive system before they can actually do the trick and may cause other health problems.

It will help mightily if you brush your longhaired cat every day. Every hair you loosen with your brush will be one that your cat doesn't swallow. In some cases, excessive grooming may indicate a medical problem. If you suspect this, talk with your vet about it.

The technical term for a hairball is trichobezoar. I thought you would want to know that.

Cats spend a great deal of time self-grooming and, during the process, they swallow lots of their own hair causing hairballs in the digestive tract. Brushing your cat regularly can help prevent this condition.

238

HELICOBACTER INFECTION

Helicobacter are spiral-shaped, gram-negative bacteria that can survive the intense acidity of the stomach by using enzymes to create their own protective layer of bicarbonate.

Causes: Numerous species cause ulcers in pets and people. In fact, various surveys show that *Helicobacter* is present in almost 100 percent of shelter and cattery cats and between 30 and 100 percent in pet cats. The route of transmission is not well understood, although body fluids and feces are suspect.

Signs: Signs include intermittent vomiting and gastritis, but it can best be diagnosed via endoscopy.

Treatment: *Helicobacter* infection can be treated with antibiotics, but treatment may not be necessary in animals showing no distress.

HEPATIC LIPIDOSIS (FATTY LIVER SYNDROME)

If you have a fat cat who suddenly stops eating for more than a day or so, call your vet. She may have fatty liver syndrome (FLS) and will die without immediate care. I hope I scared you; I meant to.

FLS is the most commonly reported liver disease in cats (although no other animals get a disease like this). It is characterized by an accumulation of fat in individual liver cells. In some overweight cats, fat is broken down in the body and deposited in the liver so rapidly that the cat's liver can't process it. Cat's livers just aren't good at this, for some reason. Anyway, the fat ends up just stored there. And that's not good either. All that fat in the liver means the liver can't function normally.

This condition can eventually lead to liver failure and death in about 90 percent of cases. However, with appropriate aggressive therapy, it is completely reversible. The earlier therapy is started, the better.

Causes: Sometimes FLS occurs with no apparent cause (idiopathic), although most cats who develop the disease are overweight. Older cats and females seem to be most at risk. In other cases, it may be secondary to diabetes or toxemia (bacteria in blood). Stress is probably also a factor. The immediate cause of fatty liver is often inappetence (failure to eat). When a cat stops eating, the fat cells in the liver are mobilized, but for some reason the liver can't use them—the problem may be a deficiency in certain proteins or perhaps arginine, one of the amino acids. Cats can't synthesize arginine on their own.

Signs: Signs of fatty liver disease include anorexia, depression, jaundice, loss of muscle mass, possible seizures, and vomiting.

Treatment: Any obese cat who refuses food for more than 24 to 48 hours

Liver Disorders

Because the liver has to do so many things (it has a role in digestion, energy metabolism, biosynthesis, immune system regulation, and waste elimination), it is very vulnerable to toxins and disease.

Disorders of the liver include various inflammatory liver diseases, infectious liver diseases, tumors, damage to the liver from toxins (cats are very susceptible to these, sustaining damage from drugs that are safe in other species), and vascular liver disease.

should be seen by a veterinarian. Treatment involves aggressive nutritional support, including appetite stimulants (Valium is used for cats, believe it or not) and usually force-feeding, perhaps through a feeding tube directly into the stomach or esophagus. (The Valium will only work, however, if the cat has at least some interest in food. Most don't.) This may be necessary for three to six weeks. A multiple vitamin and thiamine supplement is recommended, because thiamine deficiency can occur as a result of long periods of anorexia. With aggressive tube feeding or diet and fluid therapy, 60 percent of cats with primary fatty liver disease survive. The diet should be rich in protein and high in calories. Cats with hepatic lipidosis may also require supplemental vitamin K if a clotting problem is present.

Prevention of obesity seems to be the best way to avoid hepatic lipidosis. However, do *not* put your fat cat on a sudden diet. That can induce the disease. Talk to your vet about the best methods to trim down Tubby.

Fatty liver syndrome can occur in conjunction with other liver diseases.

INFLAMMATORY BOWEL DISEASE (IBD)

IBD is actually a name for a group of chronic gastrointestinal disorders. (The most common form of IBD in cats is lymphocytic-plasmacytic enterocolitis, in case you were wondering.)

Cause: The cause of IBD is unknown, although it is suspected that immunological factors play a role. Genetics and nutrition may also play a part.

Signs: The most common signs of inflammatory bowel disease are diarrhea and vomiting. Vomiting is more common when the stomach and upper portion of the small intestine are involved, while diarrhea is more frequently seen when the colon is affected. The cat may defecate more often, but each time will produce less stool. The definitive diagnostic test for the disease is a microscopic examination of small pieces of the intestinal lining. However, this is not always practical.

Treatment: While the disease is hard to cure, most cases can be managed. Treatment includes dietary management

If you have a fat cat who suddenly stops eating for more than a day or so, call your vet. She may have fatty liver syndrome, which can be fatal without immediate care.

(commercial diets are available), medical therapy (corticosteroids), and antibiotics like metronidazole or tylosin.

GALL BLADDER DISEASES

Gall bladder problems come in three general forms: obstructive bile duct disease, nonobstructive bile duct disease, and rupture of the biliary system.

Causes: In obstructive gall bladder disease, something is compressing the bile duct. It might be a swollen or inflamed pancreas, or it might be tumor. If the pressure on the pancreas is relieved, the bile can start flowing again. The gall bladder can also develop gallstones, which can get stuck in the bile duct and block the flow of bile. Nonobstructive disease such as cholecystitis (inflammation of the gallbladder) is usually caused by a bacterial infection. In rupture of the biliary system, the cause is probably trauma such as being struck by a car.

Signs: Signs of gall bladder disease include vomiting, jaundice, and lack of appetite. Fever and abdominal discomfort may also be present.

Treatment: Treatment usually involves antibiotics (for cholecystitis) and supportive therapy. Appetite stimulants are given. Many vets also recommend corticosteroids or other immunosuppressive medications. In cases of trauma, surgery is needed to keep the bile from leaking out and causing peritonitis.

MEGACOLON

Megacolon refers to extreme colonic dilation; it is a disorder of the structure and function of the colon. Cats with megacolon are always constipated. Megacolon can be primary or secondary.

Causes: Megacolon can be caused by a primary defect in the nerve supply of the colon (inherited), or it can become secondary to any lesion or disease that prevents normal defecation over a long period of time. This is more common. (Some cats get it because they will not use a dirty litter box!)

Signs: Signs include anemia, dehydration, depression, frequent nonproductive trips to the litter box, lack of appetite, less frequent defecation, passage of smaller stools than normal, straining to defecate, and vomiting

Treatment: Medical therapy with stool softeners is the first-line treatment for megacolon. Surgical removal of the colon is indicated if medical therapy has failed. Antibiotics are given short-term after surgery.

Preparing Your Cat for Surgery

Some pets are more sensitive to anesthesia than others. If you have any reason to suspect your cat may not handle anesthesia well (such as a previous bad reaction) or she exhibits exercise intolerance, unexplained weight loss, tendency to bleeding, or changes in elimination patterns, mention that to your vet. Ask him to perform complete preanesthetic blood work on your cat. Withhold all food and water for twelve hours prior to the surgical procedure. This is to prevent your cat from vomiting and inhaling stomach contents during surgery. It will also lessen nausea as your cat regains consciousness.

ANAL SAC DISEASE

I couldn't decide where to put the anal gland diseases, so I added them to the end of digestive system because they also occur at the end of the cat—at either side of the anus. (The anal glands have no real function in the digestive system, however.) These glands produce a dark, nasty-smelling fluid and are very much related to the same gland in the skunk.

Causes: Three things can go wrong with the anal sacs: They can become impacted, they can become infected, and they can become obstructed. Anal sac disease is not terribly common in cats, but can be seen in obese animals.

Signs: Signs of anal sac disease include scooting or dragging, licking at the area, pain in the area, and swelling or discharge in the area. If you see any of these signs, talk to your vet.

Treatment: If the sacs are only impacted, he can clean them out. Infected sacs need a round of antibiotics, while obstructed or abscessed ones may need surgical treatment. If your cat has recurrent problems, the glands can be permanently removed; they are not needed for your cat's health.

ENDOCRINE SYSTEM DISORDERS

The endocrine system controls hormone production and regulation.

DIABETES

Diabetes is a serious but treatable disease caused by the failure of the pancreatic islet cells to make enough insulin. The actual cells responsible are called "beta cells."

Insulin is critical to health, and has been called the "cell's gatekeeper." It attaches to the surface of cells and regulates how much glucose goes in and out. Glucose, of course, is a major energy source in the body. If there's not enough glucose, the body starts using energy from protein and fat, leading to body wasting. If too much glucose is in the blood (hyperglycemia), it spills over into the urine and causes dehydration.

About one in 400 cats has diabetes.

Causes: The exact cause of diabetes is unknown, but contributing factors are a sedentary lifestyle, too many calories, and probably too many carbs. When you take animals genetically programmed to live on a high-protein and low-carbohydrate diet and put them on a high-carbohydrate diet, their insulin resistance works against them. Their blood glucose concentrations are too high, and they start to release more and more insulin in an attempt to reduce blood glucose levels. But this strategy fails, and eventually the animals develop diabetes.

It is more common in middle-aged, overweight cats. Males are almost twice as likely to develop diabetes as females, although the reason is unclear. Burmese cats appear to be more commonly affected than other breeds.

Signs: Typically, a cat with diabetes will have the following observable signs, although not every cat will show every sign: changes in gait (hocks close to the floor), decreased activity, fierce appetite (although in some cases the cat is so sick it stops eating), increased or inappropriate urination, increased thirst, vomiting, and weight loss.

Some cats are "subclinical," meaning they have the disease, but don't show any signs of it.

To make sure the diagnosis is correct, the vet will do a blood glucose level test and a urinalysis to see if glucose is present in the urine.

Treatment: When a cat is diagnosed with diabetes, the first step is to find the correct insulin dose. In some cases, this requires hospitalization. Your vet will help you get your cat to a normal level, after which she will be put on a maintenance dose where, with luck, the condition will remain stable. However, circumstances change, and glucose levels must be regularly checked to make sure that the disease is under control. An obese cat with this condition may need to lose weight under the guidance of the veterinarian.

To keep your cat stable, you will need to give her insulin shots once or twice a day. The key is consistency—giving the correct dose at the same time every day and regulating diet. Insulin injections are given with a tiny needle

The exact cause of diabetes in cats is unknown, but contributing factors are a sedentary lifestyle, too many calories, and probably too many carbs.

just under the skin. Cats don't mind this as much as you might think. Your vet will determine the kind of insulin and proper dose needed.

You will be giving your cat a special diet that does not vary so that the glucose levels will remain the same. (No more adventurous feeding from the table!) The ideal diet is low in sugar, moderate in fat, and high in protein. Unlike people, protein is the stimulus for insulin release in cats. They have adapted to high-protein diets by being insulin resistant, which helps to maintain blood glucose during periods of fasting. This works well for cats in the wild, but not so well for pets eating a lot of carbohydrates.

High-fiber diets used to be all the rage for diabetic cats, but cats hate them. Newer research suggests a better diet is one that approximates what a cat eat would in the wild—protein and fat. Make it canned. (This should be the diet for *all* cats, not just diabetic ones.) However, some fiber is good for diabetic cats. Diets containing fermentable fiber, such as beet pulp, help with timing the release of insulin from the pancreas in diabetic animals that still maintain some pancreatic function. But don't give a diabetic cat a diet containing rice. Rice causes a spike in blood glucose. Corn, barley, and sorghum don't seem to cause as high a spike.

It was formerly thought that cats had to be fed at a specific time every day as well—newer evidence shows that diabetic cats actually do better if left to free-feed—their glucose levels stay at a more consistent level.

Most cases of diabetes are manageable. However, a very serious form of the disease is ketoacidosis. Here the ketones (products of fat) build up in the bloodstream. You may see vomiting, diarrhea, and collapse. If IV fluids, drugs to bring the potassium levels back to normal, and fast-acting insulin are not given quickly, the cat can die. With proper care, ketoacidosis can revert to the less serious and more common form of diabetes.

HYPERTHYROIDISM

Hyperthyroidism is one of the most common ailments of middle-aged and senior cats. Less than 6 percent of cases are younger than 10 years of age. The average age of onset is 12 to 13 years.

Cause: The usual cause is a nonmalignant tumor called an adenoma. In this condition, the thyroid glands are enlarged and produce excess thyroid hormone.

Signs: This is diagnosed by measuring thyroid levels in the blood. Signs include weight loss, increased hunger and thirst, restlessness, rapid heart rate, difficulty in breathing, and excessive shedding and matting of the coat. If left untreated, emaciation and severe metabolic and cardiac dysfunction result.

Treatment: Treatment options include radioactive iodine (not available everywhere), surgical removal of the gland, and treatment with anti-thyroid medications. If medication does not control the problem, other options must be considered.

Radioactive iodine treatment avoids the risks of anesthesia and surgery. However, it has a disadvantage. The patient must remain hospitalized until it no longer poses a threat to human contacts. This can be very stressful to all concerned! In places where this option is not available, surgical removal of the thyroid gland works very well. In fact, many veterinarians consider it the treatment of choice to cure hyperthyroidism.

ADDISON'S DISEASE OR HYPOADRENOCORTICISM

Addison's Disease (or hypoadrenocorticism) is a disease in which the cortisone-producing adrenal glands are not functioning properly and produce too little cortisone. As a result, the animal is not able to utilize glucose properly or to balance critical minerals like sodium and potassium. It affects primarily young cats of any breed.

Cause: The most common cause is destruction of the adrenal gland tissue by the cat's own immune system. More rarely, infections, infiltration of the adrenal glands with lymphosarcoma, or diseases of the pituitary gland may also cause Addison's disease. It can also occur when a cat is abruptly withdrawn from steroid medication.

Treatment: Medication is available, but it's a hard disease to manage. Addison's disease is fairly common in dogs but, luckily, rare in cats.

PANCREATITIS

Pancreatitis is an inflammation of the pancreas. It used to be considered rare, but is now seen more frequently, especially in older animals. Siamese cats may be more prone to the disease than other breeds, at least according to one study.

Causes: Pancreatitis can be caused by drugs (such as steroids), infections, metabolic disorders, too much calcium in the blood,

Hyperthyroidism is one of the most common ailments of middle-aged and senior cats. Signs include weight loss, increased hunger and thirst, difficulty in breathing, and excessive shedding and matting of the coat.

and trauma, such as falling. Obesity and high-fat diets may also play a role.

Signs: This disease is hard to diagnose, but signs include fever, vomiting increased heart rate, abdominal pain, and lethargy.

Treatment: Treatment is to "rest the pancreas" and provide supportive care, beginning with fasting the cat for at least 24 hours. Food is usually withheld for a day or so. Fluid therapy is also given. Most cats survive with supportive treatment. Antibiotics are frequently given. Cats who have repeated bouts may need to go on a low-fat diet.

IMMUNE SYSTEM DISEASES

Your cat's immune system is vital to her health. It protects her from disease and, when something goes wrong with it, your cat is at the mercy of every passing germ.

FELINE PANLEUKOPENIA (FPV)

FPV is a disease that, in its history, has gone by many names: feline panleukopenia (often shortened to "panleuk" in verbal discussion), FPV (feline panleukopenia virus), feline parvovirus, feline distemper, feline infectious enteritis, feline infectious gastroenteritis, feline agranulocytosis, cat plague, cat fever, show fever, pseudomembranous enteritis, maladie du jeune chat, feline typhus, feline typhoid, colibacillosis, and agranulocytosis.

Whatever you decide to call it, this is a highly contagious and often fatal parvovirus in cats and is probably very closely related to canine parvovirus. It affects the blood/lymphatic system, the gastrointestinal system, and the nervous system.

The word "panleukopenia" means a lessening of the numbers of white blood cells. Kittens are most severely affected, often dying with 24 hours of showing signs of the infection. Having built up immunity, older cats can generally avoid getting sick. Luckily, FPV is much less common in pets than it used to be, undoubtedly because of the widespread use of vaccines. However, it is still endemic in wild and feral cat populations.

Causes/Transmission: The major route of transmission is direct contact between a susceptible host and an infected animal or its secretions, especially feces. This virus also can cross the placenta to infect fetuses.

Signs: The incubation period from infection until clinical signs develop is usually from three to five days. Signs of the disease include deep depression, fever, vomiting, diarrhea, and extreme dehydration (no matter how much the cat drinks). The brain of young kittens may be affected, producing cerebellar hypoplasia.

FeLV vs. FPV

It doesn't help that it's easy to get FPV mixed up with FeLV, but they are not the same thing.

Treatment/Prevention: Quarantine and maintaining a clean environment are vital. The virus may be shed in the feces for up to six weeks after recovery. In addition, this is a tough virus; it can survive for a year in the right environment, and it can be carried around on your shoes and clothes. Bleach, however, will kill it. Interestingly, most infections are subclinical, meaning that apparently healthy cats test positive for the virus but show no signs of ill effects.

The best way to handle this disease is to get your cat immunized against it. There is no cure, and successful therapy involves fluid therapy and supportive care. A blood or plasma transfusion may help; supportive antibiotic care is sometimes given.

Many viral diseases are passed from cat to cat, so quarantine of sick animals and maintaining a clean environment are vital.

Feline Leukemia Virus (FeLV)

FeLV is a viral disease. The name feline leukemia can be misleading. While leukemia is one aspect of the disease, it can also cause immunosuppression and other kinds of cancer. This virus invades the cells of the immune system, chatting up the nuclei (where the DNA is) of the cells it gets into. It then starts bossing the cells around, making them do what it wants, which is to diminish the replication of white blood cells, specifically the T-cells (which are the center of the immune system). The weakened immune system then leaves the body open for other infections of all kinds.

It is estimated that 2 to 3 percent of healthy cats are infected with FeLV. In multi-cat homes and catteries the number is much higher—between a quarter and half of the individuals. FeLV infection is highest in cats between one and six years of age, with males more likely to be infected than females.

Causes: FeLV is transmitted from cat to cat and also from mother to offspring. Pregnant cats infected with the virus usually have stillborn or aborted kittens. FeLV is a retrovirus belonging to the same family as FIV. These things don't destroy cells—they hijack them, which is worse. Most commonly, the route of infection is through contact with infected body fluids like saliva or blood, usually through the mouth or nose. The virus is also found in tears, urine, and feces, although in lesser amounts. Not all cats exposed to the virus

Cat Scratch Disease (Cat Scratch Fever) —A Problem in People

For over a century, it has been known that cats worldwide can cause an uncommon (2.5 cases per 250,000 people) disease in human beings. Most victims are under the age of 17, or more often under the age of 12.

The disease develops at the site of a scratch (or more rarely a bite) as a small skin lesion. A couple of weeks later, the lymph nodes may swell up. About 30 percent of people will develop flu-like symptoms, including aches and fever. In most cases, the disease is mild and self-limiting, although it may take a few months for the lymph nodes to return to normal. However, some people, especially those with immune deficiencies, are more severely affected, and other conditions such as tonsillitis, encephalitis, hepatitis, pneumonia, and a variety of serious illnesses have been associated with it in vulnerable individuals. Treatment must be prescribed by a doctor.

The responsible agent has remained elusive, although it's believed that the gram-negative bacterium *Bartonella henselae* is a primary culprit. It may be transmitted from cat to cat by fleas.

become persistently infected. Either they have a powerful enough immune system to resist it, or they haven't been exposed to a sufficient number of viruses. It takes large amounts of the virus to infect an adult, so usually extended contact is necessary for transmission. Some cats exposed to these viruses can fight them off and have only a "transient infection." Others develop a hidden infection. These cats usually show no symptoms and usually do not shed virus in their saliva or other body secretions. Queens, however, may pass the virus to their kittens either before or after birth. Still others become actively ill and shed large amounts of virus.

If enough of the virus gets into the bone marrow, the cat will be infected for the rest of her life.

Signs: Affected cats show progressive deterioration in health. Signs of disease may include fever, intestinal illness, lethargy, respiratory distress, skin problems, and weight loss.

About 25 percent of affected cats develop the anemia that gives the disease its name. Sometimes the virus destroys the red blood cells in the marrow, where they originate. Sometimes the cat's own immune system destroys them. About 15 percent of cats infected with FeLV develop cancer, often lymphoma.

Treatment/Prevention: The screening test for FeLV infection is a blood test, the ELISA antigen test, and the immunofluorescent assay (IFA). Cats with hidden infections test negative, but may still develop associated disorders later in life. Currently, no treatment is available to eliminate FeLV infection. Therapy is aimed at maintaining quality of life and managing the effects of infection such as immunosuppression, anemia, and cancer. Clinically, FeLV-infected cats are treated according to the signs of disease they are showing. That said, some work is being done using new antiviral drugs. Some veterinarians who practice alternative therapies favor giving affected cats large amounts of vitamin C to help boost the immune system. Talk to your vet about the various options available.

Between 80 and 90 percent of infected cats die within three or four months after diagnosis, usually because of immunosuppression. Cats under six months of age are most at risk of chronic infection.

The virus is fragile and does not survive in a dry environment outside the cat's body. If it's moist, it can live for a day or so. Heat, drying, detergents, and ultraviolet light are its enemies.

Although FeLV vaccinations have been available for years, none are completely effective. They work by stimulating a successful immune response to the virus. In addition, these vaccines have been associated with the development of an aggressive cancer (fibrosarcoma) at the site of vaccination. Vaccination does not interfere with testing.

If you have multiple cats, have each one tested for FeLV. Separate cats who test positive from the rest, and disinfect all dishes, litter boxes, and bedding.

FELINE IMMUNODEFICIENCY VIRUS (FIV)

FIV is another nasty retrovirus, first discovered in 1986, in a California cat rescue center. Some of the cats there had been showing clinical signs similar to people with acquired immunodeficiency syndrome (AIDS). And, indeed, the viruses are quite similar. FIV infection is permanent and usually fatal. Carriers may show no signs for years, although their immune system gradually falls apart, resulting in full-blown feline AIDS (FAIDS). This particular family of viruses (lentiviruses) is known for being species-specific. It is also known for being a life-long infection responsible for slowly progressive diseases. People cannot get AIDS from cats.

FIV destroys the T helper cells, white blood cells critical to a healthy

Free-roaming cats are more likely to be infected with FIV than indoor cats. The main method of transmission is through bite wounds acquired during fighting, because the saliva contains large amounts of the virus.

Cats have a higher incidence of lymphoma than either people or dogs (and it is common in dogs). The incidence is even higher in cats who are infected with FeLV and FIV.

immune system. FIV infection is most common in middle-aged and older unneutered male and feral cats. The average age of infected cats is 3 to 5 years.

Causes: It seems that the main method of transmission is through bite wounds acquired during fighting, because the saliva contains large amounts of the virus. Kittens can also be infected at birth, presumably through virus present in the queen's milk. Interestingly, and opposite to people, sexual activity is not thought to be a major method of transmission. Nor is a shared litter box a danger. The role of fleas is not known. Unless the affected cat is a fighter, other cats in the household are not at high risk for infection (if they are vaccinated, they are completely safe).

Signs: Initial signs of infection include mild illness and fever, loss of appetite, and swelling of lymph glands. Later, there is a progressive deterioration in general health, including neurological disease, chronic renal failure, cancers (especially lymphoma), stomatitis (mouth and gum disease), respiratory conditions, diarrhea, urinary disorders, and wasting syndromes. A blood test is used to diagnose the infection.

Treatment: There is no cure, but some cats have been given improved quality of life with agents used for people with AIDS, such as AZT and interferon, drugs that stimulate the immune function. A vaccine has been available to prevent the disease since 2002. It is a killed vaccine (which does not challenge the immune system so much) reported to be 82 percent effective at preventing subtype A, with less data about its efficacy against subtype B, the subtype found on the East Coast. The virus is very fragile and cannot survive outside the cat's body.

FELINE INFECTIOUS PERITONITIS (FIP)

Feline infectious peritonitis is a poorly understood viral disease. Perhaps as many as 25 to 40 percent of household cats and up to 95 percent of cats in multi-cat households and catteries have been infected with the virus, but the fatal disease develops in only 1 in 5,000 cats in households with one or two cats. As many as 5 percent of cats die from FIP.

It can infect any cat, although young and elderly cats are most at risk. Middle-aged cats are seldom affected. It comes in two forms: the "dry" form (about 25 percent of the cases) and the "effusive" form.

Cause: The cause of FIP is a coronavirus; it is transmitted through saliva and feces. The virus can live in the environment in steadily diminishing numbers for three to seven weeks; it is killed by regular household disinfectants. Strangely, the damage is not so much due to the virus itself, but to the body's response to it. In fact, the cat's immune system, in an attempt to protect the cat against FIP, actually speeds the process of the disease. (The actual process is too complicated to go into here.)

Signs: The most common clinical signs are fluctuating fever, inappetence (loss of appetite), lethargy, and weight loss. In the effusive form, fluid accumulates in body cavities, often giving the cat a pot-bellied look. The dry form does not present this way but can pass into the effusive form (if the cat lives long enough). About half of all dry cases produce eye inflammation or neurological problems.

Treatment: Currently there is no specific treatment, and survival is extremely rare. Even diagnosis is difficult. One FIP researcher, Dr. Diane Addie, of Scotland, claims success using feline interferon omega, curing a quarter to a third of cases. Most researchers do not support her claims, however. This medication is not available everywhere. Treatment is generally limited to supportive care.

The most important thing is to interrupt the cycle of reinfection when multiple cats are involved. A preventive intranasal vaccine against FIP has been available since 1991, but neither veterinarians nor the manufacturer (Pfizer) recommend that the vaccine be given routinely. It is advised for cats in contact with free-roaming cats or for those living in households that have had a cat with FIP. Initially, two doses are given at two- to four-week intervals. It is estimated to be about 75 percent effective, although in some studies the rate was considerably lower. It is not effective on cats who have already been exposed to the virus.

LYMPH SYSTEM DISORDERS

The lymphatic system is closely associated with the cardiovascular system. It also plays a role in immunity and digestion. Problems in the lymphatic system can affect all other systems.

Leukemia vs. Lymphoma

Leukemia is a condition in which large numbers of abnormal precursors to mature white blood cells are present in the blood. Lymphoma is also a disease of the blood-forming organs, but is present as masses in various locations throughout the body. It is also often present in animals with lymphoma.

LYMPHOMA (OR LYMPHOSARCOMA)

Lymphoma is a cancer of the lymphocytes (a type of blood cell) and lymphoid tissues. These tissues are found in many places in the body, including lymph nodes, spleen, liver, gastrointestinal tract, and bone marrow. Feline lymphoma can take one of three forms: multicentric, mediastinal, and alimentary, but in all forms tumors of the lymphoid tissue are present.

Cats have a higher incidence of lymphoma than either people or dogs (and it is common in dogs). The incidence is even higher in cats who are infected with FeLV and FIV.

Causes: Typically, lymphoma occurs in younger cats who are infected with the FeLV and in older cats (about nine years old) who are *not* infected with the virus.

Signs: Feline lymphoma may appear under different guises. Because lymphocytes and lymph tissue occur throughout the body, lymphoma can appear almost anywhere and affect a wide number of organs. The symptoms of lymphoma in cats are more severe than in dogs. The precise signs depend on the location of the disease, but may include weight loss, rough coat, loss of appetite, and vomiting or diarrhea. Diagnostics includes a battery of tests including physical examination, radiographs, ultrasounds, chemistry panels, CBC counts, or fine-needle aspirates.

One of the worst cases is the so-called multicentric form, which involves several lymph nodes and perhaps several organs. This usually happens at a late stage of the disease and is the form associated with FeLV.

Another form associated with feline leukemia is the mediastinal form that attacks the thymus and lymph nodes. (The mediastinum is an aggregation of lymphoid tissue in the chest.) Cats with this type of lymphoma often have trouble breathing due to a large mass in the chest or an accumulation of fluid around the lungs.

Renal lymphosarcoma affects the kidneys. Signs are similar to those of kidney failure: increased thirst, increased urination, loss of appetite, and vomiting. Lymphoma of the external lymph nodes is less common, but tell-tale lumps may appear. The alimentary form attacks the digestive tract, including the stomach, intestines, and liver; this form is less likely to be associated with feline leukemia. Signs of this kind of lymphoma include vomiting, diarrhea, weight loss, or a decreased appetite. Bone marrow lymphoma produces leukemia. Affected cats often have anemia and bleeding.

Treatment: The treatment partly depends on where the disease

Low-Protein Diet Dangers

There is some controversy now about the wisdom of a low-protein diet for feline kidney patients. Because cats are obligate carnivores, a low-protein diet may starve the muscles and create all kind of problems. The key is to give just enough protein for the cat to maintain herself without stressing the kidneys by trying to excrete the rest. Stay tuned.

is located. The treatment of choice is chemotherapy, and about 70 percent of cats will respond well to it. In fact, remissions of two years are not uncommon. Cats do not lose their hair (although they may lose their whiskers); sometimes their fur does develop a different texture. Other side effects, such as vomiting, are rare. Surgery or radiation treatment is indicated in a few cases, usually in addition to chemotherapy. However, this is merely a therapy, not a cure, and eventually the cancer will return. However, the cat may enjoy months or years of good, quality life until then.

REPRODUCTIVE SYSTEM DISORDERS

The role of the reproductive system is obvious—it helps your cat make kittens. Even spayed and neutered animals can have problems with this important system, so don't skip it.

FELINE MAMMARY GLAND ADENOCARCINOMA (FMGAC)

FMGAC is a common tumor in cats, although it occurs less often than it does in dogs. The average age at onset is 10 to 14 years, although much younger and older cats can be affected. Siamese cats may be twice as likely to get the disease, and they are also more likely to develop the disease at a younger age. Next at risk are domestic Shorthairs. Intact females are at a much higher risk of developing mammary cancer than their spayed counterparts. Female cats who were spayed after experiencing a heat cycle, whether they had kittens or not, are at a greater risk than a cat who was spayed before her first heat cycle. FMGAC very rarely occurs in male cats.

Breast lumps in cats are malignant about 90 percent of the time, so if one is detected, it should be taken care of immediately.

Cause: The exact cause is not known, but it appears that prolonged elevated progesterone levels play an important part, so progesterone-like drugs should be avoided. Cats with cystic ovaries and other uterine disorders are more likely to develop breast cancer than are healthy queens.

Signs: Lumps in the mammary gland are apparent. This cancer is very aggressive, soon metastasizing to the lymph nodes and lungs.

Treatment: Unfortunately, most cats with the disease die within a year, partly because, by the time it is detected, the disease is far advanced. If caught early enough, two radical chain mastectomies one month apart and one year of chemotherapy may be effective.

FHV-1 (Feline Herpes Virus)

FHV-1 is an extremely common virus in cats. In fact, most cats all over the world have it. But only some get sick, and most of them do so in times of stress. The disease is very similar to the herpes virus that causes cold sores in people

Pyometra

This is a disease that affects middle-aged, unspayed females.

Causes: It used to be considered a uterine infection, but it is now known that hormones may be responsible, even when no bacterial infection is present.

Signs: The most common sign is a white, yellow, or blood-tinged discharge from the vulva. The cat will lick at the area.

Treatment: This can be a critical condition and may need immediate treatment, which usually consists of intravenous fluids, usually for several days, antibiotics, and spaying. To prevent the disease, have your cat spayed before the age of six months.

RENAL SYSTEM DISEASES

The renal system works in association with the kidneys, and its job is to eliminate toxins from the body.

Chronic Renal Failure

Feline chronic renal failure is one of the most common ailments affecting cats. The usual victim is a cat between the ages of 10 and 14 years. In kidney disease, the nephrons (filters in the kidney) begin to fail. Normally, their job is to remove toxins from the blood. Efficient kidneys can make highly concentrated urine, so that a large amount of toxins can be excreted in a relatively small amount of water. In kidney failure, urine is usually produced in excessive quantities. It takes more and more water to filter the same amount of toxins as previously. Ultimately, the cat just can't drink enough water to support the failing kidneys, and toxin levels begin to rise. That's what kills the cat.

Causes: Causes can include age, infections, parasites, cancer, amyloidosis, inflammation, autoimmune disease, trauma, toxic reaction to drugs, and congenital or genetic problems.

Signs: Signs include bad breath, blood in urine, constipation, increased thirst and urination, lack of appetite, lethargy, nausea, poor coat, and weight loss.

These are pretty vague signs that could mean almost anything. The official diagnosis is made by determining the level of two waste products in the blood: blood urea nitrogen (BUN) and blood creatinine.

Treatment: The disease is progressive, terminal, and occurs in all breeds of cat. Despite this gloomy prognosis, there are many things you can do to help your cat achieve a good quality of life for months or even years.

And while it's important to know that chronic renal failure is largely a product of aging, it can also result from numerous other causes, some of which are quite curable if caught in time.

The goal of therapy is to reduce the amount of waste products in the system. Treatment begins with an attempt to get the kidneys working again by administering intravenous fluids to flush out the kidneys. Not only water but important electrolytes like potassium are included. This is called diuresis. Mild, early cases can be treated with subcutaneous fluids at home. After this, the vet will put the cat on a special reduced-protein, low-phosphate diet, potassium supplementation, a phosphate binder, drugs to help nausea and regulate calcium levels, and possibly a medication for high blood pressure.

Kidney transplants are another option for some cats. First performed in the mid-1980s at University of California at Davis, they are no longer considered experimental. Today, at least nine veterinary hospitals are available, with

Your cat's immune system is vital to her health. Just as with humans, maintaining a healthy lifestyle with a nutritionally-balanced diet, daily exercise, stress avoidance, a controlled weight, and routine veterinary preventative health care can help keep your feline in the best shape possible to fight infections.

surgeons capable of performing kidney transplants on cats. The success rate of the surgery is about 90 percent, but the procedure is not cheap. In addition, the cat must still be in good condition. Extremely sick cats would not survive the surgery.

Feline Urologic Syndrome (FUS) or Feline Lower Urinary Tract Disease (FLUTD)

Cats are frequent sufferers of lower urinary tract diseases. Most of these affect the bladder or the urethra, the tube that carries urine from the bladder to the outside of the body. Urinary stones, or uroliths, can form in the urinary tract and cause signs of lower urinary tract disease. The technical term is urolithiasis. The two most common types of stones in cats are made from struvite (magnesium ammonium phosphate) and calcium oxalate. Male cats are at greater risk because their urethra is longer and narrower. This can be life-threatening. The urethra may be plugged by a stone (usually struvite) or by a plug made from soft compressible material. These plugs can be formed by minerals, cells, and all kinds of other stuff. You don't want to know.

Causes: Many agents can contribute to this problem, including infections of bacterial, fungal, parasitic, or viral origin. Urinary stones, urethral plugs, cancer, and other disorders may be present. Some research even suggests that high levels of magnesium in foods and constant stress are other possible triggers. And sometimes, the cause remains unknown.

Signs: Signs include straining and making unsuccessful attempts to urinate. Cats will frequently lick the genital area. Blood may be present in the urine.

Treatment: Management of the condition depends on the stone type. Surgical removal is usually required. Special diets designed to dissolve struvite stones are available from your veterinarian. If fed over a period of time, such diets are often successful.

If the cat's urethra becomes blocked, you have a veterinary emergency. A cat with a true obstruction is very distressed and in a great deal of pain. Get her to your vet right away; otherwise your cat can die in agony.

RESPIRATORY SYSTEM DISORDERS

Without the respiratory system we can't breathe. Unfortunately, this major system is under frequent attacks in cats.

What's the FUS?

In many cases, there seems to be a similarity between feline urologic syndrome (FUS) and a bladder problem in people called interstitial cystitis (IC).

DISEASES OF THE NOSE AND MOUTH

Oropharyngeal conditions may be a consequence of underlying, generalized disease, particularly chronic kidney failure, leucopenia (depressed white blood cell count), immunosuppression secondary to FeLV or FIV infections, or even diabetes. In such cases, the oral problem will not resolve unless the underlying problem is treated.

ASTHMA

Feline asthma is an intermittent airflow obstruction (a muscle spasm in the bronchi). An acute asthmatic crisis can arise at any time and become life-threatening. Unfortunately, the inability to clear the bronchi of mucus leaves the cat susceptible to secondary infections as well.

The most common victims are female cats between the ages of one and eight years. Siamese and Himalayan cats may be especially susceptible. About 1 percent of all cats will develop the disease.

Causes: The exact causes are not always known (a genetic component may be present), but it is apparent that a chronic inflammation of the tissues in the bronchial walls occurs, which seem to react to allergens such as smoke, aerosol sprays, and ragweed, along with viruses and infections. All these agents in turn

Respiratory infections such as feline rhinotracheitis virus and calicivirus are usually spread through cat-to-cat contact with the discharge from the eyes and nose of an infected animal. Sharing food dishes, litter boxes, bedding, etc., that have been contaminated with infected discharge can transmit these viruses to healthy cats.

257

cause increased mucus production. Some cats may also have asthma attacks following the ingestion of certain foods, especially fish; fish seem to be high in histamines.

Cats, especially Siamese and Himalayans, can be prone to allergic-reaction asthma. One suspect is the dust from litter boxes. Because this can be a life-threatening emergency, contact your vet at once if your cat is having difficulty breathing.

Signs: Signs include coughing, wheezing, and in more severe cases, open-mouthed breathing. Sometimes it appears as if the cat is trying to cough up something, and she may vomit after an attack. (Too many cat owners just assume the cat is trying to cough up a hairball.) The cat's ears and gums may become blue.

Treatment: The first approach in dealing with this condition is to try to make lifestyle and diet changes. It helps to clear the home of any substances that may be causing the problem. It might be as simple as changing your cat's brand of litter or as hard as giving up smoking. Also, the diet should be reviewed for allergy-provoking substances, and obese cats should be put on a weight-reduction diet.

The medical treatment of choice is corticosteroid therapy. Some cats will need this therapy for the rest of their lives; others can get by with being treated only during flare-ups. Some veterinarians also use injectable or oral terbutaline to help bronchodilatation. Inhalers for cats have recently become available. Regular treatment with inhalers is recommended for cats with mild symptoms.

Antihistamines that block serotonin and smooth muscle contraction in the bronchioles are also used. Side effects include increased appetite and tranquilization.

BORDETELLA (OR URTD)

Feline infectious upper respiratory tract disease (URTD) is a frequent disease

Cats are subject to many diseases affecting the nose and nasal passages.

among cats, especially in animals under stress or living in close quarters, such as in catteries. While some people believe it to be rare, it may actually be that many cats don't show signs.

Causes: Formerly, the organisms blamed for the condition were FCV, FHV-1, and *Chlamydophila felis* (previously known as *Chlamydia psittaci*). However, because vaccinations did not prevent the disease and the condition will often respond to an antibiotic, attention has shifted toward *Bordetella bronchiseptica*, the same bacillus that causes tracheobronchitis (kennel cough) in dogs. In fact, cats and dogs can pass the disease to each other. Studies have shown that *B. bronchiseptica* can cause URTD in experimental cats known to be free of all other known respiratory pathogens.

Signs: Signs of the disease include coughing, fever, labored breathing, lack of appetite, nasal discharge, and sneezing.

In otherwise healthy cats, the disease is usually mild and clinical signs disappear after about ten days. Young kittens, however, are at risk of developing bronchopneumonia. In them, the disease can be life-threatening.

Cats who are reluctant to eat must be force-fed, or risk developing feline hyperlipidosis, a potentially fatal disease. Some cats may become carriers and continue to shed bacteria for at least 19 weeks after developing the disease.

Treatment: *B. bronchiseptica* infection can be treated with antibiotics. Usually, a course of 21 days is required.

Not Just the Sniffles

Various organisms can cause different kinds of upper respiratory disease in cats. If your cat develops the sniffles, has watery eyes, and nasal discharge, head for the vet because the disease is probably much more serious than a common cold in people.

259

Nasal Disease

Cats are subject to many diseases affecting the nose and nasal passages.

Causes: Chronic viral nasal disease can develop from both feline rhinotracheitis virus (FVR) and FCV. Both are extremely contagious.

Signs: Signs include sneezing, bilateral nasal discharge, increased breathing sounds, and discharge from the eyes. If severe bleeding is present, nasal tumor is indicated. Nasal tumor, tooth abscess, or a foreign body are suspected if discharge occurs from only one side of the nose.

Treatment: Treatment depends on the cause, as is so often the case. Supportive treatment is usually sufficient, with antibiotics administered if a secondary infection develops.

Feline Calicivirus (FCV)

Calicivirus is part of the feline upper respiratory infection (URI) complex, a group of viral and bacterial infections (e.g., FHV, chlamydiosis) that cause discharge from the eyes and nose. Calicivirus and FHV account for 85 to 90 percent of all URIs in cats.

FCV is a viral disease characterized by upper respiratory symptoms, pneumonia, oral ulceration (sores in the mouth), and occasionally arthritis. It usually affects the throat and sometimes the lungs; it can also infect the intestines, and it has been isolated from feces.

Calicivirus occurs worldwide and affects all breeds of cat. Vaccination has reduced the incidence of clinical disease (the animals who actually get sick), but it hasn't decreased the prevalence of the virus. The virus is spreading, even though fewer cats show symptoms. Even when they do, it's a fairly mild, flu-like disease that seldom causes serious complications. More recently however, a more virulent strain of FCV has been identified in the US.

Calicivirus is most common in kittens, multi-cat households, and pet adoption shelters. Outbreaks can occur in overcrowded, poorly ventilated, or unsanitary conditions; and situations in which cats are poorly fed or stressed, either physically (e.g., extreme temperatures) or psychologically (e.g., introduction of a new cat). Several strains of FCV exist, and different strains cause different symptoms. (For example, one particular strain can cause ulcers on the paws as well as in the mouth.)

Calicivirus often occurs with another upper respiratory infection, such as FHV, rhinotracheitis virus, or chlamydiosis

Causes: Calicivirus is spread through direct contact with the saliva, eye and nose discharges, and sometimes the feces of an infected cat.

Signs: Characteristic mouth ulcers (tongue, nose, and roof of the mouth)

may be the only sign of infection. The new, more serious strain causes severe swelling of the face and paws and has a deleterious effect on the whole body, with a high mortality rate (40 percent). Further investigation into this strain is ongoing.

Treatment/Prevention: FCV can survive outside the cat's body for as long as eight to ten days, so it may be present in dishes, litter boxes, and clothing, even after a thorough cleaning. Many cats remain contagious for years, even though they may not show signs of disease. Healthy (i.e., asymptomatic), contagious cats are known as latent carriers. Most cats infected with FCV shed the virus continuously only for a short time after recovering. However, in a few cats, FCV shedding continues for several years.

CHYLOTHORAX

Chylothorax is an accumulation of lymph and other fluids in the chest. A build up of these fluids around the lungs makes it difficult for the cat to breathe, and the disease can be life-threatening. The disease is fairly uncommon; Siamese and Himalayan may be at increased risk. Both sexes are equally affected.

Many respiratory disorders are caused by unsanitary conditions or poorly ventilated, overcrowded conditions.

Cause: The cause is not always known; in some cases, it can be traced to trauma. Underlying causes may also include lymphoma associated with FeLV, cardiomyopathy, heartworms, and chest tumors. Cats whose disease has been caused by trauma will usually recover with proper care. However, the prognosis for idiopathic disease is guarded, even with the best care. Some cats can recover completely, especially with surgery.

Signs: Signs of the disease include appetite loss, coughing, increased respiratory rate, lethargy, and open-mouth breathing.

Treatment: Medical management includes monitoring fluid in the chest and removing it when necessary. Chylothorax in cats is somewhat responsive to low-fat diets. In other cases, surgical correction of the condition is indicated. If that doesn't work, surgery to open the chest and sew the lymph ducts shut may be necessary. (These ducts are similar to arteries and veins. But instead of carrying blood, they carry lymph fluid from the tissues to the heart.)

FELINE UPPER RESPIRATORY DISEASE COMPLEX

This condition affects the mouth, nasal passages, sinuses, and upper airway in cats and kittens. Most animals infected with FHV or calicivirus will become chronic carriers of the virus.

Cause: In most cases, the causative agents are FHV (formerly called feline rhinotracheitis virus) and calicivirus. It is spread through contact with the discharge from the eyes and nose of an infected cat.

Alternative Health Care

Many pet owners decide to try an additional route to maintaining their cat's wellness or to restoring a sick animal to health. Some have had poor experience with standard medicines, some are looking for a miracle, and some are open-minded people willing to try new options. However, if you decide to go with alternative treatment, discuss it with your veterinarian first, and get referrals. In some states, a person may need to be a licensed veterinarian to legally treat the animal.

Varieties of alternative health care include aromatherapy; flower remedy therapy; energy therapy; low-energy photon therapy; magnetic field therapy; orthomolecular therapy; veterinary acupuncture, acutherapy, and acupressure; veterinary homeopathy; veterinary manual or manipulative therapy (similar to osteopathy, chiropractic, or physical medicine and therapy); veterinary nutraceutical therapy; and veterinary phytotherapy.

The scientific evaluation of these therapies has produced variable results. Some have been shown to be useful adjuncts to modern Western care; others have not. Some, especially aromatherapy, can be dangerous to cats, who are highly sensitive to certain aromatic oils, just as in regular medicine, pyrethrum, which is great for dogs, is toxic to cats. Do not attempt any alternative care without your veterinarian's advice and approval.

My own feeling is that modern Western veterinary care is the single best modality for treating a sick animal. But it is not the only one. Acupuncture is probably very effective in some cases. Herbal medicine can be powerful (after all, many modern medicines are based on

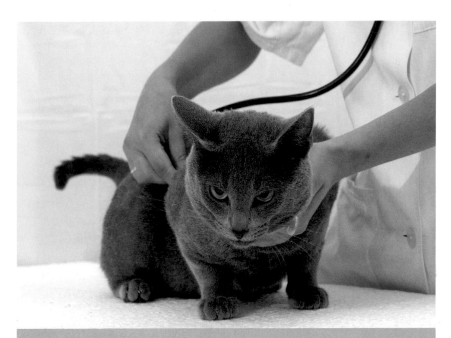

A holistic veterinarian can discuss alternative health care treatment options with you in detail and help you to determine which would be appropriate for your cat.

herbs), but the dosages are impossible to standardize and the results are wildly variable. They can be dangerous in the wrong hands, and many herbalists are not veterinarians. Some have had extensive practice with people, but cats often respond very differently.

Chiropractic care has a place (a narrow one, I think) in veterinary medicine. I believe aromatherapy not only does not work, but can be positively harmful to cats when certain essential oils are used. Some people believe that other alternative therapies have yielded good results (what the scientific community would call "anecdotal evidence"), but so far no scientific studies have indicated a benefit for these methods. I, myself, do not believe that homeopathy, flower essences, and crystals work at all, except to perhaps calm down the owner and change her perceptions of the animal's illness. At least they do no harm, unless the owner puts off getting real help for her pet. However, I am willing to be convinced otherwise, and I have included some standard alternative medicines in my treatment of the diseases discussed in

Many pet owners prefer alternative veterinary medicine because it does not use drugs, chemicals, chemotherapy, or other treatments they believe harm the system. If you decide to go with alternative treatment, discuss it with your vet first.

this chapter. I have seen plenty of scientific evidence, however, showing the benefit of acupuncture and of chiropractic, although the latter can be harmful in the wrong (unskilled) hands.

Alternative therapies such as acupuncture, acupressure, aromatherapy, botanical medicine, herbs, homeopathic medicine, massage therapy, and chiropractic therapy are designed to help return the body to a natural state of balance. Many are used to treat chronic pain, behavioral disorders, and degenerative diseases. A holistic veterinarian can discuss the different treatments options with you in detail and help you to determine which would be appropriate for your cat.

A holistic veterinarian, by the way, uses both standard and alternative medicine. One who refuses to use standard Western medicine is not a holistic vet, but an alternative one. The word "holistic" means "whole."

ACUPUNCTURE

If any medical treatment has withstood the test of time (lots of it), it's acupuncture. First practiced in China on horses over 3,500 years ago, acupuncture is an accepted modality of treatment for many animals, as well as human beings. There's also a record of an elephant being successfully treated for bloat with acupuncture. While it's not necessarily true that what works on an elephant will work on a cat, it happens to be so in this case.

Acupuncture is the examination and stimulation of specific points of the body through the use of fine needles, pressure, and heat. It is based on the principle that the life force or *qi* (pronounced *chee*) flows through 14 invisible energy channels in the body called meridians. Along these meridians are specific points that, when stimulated, enhance the body's natural healing capacity. These are the acupuncture points.

In classical acupuncture theory, animals tend to become ill if these energy channels are blocked by stress or subtle injury. Complementary forces within the body, called yin and yang, must be kept in balance. The goal of acupuncture is to open the channels so that the balancing flow of *qi* can be released and restore the body to its natural balance.

Even Western medicine can provide a rationale as to why acupuncture works. It stimulates nerves, increases blood circulation, relieves muscle spasms, and encourages the release of pain-relieving hormones like endorphins. (The fancy name for this is the neural opiate theory.) Acupuncture is recognized by the American Veterinary Medical Association as "an integral part of veterinary medicine."

What's more, it's painless. Believe me, if it hurt, the cat would let you know. The depth of the needle, insertion, type of stimulation, and duration of treatment vary according to the condition being treated. Although not used as often, more modern methods include electrical or laser stimulation, gold beads, surgical staples, or magnets to provide permanent stimulation.

Acupuncture is most effective for functional problems such as those that involve paralysis, noninfectious inflammation (like allergies), and pain. In cats, some conditions that may be treated with acupuncture include:

- gastrointestinal problems (for example, diarrhea)
- musculoskeletal problems (for example, arthritis or vertebral disc disease)
- respiratory problems (for example, feline asthma)
- skin problems (for example, obsessive-compulsive grooming)

Any particular stimulation of an individual acupuncture point may take as little as 10 seconds or as long as 30 minutes. A simple acute problem, such as a sprain, may need only one treatment, while severe or chronic conditions may require repeated visits.

Acupuncture can be used with standard Western medicine. It has no side effects or contraindications. In fact, many people believe that it will actually enhance conventional veterinary therapy.

It's amazing to watch an acupuncture treatment. Even a highly nervous cat will start to relax and even fall asleep until the needles are removed.

One of the greatest advances in acupuncture is the use of the laser beam. The laser avoids even the slightest discomfort, and the practitioner does not have to develop the fine-tuned skill that a manual acupuncturist must have. The use of the laser also eliminates even the slightest chance for infection. The treatment takes less time that conventional acupuncture, and the equipment is relatively inexpensive.

A veterinary acupuncturist must be a licensed veterinarian who has been

Just as many houseplants are toxic to cats, many herbs used in herbal therapy may not be safe for them because they are sensitive creatures reacting very differently to them than do people or dogs.

certified by the International Veterinary Acupuncture Society, currently the only accredited certification program for veterinary acupuncturists. To find a certified practitioner in your area, check the International Veterinary Society directory at http://www.komvet.at/ivadkom/vapsocs.htm.

Currently, there is no official AVMA listing for specialty certification in acupuncture.

HERBAL THERAPIES

Herbs are the mothers of medicine. Many modern medications are ultimately derived from herbs, but herbalists assert that these pharmaceutical derivatives are very different from the mother plant. They contend that the original herbs have unique properties that the drugs derived from them lack. They believe whole herbs create a healthful synergistic effect in the body. Even herbalists, however, often don't use whole herbs because they can be hard to find—and because it may be very difficult to get a cat to eat most of them. Therefore, many are compressed into pill form.

Although herbal therapy is undeniably effective for many animals, the truth is that many herbs may not be safe for cats because they are sensitive creatures reacting very differently to them than do people or dogs. In fact, it's probably smart to assume that, unless you specifically know otherwise, all herbs are unsafe for your cat without prior approval from your vet. However, seven widely used herbs are considered safe for cats and these have a variety of uses. These are:

- bugleweed: a mint helpful to cats with an overactive thyroid
- catnip: when ingested, it can help remedy stomach and digestive problems, especially flatulence
- couchgrass or quackgrass: this grass can be used to disinfect the urinary tract
- cranberry: to aid animals with feline lower urinary tract disease (FLUTD)
- dandelion leaf: a powerful diuretic for chronic kidney failure
- slippery elm bark and marshmallow root: for cats with digestive problems including vomiting, diarrhea, and inflammatory bowel disease

Herbalists believe that whole herbs and grasses, like wheatgrass, create a healthful synergistic effect in the body.

Essential oils can be dangerous for cats, whether ingested, inhaled, or applied to the skin.

- stinging nettle: for sneezing and hay fever

Several other herbs may have medical uses in cats if administered properly, but this should really be prescribed by a competent herbalist.

Herbs potentially toxic to cats include white willow bark, feverfew, meadowsweet, mistletoe, pennyroyal, rue, wormwood, comfrey, chaparral, and lobelia.

Because herbs are strong medicine, don't use them at all without consulting your vet, especially if your cat is on a conventional medication. The biggest drawback of herbs is that the amount of active ingredient in an herb can vary wildly depending on growing conditions and other factors.

ESSENTIAL OILS: DANGEROUS TO CATS

Essential oils, while useful in equine care, can be dangerous to cats, whether ingested, applied to the skin, or even just inhaled. Don't use them around cats. They are hard on the cat's liver, which simply cannot metabolize them. If you want the technical reason, it's because cats lack the enzyme glucuronyl transferase, which helps in eliminating compounds through hepatic glucuronidation. (Glucuronidation is the process of attaching glucose [a kind of sugar] to toxins to make them more water soluble and easier for the kidneys to excrete.) Most other animals can handle glucuronidation with ease, but not cats for some reason. As a result, it's easier for them to build up toxic levels of stuff that other animals just shrug off, so to speak. Some of the most dangerous are:

- birch oil
- cinnamon bark oil
- lavender oil
- lemon oil
- melaleuca oil
- peppermint
- tea tree oil
- thyme oil
- wintergreen oil
- other oils containing phenol

The most popular flower essence for cats, dogs, horses, and people is Rescue Remedy. It is supposed to help in cases of shock or traumatic emergency.

HOMEOPATHY

Homeopathy is a system of remedies devised and formalized by a German physician, Samuel Hahnemann, in the late 1700s. It is based on the principle that you can cure a disease by imbibing (or in some cases just rubbing an ear with) an extremely dilute solution of the agent that caused the disease. The more dilute the substance, the more powerful it is and the less frequently it needs to be given. These remedies are believed to boost the immune system and stimulate the body's natural defenses to heal itself.

Many people have had excellent success using homeopathy, which is especially popular in England and Europe (it is much cheaper than standard care.) However, its benefits have no scientific backup, and even its ardent supporters agree that homeopathy is more suited to mild chronic diseases than acute or serious ones. Again, use caution. I know many people whose pets died under homeopathic care because they refused to get regular veterinary treatment along with "alternative treatment."

FLOWER ESSENCE THERAPY

Flower essences are liquid flower extracts, usually administered orally. They are made from a sun infusion of blossoms in a bowl of pure water; then further

269

Flower essence therapy is designed to help primarily with emotional and psychological rather than physical trauma. Animals who are in fear or shock (emotional states) because of pain (a physical state) can benefit.

diluted and potentized (as in homeopathy). The essences are usually preserved in brandy or another form of alcohol. This alone should give one pause. Alcohol is not really good for cats in any amount, in my opinion.

Flower essence therapy is designed to help primarily with emotional and psychological rather than physical trauma. Of course, the two often go together, and animals who are in fear or shock (emotional states) because of pain (a physical state) can benefit. People who use flower essence therapy find it useful for the following conditions: abuse, grief, neglect, jealousy, aggression, litter box problems, hyperactivity, excessive grooming, and fear. They are said to work through vibrational impulses, but that phrase seems really unclear to me.

Other popular remedies are:

- aspen: to reduce unknown fears in "fraidy cats"
- mimulus: to reduce known fears
- larch: to improve self-confidence in shy cats
- snapdragon: to reduce aggression
- water violet: to help make an aloof cat more friendly

- chestnut bud: to help break bad habits
- beech: to help a cat accommodate to change
- quaking grass: for cats who live in a group and experience tension
- red clover: for cats experiencing the crazies when taken to the vet
- impatiens: to calm nervous cats
- bleeding heart: for cats who have lost a companion
- crab apple: for cats who groom excessively
- chicory: to curb possessiveness
- white chestnut: to reduce worrying

No studies have ever been done to show that these remedies are actually effective, nor is there a scientific rationale as to why they might be. These remedies were originally designed for human beings, and people have adjusted them for use with cats and dogs. Different sources suggest different essences for the same ailment.

The word "chiropractic" comes from the Greek and means to "practice with the hands."

CHIROPRACTIC CARE

Chiropractic care is based on the relationship between the spine and the central nervous system. Practitioners believe that ill health results from misalignment of various body parts, particularly the vertebrae. Misalignment can cause damage to the joints, muscles, nerves, connective tissues, blood flow, and functions of the body. In chiropractic lingo, these misalignments are called subluxations. The manipulation of the spine is called "adjustment."

Contemporary animal chiropractors may use an instrument called an "activator," a spring-loaded device that applies a high-velocity, short stroke to the affected area. It seems to create less apprehension for dogs and cats than traditional chiropractic manipulation; it also allows multiple adjustments to be performed easily.

Currently, there is no AVMA-recognized specialty status for veterinary chiropractic. However, there is an organization of practitioners called the American Veterinary Chiropractic Association (AVCA). Members are licensed doctors of chiropractic or veterinary medicine. Graduates complete 150 hours of course work.

MASSAGE THERAPY

Massage means applying gentle, rolling pressure to various parts of the body. The benefits of massage are well known. It produces a sense of well-being and relaxation, and can soothe muscles and help them heal. It may be especially

If your cat is unable to exercise due to old age or injury, you can stimulate circulation and healing as well as help your cat's joints and muscles stay supple by flexing and massaging them everyday.

useful for aging cats, who tend to have stiffer joints and muscles. Several different types of massage are practiced.

Effleurage: This term refers to the movement of blood. Techniques include rotary, one-hand, and hand-over-hand massage to improve circulation and warm the tissue. It can be used from head to tail, over the trunk, and down the outside limb and up the inside of the limbs.

Passive touch: Here the hand is merely held in place for 30 to 90 seconds to warm the tissue and calm the animal. It is often used during the massage as a break from other motions.

Kneading: Kneading techniques are said to improve circulation and flow. Deep kneading affects the muscle fibers. It is applied directly to the muscle not to the bone. It is said to release toxins.

Tapotement: Tapotement refers to tapping or cupping. This is a stimulating rather than soothing massage. Hacking is sometimes used on large muscle areas (never on the spine). Tapping may be used over the body and head. Tapping is applied three times only, for 30 seconds or less.

Stroking: Stroking is used to calm and quiet the animal.

Passive joint movement and stretching: Passive joint movement and stretching is a range-of-motion physical therapy for the moveable joints. However, avoid this unless you are extremely familiar with feline anatomy. A mistake could cause trauma to the joint and tissue.

There is nothing particularly mysterious, new-age, or "holistic" about massage therapy; it's been standard for years in human medicine. A well-done massage can improve flexibility, reduce pain, and possibly decrease recovery time after surgery. However, it is not a substitute for veterinary care. It should not performed on cats who are feverish, nor should massage be performed near wounds.

Cats like a gentle massage, too, as long as you don't overdo and tax their hair-trigger temperaments. While the ideal average session is said to be about 30 minutes, your cat may suddenly decide she's had enough at any point. If she decides to terminate the massage session, don't argue with her.

Health problems can range from something minor to a major life-threatening situation. Being fully informed and prepared is vital to your cat's proper care.

Part 4

GOOD
SENSE

Chapter Ten

First Aid & Emergency Care

"We should be careful to get out of an experience only the wisdom that is in it and stop there, lest we be like the cat that sits down on a hot stove-lid. She will never sit down on a hot stove-lid again, and that is well; but also she will never sit down on a cold one anymore."

- Mark Twain

A medical emergency is a situation that may result in the death or serious disability of your pet unless you get immediate help. Not every emergency is life-threatening, and some very serious diseases like cancer are not really "emergencies."

Sometimes, you will be able to provide part or all of the help your pet needs. In other cases, you will need immediate veterinary assistance.

In all cases, you need to work fast, safely, and efficiently. But don't play doctor. In an emergency, take your cat to the nearest vet, even if your regular vet is ten minutes further away. In a life-or-death situation, a few minutes can make the difference. Even the best-kept cat can get sick or have an accident. In that case, your appropriate response can make the difference between life and death.

The following conditions should be deemed emergencies in which you should call your vet:

- acute abdominal pain
- breathing problems
- broken bones
- burns
- car accidents (even without obvious injury)
- collapse or fainting
- diarrhea that goes on for more than a day, especially in young animals
- diarrhea with blood
- electrical shock
- eye swelling or injury
- frequent vomiting
- frostbite
- loss of consciousness
- neck injury
- paralysis or lack of coordination
- poisoning
- seizures
- smoke inhalation
- uncontrolled bleeding or bleeding from the chest

Emergencies make up about 60 percent of veterinary hospital admissions.

First Aid

Every pet owner needs a first-aid kit specifically designed for their animal. Keep the kit in an easily accessible place, and write your vet's phone number on the outside. Also write down the age and weight of each of your cats. For obvious reasons, choose a durable, waterproof box with a handle. In it, you should have:

- plant/spider/snake/amphibian identification book: to help you identify and explain to your vet what the "culprit" may have been (if you saw it)
- first-aid booklet
- copy of vet records and vaccinations, especially rabies
- hydrogen peroxide (3 percent solution) to induce vomiting for poisoned cats; keep it fresh and always check the expiration date
- activated charcoal, available in capsules and powder form, to help absorb poisons
- Benadryl for bites and stings
- cotton balls for cleaning away pus and discharges
- emergency ice pack
- styptic powder for bleeding nails
- two rolls of large gauze bandages
- nonstick tape (to use with bandages)
- large gauze sponges
- eye dropper or syringe
- box of exam gloves
- antibiotic ointment for minor cuts
- scissors and tweezers to remove ticks and splinters

In an emergency, your appropriate response can make the difference between life and death for your pet.

279

- towels or blankets to keep an injured animal warm and to avoid shock; also for wrapping the animal for your protection
- thermometer (rectal, for animals)
- water-soluble lubricating jelly
- eyewash
- a box of baking soda
- paper towels for clean up

Approaching an Injured Cat

Injured cats, even your own, may become aggressive. Move slowly, large towel in hand, and don't stare at your cat. Drop the towel over as much of the cat as possible (especially the front end). Quickly pick her up and hold her firmly in your arms.

Emergency Care

Knowledge of symptoms and treatments could be the difference between saving your cat's life and losing her to an emergency. Many potential hazards are found in and around a typical household, and knowing what to do if your cat has met with an accident, has ingested something she shouldn't have, or is having a sudden physical or allergic reaction you can't explain can save your pet's life. Remember that at-home care is never a substitute for professional veterinary care, and that it is always best to get immediate veterinary advice and attention as soon as possible.

ANAPHYLAXIS

Anaphylaxis is an extreme reaction to an allergen, usually something injected, like a bee sting. The most common signs include sudden-onset diarrhea, vomiting, shock, seizures, coma, and death. The cat may go into shock (pale gums, cold limbs, rapid weak pulse). Usually, no facial swelling occurs. This is an extreme emergency: You generally have only minutes to get the cat to a vet.

BACK AND NECK INJURIES

These require immediate professional attention because the spinal cord may be involved. Move the animal carefully in a pet carrier with a removable top or strap her to a board to reduce movement and consequent injury while being transported to the veterinary hospital.

Taking Your Cat's Temperature

To take your cat's temperature, first lubricate a feline thermometer with water-soluble lubricating jelly, and then insert it about 1 inch (2.5 cm) into the anus (you may need someone else to hold the cat) and wait about 2 minutes. Remove and read. The normal temperature is between 100.5° and 102.5°F (37.8° to 39°C).

BITE WOUNDS

Bite wounds are often puncture wounds and can be more serious than they look. They may be accompanied by lacerated skin, swelling, and bleeding. Clip hair from around the wound and wash it for several minutes. Apply warm compresses to promote drainage and an iodine solution to disinfect it. An abscess may form. If it ruptures, keep it open and clean. Prescription antibiotics may be needed.

At-home care is never a substitute for professional veterinary care; it is always best to get immediate veterinary advice and attention as soon as possible.

BLEEDING

Locate the source of the bleeding. Arterial bleeding is the most serious. It can be recognized by its bright red color and spurting with each heartbeat. Stop it by applying firm direct pressure to the wound for at least five minutes. Don't pull off the bandage because you may be interfering with clot formation. Instead, keep adding bandages. Try to estimate the amount of blood lost for the vet's information. Monitor your cat's vital signs every 15 minutes.

Here are some possible causes for bleeding:

- blood in the mouth: may be due to poison, trauma, or autoimmune disease, especially if there is blood from another area of the body as well

- blood in the stool: collect a sample and call your vet for further instructions

- blood in the urine: suggests a urinary tract infection

- bloody nose: could be a bleeding disorder (bleeding excessively from minor wound or accompanied by bloody urine or skin bruising), poisoning (rodenticide), trauma (profuse bleeding), a foreign body (accompanied by sneezing and pawing), or a tumor

To be safe, always seek veterinary advice about any of these conditions.

BREATHING PROBLEMS

The normal breath rate of a cat is 20 to 40 breaths per minute. Count the breaths by watching the chest rise or fall (not both—you'll get a double count). Normally, the respiration of a cat is silent (except in some short-snouted breeds like Persians).

In general, something is wrong when:

- the cat's breathing is labored or abnormal (wheezing) (may mean a restricted airway)
- the cat seems "short of breath" and is gasping (may mean cardiac problems or heatstroke)
- the cat gurgles when she breathes (indicates fluid in the lungs or throat)
- the cat's respiratory rate is faster than normal
- the cat is hyperventilating
- the cat is panting (unlike dogs, panting is not normal in cats)
- the cat is breathing too shallowly or stops breathing for a period
- an increase in respiratory distress occurs when the animal is lying down

    With any of the these symptoms, get your cat to the vet immediately.

BURNS

We all know how terribly painful burns can be. And cats are so sensitive that they must feel even worse coping with them.

If your cat has been burned, wash the area with cool water. Don't pack ice on it. Don't pick at any blisters. Cover closed blisters with a dry bandage; let open ones heal in the air. Small surface burns can be treated at home, but any burn or blister more than a couple of inches (cm) in diameter should be seen by a vet, even if it seems as if it only affects surface tissue.

All chemical burns should be immediately treated by a professional. If your cat has suffered a burn from a liquid chemical, rinse it off with warm water. If the substance is a powder, brush it off (wearing gloves of course). Then take your cat to a vet. If possible, take a sample of the substance, including the package label, with you.

Cats have been known to go into shock or become dangerously dehydrated as a result of burns. Also, burns are not only painful and damaging in themselves, but they can also lead to a secondary infection.

Understanding Burns

Different degrees of burns require specific care, so you should learn what to look for and know when professional help is needed.

Burns are sometimes divided into three categories. First-degree burns are minor and produce only redness. Second-degree burns produce blisters, and third-degree burns actually char the flesh. All third-degree burns require urgent professional care.

An effective herbal remedy for burns is pain-relieving aloe vera. Just crush a leaf from a plant and squeeze it over the burn to soothe it. Using honey as poultice is also very effective (it's the sugar that heals). Some herbalists have achieved success with infusions of calendula, or stinging nettles. It may seem odd that stinging nettles help burns, but they do.

During the healing process make sure the cat has ready access to clean fresh water. You don't want the animal to become dehydrated.

CAR ACCIDENTS

A car accident usually involves serious trauma. Even if your cat appears to walk miraculously away uninjured, don't assume that to be the case. She may be suffering from internal bleeding or a fracture that may suddenly get worse. Always transport a struck pet to the vet for a full evaluation and X-rays. Most vets will want to monitor the animal's behavior for at least 24 hours. You may need to wrap your cat in a towel to keep her still during transport.

Signs of major injuries include weakness, lameness, bleeding, difficulty breathing, or off-color gums (pale or purple). Keep your cat as quiet as possible during transport.

If the animal's major symptom is difficulty in breathing, keep her upright if possible on the way to vet. If profuse bleeding is present, put a clean cloth and pressure on the wound on the way to the clinic.

CHOKING

If your cat is choking, it may be necessary to use the Heimlich maneuver. Here's how to perform this technique on your cat:

- Place your cat on her side on a hard surface.
- Put both hands behind the last rib and press down and slightly forward quickly and firmly.
- Release quickly.
- Repeat several times.

Pet CPR

Every owner should know how to perform mouth-to-nose resuscitation on their pet. One of the best ways to practice CPR technique is by using a stuffed animal. You can also attend one of the many clinics offered by your local Red Cross, some of which target veterinary CPR. Here are the basics:

- Close the animal's mouth and breathe gently but firmly into her nose (with your mouth over the nose or by using your hand in an air-tight cupped position). The animal's chest should rise and fall with each of your breaths. After each breath, release your mouth to allow lungs to deflate. The amount of air you blow in should be just enough to cause the chest to rise and fall.
- If your breath still does not go through, hold the nose shut with one finger and blow into the mouth holding the sides of the mouth as air-tight as possible.
- If the animal begins breathing, do not continue. Further forced breathing or CPR could hurt the animal. If breath still does not go through, perform the Heimlich maneuver.
- If this too does not work, repeat the process until a passage is clear. A passage must be clear for the breathing/chest compression cycle to be successful.

Depression is not just an emotional disorder; it is also a sign of dozens of diseases in cats. Have your feline examined by a vet if the condition persists.

COUGHING

Coughing can indicate dryness in the air, allergic reaction, asthma, fluid in the chest, tracheal disease, cancer, heart failure, parasites (such as roundworms), or infectious disease. If more than one cat in the house is coughing, especially with a dry gagging cough followed by expulsion of mucus, suspect *Bordetella* or another infectious disease. Cats with a gagging cough may have hairballs.

DEPRESSION

Depression is a sign of dozens of diseases in cats.

- If accompanied by increased thirst and urination, it could mean kidney or liver disease, pyometra (uterine infection), or diabetes.
- If accompanied by a raised temperature and lack of appetite, it could mean an infection in the kidneys, joints, or blood.
- If accompanied by a reluctance to move, it could indicate a joint disease, muscle inflammation, neck, back, or abdominal ailment.
- If accompanied by weakness and pale gums it could mean anemia or shock.
- If accompanied by vomiting and diarrhea it could mean any number of serious diseases.

    In all cases, seek veterinary advice.

DIARRHEA

Diarrhea can stem from dietary indiscretion, enteritis, worm infestation, food intolerance, inflammatory bowel disease, cancer, liver disease, infectious disease, or poison. It is most serious in kittens, who have little "reserve." Mild cases of diarrhea can be treated by withholding food (not water) for 24 hours. Then give a bland diet of chicken and rice. Adding canned pumpkin (not the pie filling) adds fiber and may be helpful. Cooked pasta may

Diarrhea Warning

Kittens and older cats are less hardy than adults, and diarrhea can cause life-threatening dehydration in them. If your cat has diarrhea, give her plenty of water and take her to the vet as soon as possible.

also help. Diarrhea accompanied by vomiting, bloody stools, obvious distress, or lethargy can be life-threatening; take your cat to the vet immediately.

DROWNING

If your cat has drowned, hold her upside down by the rear legs to let the water run out of the windpipe. Pounding her on the chest may expel the water faster. Then place the cat on a firm surface (with the head lower than the chest) and begin artificial respiration. You may need to use mouth-to-nose breathing. With heart stoppage, try chest compressions.

Once the immediate crisis is over, take your cat to the vet. Water left in the lungs (even a little) can cause pneumonia.

EYE PROBLEMS

All conditions affecting the eyes should be considered an emergency. Seek immediate veterinary advice.

Eyelid cuts must be sutured or the eyeball will not be properly protected. This must be done by a vet with the cat under sedation. Do not force the eye open. Place some ice in a plastic bag between layers of clean cloth to reduce inflammation. Eyelid wounds usually heal well.

An eyelid drooping on one side may indicate a problem in the nerve supply to the head. Abnormal pupils could mean brain injury, rabies, encephalitis, concussion, or eye injury like cataracts, optic nerve damage, or retinal damage. Red eyes indicate an inflammation. If the eyes are cloudy and swollen, this is an emergency. Squinting may indicate injury, infection, or a foreign body.

FEVER

Fever usually indicates a bacterial or viral infection. Call the vet.

FRACTURES

Even indoor cats are subject to fractures. My housemate sat on our small kitten by mistake and fractured her femur (she's fine now). Fractures come in four varieties: closed (in which the skin is

Take your cat to the vet immediately if she has been in an accident. Even if she appears to walk miraculously away uninjured, don't assume that to be the case—she may be suffering from internal bleeding or a fracture that may suddenly get worse.

not broken), compound (in which the skin is pierced by the broken bone), epiphysis (in which the soft ends of young growing bones are broken), and greenstick or hairline (mere cracks in the bone). Most fractures are simple fractures, meaning that the bones break in only two or three pieces but, in some cases, the fracture is *comminuted*, meaning that the bone is shattered.

Treatment depends on the type of fracture and the age of the cat. Options include splints, casts, screws, or, in the case of my kitten, just pain medication and rest. Your veterinarian will evaluate your cat and make the best treatment choice.

INSECT BITES AND STINGS

If your cat does not have a serious allergic reaction to bites and stings, they are usually pretty easy to handle at home. Stings generally produce only local reaction, swelling, and inflammation, which should subside within an hour.

Signs of a serious allergic reaction include shock, chilled body, unconsciousness, pain, difficulty breathing, and perhaps hives over the body or a swollen tongue (this is an emergency situation—get the cat to a vet right away).

In other cases, remove the stinger by scraping it out with a disinfected credit card or even your fingernail. To relieve the pain of the sting, use a little ammonia or a paste of baking soda and water to stop the itching. Follow with a cool compress or some aloe vera.

FROSTBITE

Frostbite affects the toes, ears, and scrotum. The skin appears first white, then red, blistered, swollen, and peeling, like a burn. Warm frostbitten parts with warm (about 90°F /32.2°C) water for 15 to 20 minutes. Don't rub. Apply antibiotics. Frostbitten tissue will eventually scar or slough off.

Cold Feet

Cats can suffer frostbite in cold weather. The ears, tail, and feet are affected first. If you have an outside cat, make sure she has access to a warm area during the winter months.

GUMS (OFF COLOR)

Gums that are not the normal healthy pink color are a clue to many conditions:

- normal gums: pink
- dark or muddy gums: blood poisoning
- purple gums: heart failure
- yellow gums: liver, gall bladder, or kidney trouble
- pale gums: anemia or shock

GUNSHOT WOUNDS

Do not attempt to remove the pellet or bullet. Locate the source of the bleeding and apply pressure for 5 to10 minutes. Place a nonstick bandage on the wound and wrap it. Monitor the cat's vital signs on the way to the vet. Estimate the amount of blood lost for the vet's information.

HYPOTHERMIA

Hypothermia occurs when body temperature goes too low. It may or may not be accompanied by frostbite. Exposure to wet conditions increases the chance of hypothermia developing, and smaller pets with short hair are more at risk.

Signs include violent shivering and disorientation. More advanced cases include weakness, disorientation, and lethargy. The rectal temperature will fall below 98°F/36.7°C.

Bring your pet indoors immediately. If your cat is wet, place her in a warm bath first. Dry her, wrap her in blankets, and turn up the heat. Place warm (105° to 108°F/40.6° to 42.2°C) packs to the "armpits" and abdomen until her temperature reaches 100°F/37.8°C. (In a pinch, use a large plastic bottle filled with warm water.) A hairdryer may also work. Check the temperature every 5 minutes. When your cat begins to recover, give her glucose (4 tablespoons of sugar to a pint of water). Seek veterinary advice, because shock may develop. (Also see frostbite.)

LETHARGY

Lethargy can be a generalized response to a variety of conditions including constipation, diarrhea, intestinal blockage, poisoning, or an illness like heartworm. If your cat doesn't snap out of it in a day or so, or other signs such as drooling, vomiting, coughing, or breathing difficulty appear, it's time for a trip to the vet. It is also a good idea to check the color of the gums, appearance of the eyes, and condition of the coat.

Cats can find any number of ways to get into trouble—indoors or out. As a responsible owner, you must do all you can to ensure the health and safety of your pet.

NASAL DISCHARGE

Nasal discharge can be a sign of infectious

disease (especially if accompanied by fever, lethargy, severe diarrhea/vomiting, and runny eyes), a foreign body in the nose (accompanied by scratching), oral-nasal fistula (discharge may contain food particles), a fungus, tumor, or an abscessed tooth (discharge crusty or pus-filled). A bloody discharge on both sides, with tiny gum hemorrhages may indicate a clotting problem due to drugs or rat poison.

In cats, a yellow discharge may indicate a sinus infection, which can be treated with antibiotics. A runny nose in cats may be an upper respiratory infection, which is especially dangerous in kittens. If you suspect a contagious disease, isolate other cats and disinfect your hands and clothes before touching other pets.

POISONING

DRUG TOXICITY

Never give your cat a nonsteroidal, anti-inflammatory medication such as aspirin or acetaminophen unless directed by your vet. Acetaminophen is toxic to cats—two extra-strength tablets are likely to kill a cat, and even aspirin is extremely easy to overdose. Cats can't metabolize this drug very efficiently, so high levels can build up in the blood. Signs of aspirin toxicity are loss of appetite, abdominal pain, nausea, vomiting, black stools, and lethargy.

Aspirin toxicity can also cause acute kidney failure. While some diseases can be treated with aspirin, your cat must be under the supervision of a vet while undergoing therapy. A specific antidote to counteract the effects of aspirin is not available. Don't give your cat aspirin on your own.

Poison Hotline

If you think your cat may have become accidentally poisoned, call the vet and the ASPCA Poison Control Center at (888) 426-4435. Be prepared with the name of the product if possible (and have your credit card in hand).

ANTIFREEZE POISONING

Most antifreeze contains ethylene glycol, whose rapidly forming metabolites cause deadly kidney damage. Signs of poisoning include increased thirst, vomiting, diarrhea, and acting "drunk." Induce vomiting with hydrogen peroxide and get immediate veterinary help. An antidote is available.

LEAD POISONING

Cats who ingest lead-based paint chips, swallow drapery or fishing weights, or drink from improperly glazed ceramic bowls may become victims of lead poisoning. Signs include appetite loss, vomiting, chomping of the jaws, seizures, blindness, or behavior changes. Treatment involves removing the ingested lead by chelation therapy using EDTA and perhaps penicillamine or thiamine.

SHOCK

Shock is an emergency situation in which not enough oxygen is being supplied to the cells. It usually occurs due to lack of blood flow. The immediate cause is often hemorrhage or tissue trauma. If not addressed, it will kill your pet.

To check for shock, lay your cat on her side and expose the gums. Press your finger against the gum for a second or so. Observe how long it takes for the color to return to the area after your remove your finger. This is the capillary refill time. Anything over a second or two may indicate shock. Animals in shock also have a rapid, weak pulse.

Pets in shock need these three measures, sometimes called VIP, for ventilation, infusion, and pumping:

- immediate ventilation to make sure the oxygen is getting to the bloodstream
- an infusion of fluids to restore blood volume
- maintenance of the heart pumping action

Always assume shock is a probable concomitant of any serious trauma or injury.

SKUNKED!

Skunk spraying can be painful and serious. While most cats (unlike dogs) are too smart to run afoul of skunks, it does happen. If your cat gets hit in the eyes, wash them thoroughly with water. To get rid of the smell, use a commercial product made for the purpose. In an emergency, you can use a vinegar douche product, or mix a quart of hydrogen peroxide with 1/4-cup of baking soda and a teaspoon of dishwashing liquid. Apply on the fur, let it sit, and rinse. If you believe your cat has been bitten by a skunk, take her to the vet immediately.

SMOKE INHALATION

Animals trapped in fires may experience difficulty in breathing and shortness of breath even after being rescued. Their gums

Pain Control

If your previously social feline begins hiding, it's a good sign she is in pain.

Cats are generally reluctant to let on when they are in pain and, because they often hide their suffering, pain can go untreated. Fortunately, over the past decade, both vets and owners have become more sensitive to this issue. Discomfort from illness, injury, or surgery can be treated with safer, more effective medications that have become available for veterinary practice.

If your cat is ill or injured or has had surgery, don't let her suffer in silence. Ask your vet about pain control.

may be pale or blue. If the cat is not breathing, establish an airway and begin CPR. If the cat is breathing, keep her calm and upright (belly down) to improve breathing. Fill a large bottle with warm water and place it against the cat. Transport her to the vet right away. Some very serious injuries may not appear for a day or so.

SCORPION AND SNAKE BITES

There are two basic kinds of poisonous snakes in the United States: pit vipers (including rattlers, moccasins, and copperheads) and elapids (coral snakes). First and foremost: Do not get bitten! Do not attempt to make a tourniquet, or suck out the poison (either by mouth or with a suction device). They don't work and only take up precious time. Call the nearest vet clinic to direct you, and identify the snake if possible. Not all clinics routinely carry antivenom. Time is of the essence.

Bites by pit vipers leave tell-tale fang marks. Bites by coral snakes do not. Many bites, even by poisonous snakes, are "dry," which means that no venom was injected. Envenomated bites are usually swollen, red, and extremely painful.

Nonpoisonous snakes do not have fangs, but rather many small teeth. They generally leave a U-shaped mark.

SPIDER BITES

While all spiders are somewhat poisonous, usually only bites from the comparatively rare black widow, hobo, and brown recluse spiders are truly dangerous. In some cases signs appear immediately; in others, several days may pass.

Common signs include an irritated area or an open sore on the skin, muscle pain, fever, difficulty in breathing, and vomiting. Put ice on the wound. (If you don't have an ice pack, use a bag of frozen peas or lima beans.) Call your vet.

SWELLING OF THE FACE

Swelling or thickness on the skin around the face, eyelids, or lips may be a sign of hypersensitivity, and it may be the first sign of anaphylactic shock. First, get your pet fresh air and try to reassure her. While en route to the vet, try to determine what may have caused the reaction.

 Be Prepared

As curious as cats can be, your own feline could become victim to any number of mishaps throughout her long and mischievous lifetime. The important thing is to be prepared. If your cat does become injured, you will be ready to act in a calm manner and to provide appropriate medical care immediately. Your cat is depending on you!

Emergency Hotline

Provided by the American Humane Association, the Emergency Disaster Hotline is your first point of call in disaster preparedness, including what to do and where to go. Call the following phone number for assistance: 1-800-227-4645.

They can provide support and disaster-relief information.

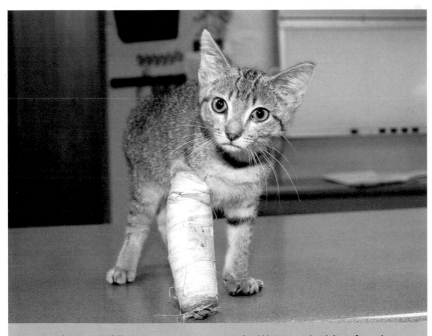

Many mishaps may befall a curious cat, so every owner should be prepared with basic first aid knowledge and the tools needed to assist a pet in the case of an injury or an emergency.

Chapter Eleven

Hard Things:
Death,
Divorce & the Law

"Another cat? Perhaps. For love there is also a season; its seeds must be resown. But a family cat is not replaceable like a worn out coat or a set of tires. Each new kitten becomes its own cat, and none is repeated. I am four cats old, measuring out my life in friends that have succeeded but not replaced one another." - Irving Townsend

Cats themselves don't have responsibilities. They don't owe you love, respect, or good behavior either. (It's your responsibility to earn them.) It is actually your job, as a pet owner, to be responsible for your cat's good care, her behavior toward you, and her behavior toward other animals, people, and their property. You are responsible to her and for her. You also owe it to your feline and yourself to be prepared for the unpleasantries that life sometimes has to offer, such as divorce and other legal hassles.

Then there's the really hard stuff: Cats may have nine lives, but like the rest of us, the time comes when even they must pass on to a better world. You owe it to your cat to know when that time has come.

Hard Decisions

The great universal concern is quality of life. In the olden days, when cats lived mostly outdoors, they seemed to know when the hour arrived and disappeared quietly into the woods to die. Today, most cats don't have that option, and it is left for their hapless owners to decide when their beloved pet has reached the end of the road.

Listen to your heart. Does your cat still enjoy eating, being petted, and the comfort of her bed? Or do you have to force-feed her and watch her slip further into decline with each passing hour? If you are still uncertain what is best, it's time to sit down for a heart-to-heart with your veterinarian. Ask for his honest opinion.

When this time comes, the most difficult part of the process may be to make the appointment. If that's the case, ask a friend to help. The receptionist will be very sympathetic and help you pick a time, usually at the beginning or end of the day, when the vet can spend the necessary amount of time with you and your cat. Some vets will also come to your home, which is much less stressful for your feline friend.

The actual procedure is simple and painless. It mostly involves giving a large overdose of an intravenous anesthetic that will simply cause the animal to lose consciousness and then die very

Your cat's overall quality of life should be the first and foremost thing to consider as she advances in age.

peacefully and quickly. You do not have to be present, although some owners wish to be. You can also have your cat heavily sedated or put into a sound sleep while you say good-bye, and then leave prior to the actual procedure. Whatever decision you make will be all right. While it is wonderful if you can be there until the end, you may do more harm than good if you are extremely upset. Afterwards, you may take your cat home for burial or opt for cremation or disposal at the veterinary facility. Whatever you decide, be assured that your cat's elusive spirit has escaped the confines of her sick body and now roams free throughout the universe. I expect that she may stop by now and again to pay you a quiet and unseen visit.

It is also up to you to decide how to handle your cat's remains. You may want to leave your cat at the clinic for them to handle, or you may wish to have your cat buried or cremated. Most areas have services for all these options, and your vet will be able to advise you. Some people simply want to take their cat home and bury her under a favorite tree.

 Grief

Of course you will grieve, but you will do it in your own way, a way that best honors your relationship with your cat. Don't worry about "stages of grief" or any other bits of psychobabble that try to tell you how you should feel and in what order. Some people wish to donate to a rescue in their cat's name. Others write poems, make art, write in a journal, or find some other way of memorializing their pet. Your grief will be right for you, and so will your healing.

Some people wish to fill their lives immediately with another cat, perhaps deciding to honor their lost friend by saving the life of a doomed cat at the shelter. Others need more time, but know that eventually another cat will appear in their lives. What is life without a cat, after all?

If you feel completely overwhelmed by the loss of your cat to the point where you cannot cope, please call a mental health professional. It doesn't mean you're crazy—it means you are smart enough to get the help you need.

Explaining Pet Loss to Children

Obviously, explaining death and loss to a young child is difficult. It's also an individual matter that depends on your child's age, your own religious beliefs, and other circumstances.

The important thing is to be honest with your child. Children should understand that their beloved pet is not away on a trip or living with another family. They can accept the permanence of death only if you explain it to them. However, if you believe in a life beyond this one, and your religious faith

When a beloved family pet dies, encourage children to talk about their feelings, and answer any questions honestly.

Losing a beloved pet can be a difficult experience. If you don't know anyone who can help you through this time, don't hesitate to call one of the many pet-loss support services available. Here are just a few:

- Cornell University Pet Loss Support Hotline: (607) 253-3932, Tuesday–Thursday 6–9 pm, ET; http://www.vet.cornell.edu/Org/PetLoss/; staffed by Cornell University veterinary students.

- Michigan State University Pet Loss Support Programs: (517) 432-2696, Tuesday–Thursday, 6:30–9:30 pm, ET; http://cvm.msu.edu/petloss/index.htm; staffed by Michigan State University veterinary students.

- Tufts University Pet Loss Support Hotline: (508) 839-7966, Monday–Friday, 6–9 pm, ET; voicemail messages will be returned daily; collect outside Massachusetts; http://www.tufts.edu/vet/petloss/; staffed by Tufts University veterinary students.

- UC Davis Pet Loss Support Hotline: (530) 752-3602 or toll free (800) 565-1526 weekdays, 6:30–9:30 pm, PT; http://www.vetmed.ucdavis.edu/petloss/index.htm; staffed by University of California-Davis veterinary students.

- University of Illinois Veterinary College C.A.R.E. Pet Loss Helpline: (217) 244-2273 or toll-free (877) 394-2273(CARE), Sunday, Tuesday, and Thursday evenings, 7–9 pm, CT; http://www.cvm.uiuc.edu/CARE/; staffed by University of Illinois veterinary students.

- Washington State University, College of Veterinary Medicine Pet Loss Hotline: (509) 335-5704, Monday, Tuesday, Wednesday, and Thursday 6:30–9:00 pm, and Saturday 1:00–3:00 pm, PT. http://www.vetmed.wsu.edu/plhl/index.htm; staffed during the semester by Washington State University veterinary students.

Pet Grief Counseling

If you have other pets, they may react emotionally to the loss of their feline friend and experience profound grief.

permits, you can certainly comfort your child with the thought that your cat is enjoying a wonderful existence in heaven. If you do not believe that, you can at least assure your child that your cat is no longer suffering.

It is better to use words like "death" and "dying" rather than "go to sleep," which implies the animal will wake up. It's far better to honestly explain that neither you nor anyone knows why pets or people get sick and die, and assure your children that you will be around for a very long time to take care of them.

Young children may regress in development in response to a pet's death, and older ones may become remote or depressed. Encourage your children to talk about their feelings, and don't judge them. Some children even feel guilty, deciding that their pet's death was somehow their fault. They believe that if they had done one small thing differently, everything would have been okay. In the rare circumstance that something your child actually did caused the death of a pet, even by accident, I recommend professional counseling. When I was a kid, my cousin saw the family dog across the street and called her to come home. The dog obeyed and was hit by an oncoming car and killed. It was a very bad time.

Resist the urge to go out and get another pet immediately to soothe your child's feelings, even if this is what you would do if you had only yourself to consider. A child might get the wrong message—that pets are commodities to be thrown away when they are used up and replaced with something new and cute. It's also often a good idea to choose a pet that is somewhat different from the first in size and color so that neither of you will be subconsciously comparing the new pet with the old, which is not fair to either the animal or the child.

Reaction of Other Pets

Other pets may react to the loss of one of their own, but they may not always react in the way you expect. I once had two feline siblings, one much more dominant than the other. They seemed inseparable and when one (the more dominant one) died, I feared the other would go into a decline. Just the opposite happened. She seemed relieved that her bossy sister had fled to greener pastures, and really came into her own. Some cats may seem disturbed by the simple change in the environment (cats are conservative and don't really like change); others may respond to your own feelings of upset and grief. A few may sincerely grieve, and others may remain completely unaffected by it all.

Because most cats are basically loners, they usually do not form intense attachments the way dogs do. This is part of their survival strategy.

If you have other pets in addition to cats, they too may react emotionally to your cat's death. And if she had a special friend (cat or other), that animal may experience profound grief. These changes usually resolve themselves in a few days. Occasionally, a pet's grief can turn into depression. This is most common when the deceased pet is survived by an animal with whom she spent most of her life, or with whom she was especially close. The animal may withdraw from normal activities, be lethargic, and may

sometimes show loss of appetite. If symptoms last more than a few days in one of your surviving pets, speak to your vet. A short course of medication may help.

 ## Ah, But What If You Die First?

"But thousands die, without this or that,
Die, and endow a college, or a cat"—Alexander Pope

In the event that a cat outlives her human companion, the responsible pet owner has made preparations in advance to ensure that his or her animal will be well provided for.

If a cat outlives her human companion (and it's always a possibility), the responsible pet owner makes sure his or her animal will be well provided for. To that end, you can set up a trust fund for your beloved feline. The trustee can be a particular person or an organization. Be certain that the trustee is made aware of this arrangement ahead of time and that caring for a pet is a viable option for the chosen individual. You certainly don't wish to entrust your pet's welfare to someone who doesn't want her. Remember, also, that a pet animal is considered tangible personal property that can be disposed of in a person's estate plan in the same way as a car, antique vase, or recliner; so plan accordingly and speak to your lawyer if necessary.

When planning for your pet's care, educate yourself. It's important to know the implications of the various options available to you. For example, a trust is not the same as a will. If you give money in your will to someone solely for use in providing care for your pet, there is no way to enforce it. Resist the temptation. A trust is more difficult to set up, but your cat is worth it. The invested money is called the principal, and it should be enough to provide food and veterinary expenses for the estimated remainder of your cat's life. It's usually best just to state that the trust is for any animals you have at the time of your death rather than naming them one at time. The trust should also provide for what will happen to the remainder of the money after your pet(s) dies. That beneficiary is called the remainderman and should probably be someone other than the trustee (who should also be compensated for her care of your pets).

It's often a good idea to add an *in terrorem* clause to the trust, which specifically states that any beneficiary who challenges the fund because of excessiveness will receive nothing. (Some people take it upon themselves to decide that you have provided way too much for the cat, and that they would make better use of the money themselves.) The old *in terrorerm* clause should make them stop and think.

 ## Divorce

In many states, pets are treated like property, even though we all know they are living beings with feelings and preferences. If you and your divorcing partner can agree on nothing else, at least make an effort to agree on who gets the cat. Judges get really annoyed if you leave it up to them. Put the cat first. And if you're not married yet, consider a prenuptial agreement. It's not romantic, but it could save you a lot of heartache later on.

Bending the Rules

Many states are recognizing the special place pets play in the lives of many people. If you are a senior citizen, for example, your locality may grant an exemption to the regular landlord/tenant rules.

This situation may also apply to circumstances tenants face in subsidized housing, where the government may play a role in permitting or disallowing pets.

Your Rights as a Renter

Most of us are passionate about our pets. In fact, one recent survey showed that over 85 percent of pet owners declared that the ability to have a pet dictated the choice of where they might live, a kind of "Rent to me, rent to my pet" philosophy.

Landlords are not compelled to rent apartments to people with pets. Some pet owners have successfully managed to bring suit against landlords in order to have a pet if they can medically prove that the cat is an emotional support—a sort of mental health pet. But that is a long and difficult route.

You are much better off finding a pet-friendly apartment to begin with. Websites such as www.peoplewithpets.com/, www.rentnet.com/apartments/mme/pets, or www.petrent.net/ are designed to help you locate appropriate resources.

In any case, never sign a lease that says "No pets allowed," even if you get verbal assurance from the landlord or manager that it would be okay to have a cat. If the landlord changes his mind later, you don't have a leg to stand on. It is better if you make sure the right to keep a cat is clearly written into the contract, even as an addendum. That could save a lot of trouble later on and puts the burden onto the landlord if he changes his mind. The contract might even specify the name and color of the cat, such as: "The tenant is permitted to keep two cats, Ike and Tina, both Siamese, on the premises, and no other animals," or something of that nature. A security deposit may be required.

It is also wise to learn the difference between a lease and a rental agreement. The latter is open-ended and usually runs from month-to-month; a lease exists for a certain period of time. Know what you are signing! If you have a rental agreement, the landlord may be free to change the terms of the agreement every month; however, the good news is that if you've owned a cat for a long time and there have been no documented problems, the courts may well uphold your right to keep the cat even if the landlord changes his mind.

Sometimes you can convince an ambivalent landlord to accept your cat if you bring her with you and show the landlord how clean and well-behaved she is. Bring her vet records as well, or even letters of reference.

At any rate, under no circumstances should you try to "sneak" a cat into your apartment or condominium. If you are found out,

Ensuring that your cat enjoys her final years in comfort and peace is the best thanks you can give her for her many years of loyalty and companionship.

you will have to move or find another home for your cat. As someone who has worked with animal rescue for many years, I can't tell you how many times we have had to take in an animal who was given up just for this reason. It is not a responsible act for anyone to break a contract in this way.

For a Lifetime...

As every pet owner knows, a cat is much more than a pet, or even a companion. A cat is smoke and mirrors, magic and mystery, tabby and tiger. She is equally at home in Manhattan and Manitoba, the backwoods and the front porch. She bears in her little body the wild genes of her ferocious ancestors, but is more sophisticated and urbane than most humans. She is capable of great tenderness and of terrible ferocity. She is kind to her owners, but won't shed a tear for you. She will never kowtow to your whims, but she may indulge them—if she feels like it. To enter into a relationship with a cat is like walking in the mist—you never really know where you are—but it's beautiful. And it's cool.

Resources

REGISTRY ORGANIZATIONS

American Association of Cat Enthusiasts (AACE)
P.O. Box 213
Pine Brook, NJ 07058
Phone: (973) 335-6717
Website: http://www.aaceinc.org

American Cat Fanciers Association (ACFA)
P.O. Box 1949
Nixa, MO 65714
Phone: (417) 725-1530
Website: http://www.acfacat.com

Canadian Cat Association (CCA)
289 Rutherford Road South
Unit 18
Brampton, Ontario, Canada
L6W 3R9
Phone: (905) 459-1481
Website: http://www.cca-afc.com

The Cat Fanciers' Association (CFA)
1805 Atlantic Avenue
P.O. Box 1005
Manasquan, NJ 08736-0805
Phone: (732) 528-9797
Website: http://www.cfainc.org

Cat Fanciers' Federation (CFF)
P.O. Box 661
Gratis, OH 45330
Phone: (937) 787-9009
Website: http://www.cffinc.org

Federation Internationale Feline (FIFe)
Penelope Bydlinski, General Secretary
Little Dene, Lenham Heath
Maidstone, Kent, ME17 2BS
ENGLAND
Phone: +44 1622 850913
Website: http://www.fifeweb.org

The Governing Council of the Cat Fancy (GCCF)
4-6, Penel Orlieu
Bridgwater, Somerset, TA6 3PG
UK
Phone: +44 (0)1278 427 575
Website: http://ourworld.
compuserve.com/homepages/
GCCF_CATS/

The International Cat Association (TICA)
P.O. Box 2684
Harlingen, TX 78551
Phone: (956) 428-8046
Website: http://www.tica.org

Traditional and Classic Cat International (TCCI)
(formerly known as the Traditional Cat Association)
10289 Vista Point Loop
Penn Valley, CA 95946
Website: http://www.tccat.org

VETERINARIAN SPECIALTY/ MEMBERSHIP ORGANIZATIONS

American Animal Hospital Association (AAHA)
P.O. Box 150899
Denver, CO 80215
Phone: (303) 986-2800
Website: http://www.aahanet.org

American Association of Feline Practitioners (AAFP)
200 4th Avenue North, Suite 900
Nashville, TN 37219
Phone: (615) 259-7788
Toll-free: (800) 204-3514
Website: http://www.aafponline.org

American Holistic Veterinary Medical Association (AHVMA)
2214 Old Emmorton Road
Bel Air, MD 21015
Phone: (410) 569-0795
Website: http://www.ahvma.org

American Veterinary Medical
Association (AVMA)
1931 North Meacham Road,
Suite 100
Schaumburg, IL 60173
Phone: (847) 925-8070
Fax: (847) 925-1329
Website: http://www.avma.org

The Academy of Veterinary
Homeopathy (AVH)
P.O. Box 9280
Wilmington, DE 19809
Phone: (866) 652-1590
Website: http://www.theavh.org

The American Association for
Veterinary Acupuncture (AAVA)
P.O. Box 419
Hygiene, CO 80533
Phone: (303) 772-6726
Website: http://www.aava.org

ASPCA Animal Poison
Control Center
1717 South Philo Road, Suite 36
Urbana, IL 61802
Telephone: (888) 426-4435
www.aspca.org

International Veterinary
Acupuncture Society (IVAS)
P.O. Box 271395
Ft. Collins, CO 80527
Phone: (970) 266-0666
Website: http://www.ivas.org

ANIMAL WELFARE GROUPS AND ORGANIZATIONS

American Humane Association
(AHA)
63 Inverness Drive East
Englewood, CO 80112
Phone: (800) 227-4645
Website: http://www.
americanhumane.org

American Society for the
Prevention of Cruelty
to Animals (ASPCA)
424 East 92 Street
New York, NY 10128
Phone: (212) 876-7700
Website: http://www.aspca.org

Best Friends Animal Sanctuary
Kanab, UT 84741-5001
Phone: (435) 644-2001
Website: http://www.bestfriends.
org

Cats Protection
17 Kings Road
Horsham, West Sussex RH13
5PN UK
Phone: +44 (0) 1403 221900
Website: http://www.cats.org.uk

Feral Cat Coalition
9528 Miramar Road, PMB 160
San Diego, CA 92126
Phone: (619) 497-1599
Website: http://www.feralcat.com

The Humane Society of the
United States (HSUS)
2100 L Street, NW
Washington, DC 20037
Phone: (212) 452-1100
Website: http://www.hsus.org

The Winn Feline Foundation,
Inc.
1805 Atlantic Avenue
P.O. Box 1005
Manasquan, NJ 08736-0805
Phone: (732) 528-9797
Website: http://www.
winnfelinehealth.org

WEBSITES

Acme Pet Feline Guide
(http://www.acmepet.com/
feline/index.html)
A leading figure in the pet
products industry, Acme Pet
has put together an extensive
site. At the feline site, you can
access the feline marketplace,
which has places to shop for cat
products as well as a pet library,
reference materials and articles,
questions and answers about
cats, an extensive list of rescue
organizations, clubs and shelters,
and the ever popular "cat chat"
room.

Cat Fanciers Website
(http://www.fanciers.com)
In 1993, the Cat Fanciers
mailing list was started on the
Internet as an open forum for
breeders, exhibitors, judges, or
anyone interested in the world
of the Cat Fancy. The on-line
discussion group has thousands
of members from all over
the world. The group's focus,
however, is to make life better
for felines around the globe. The
site offers general information
on cat shows, breed descriptions,
veterinary resources, and much
more.

The Daily Cat
(http://www.thedailycat.com)
The Daily Cat is a resource for
cats and their owners. The site
provides information on feline
health, care, nutrition, grooming,
and behavior.

Healthypet
(http://www.healthypet.com)
Healthypet.com is part of the
American Animal Hospital
Association (AAHA) an
organization of more than
25,000 veterinary care providers
committed to providing
excellence in small animal care.

Petfinder
(http://www.petfinder.org)
On Petfinder.org, you can search
over 88,000 adoptable animals
and locate shelters and rescue
groups in your area who are
currently caring for adoptable
pets. You can also post classified
ads for lost or found pets, pets
wanted, and pets needing homes.

Pets 911
(http://www.1888pets911.org)
Pets 911 is not only a website;
it also runs a toll-free phone
hotline (1-888-PETS-911)
that allows pet owners access
to important, life-saving
information.

ShowCatsOnline
(http://www.showcatsonline.
com)
ShowCatsOnline.com is an
online magazine devoted to all
breeds of pedigreed cats. They
provide information on the
breeding and showing of all
breeds of pedigreed cats and
update their members on the
latest developments in medical
care, breeding, grooming, and
showing.

21cats.org
(http://21cats.org)
21Cats provides information
that will help cats live longer,
healthier lives. The site contains
an online Health and Care
InfoCenter, an "Ask the Kitty
Nurse" Hotline, and a free
monthly newsletter. One of
their goals is to raise awareness
of successful methods used to
reduce the cat overpopulation
problem.

VetQuest
(http://www.vin.com/vetquest/
index0.html)
VetQuest is an online veterinary search and referral service. You can search their database for over 25,000 veterinary hospitals and clinics in the United States, Canada, and Europe. The service places special emphasis on veterinarians with advanced online access to the latest health care information and highly qualified veterinary specialists and consultants.

PUBLICATIONS

Animal Wellness Magazine
PMB 168
8174 South Holly Street
Centennial, CO 80122

ASPCA Animal Watch
424 East 92nd Street
New York, NY 10128

Cat Fancy Magazine
P.O. Box 52864
Boulder, CO 80322

Catnip
P.O. Box 420070
Palm Coast, FL 32142

CatWatch
P.O. Box 420235
Palm Coast, FL 32142

Whole Cat Journal
P.O. Box 1337
Radford, VA 24143

Your Cat Magazine
1716 Locust Street
Des Moines, IA 50309

Index

Note: Boldfaced numbers indicate illustrations.

About the Author

Diane Morgan is an award-winning writer who is the author of many books on pet care, including *The Sneeze-Free Cat Owner*, *Good Dogkeeping*, *The Quick and Easy Guide to Bird Care*, and *Feeding Your Horse for Life*. She is a college professor of philosophy and literature and resides in Williamsport, Maryland.

Dedication

To Tammy Snyder of Cumberland Valley Veterinary Clinic in recognition of her loving care of homeless cats and her tireless efforts to find them homes.

Acknowledgments

Special thanks to Mary Grangeia for her superb editing of this manuscript, and to all my "cat friends" everywhere, especially Bette Pierson, Nancy Mandowa, and Rosie Houston.

Photo Credits:

Gregory Albertini (Shutterstock): 41; Trevor Allen (Shutterstock): 100-101, 116; Galyna Andrushko (Shutterstock): 204; ANP (Shutterstock): 217; Joellen L. Armstrong (Shutterstock): 299; Wesley Aston (Shutterstock): 80, 303; Joan Balzarini (Shutterstock): 36, 68; Heather Barnhart (Shutterstock): 76; Laurie Barr (Shutterstock): 234; Cristi Bastian (Shutterstock): 249; Linda Beatie: 188; Mario Beauregard (Shutterstock): 129; Paul Andre Belle-Isle (Shutterstock): 295; Hagit Berkovich (Shutterstock): 230; Mary Bingham (Shutterstock): 267; Joy Brown (Shutterstock): 89, 228, 240; Katrina Brown (Shutterstock): 26, 64, 180; Sherri R. Camp (Shutterstock): 45; Tony Campbell (Shutterstock): 29, 67, 70, 90, 99, 115, 183; Carolina (Shutterstock): 193; Lars Christensen (Shutterstock): 38, 49, 196, 289; Tan Chuan-Yean (Shutterstock): 166; Heather Coleman (Shutterstock): 298; Diane Critelli (Shutterstock): 12; Hermann Danzmayr (Shutterstock): 98; Geoff Delderfield (Shutterstock): 197; Arturs Dimensteins (Shutterstock): 174; Sebastian Duda (Shutterstock): 53, 144, 276; Dean Evangelista (Shutterstock): 294; Lakis Fourouklas (Shutterstock):250; Isabelle Francais: 46, 108, 121, 125, 132, 155; GeoM (Shutterstock): 28; Jurgita Genyte (Shutterstock): 273; David Gilbey (Shutterstock): 14; Michael Gilroy: 177; Stefan Glebowski (Shutterstock): 56, 85, 201, 218; Johanna Goodyear (Shutterstock): 151, 229, 243; Esther Groen (Shutterstock): 266; Tim Harman (Shutterstock): 284; Ben Heys (Shutterstock):114; Shawn Hine (Shutterstock): 1; Ingret (Shutterstock): 18, 40, 83, 158, 174, 224, 236; iofoto (Shutterstock): 199; Eric Isselee (Shutterstock): 24, 43, 69, 91,134, 179, 205, 269, 301; Dmitry Kosterov (Shutterstock): 9, 184, 213; JC (Shutterstock): 148; Shazia Jameel (Shutterstock): 264; Milos Jokic (Shutterstock): 255; Elena Kalistratova (Shutterstock): 203; Julie Keen (Shutterstock): 291; Robert Kirk (Shutterstock): 147; James A. Kost (Shutterstock): 74; Eric Lam (Shutterstock): 153; Theodore Littleton (Shutterstock): 194; Paulina Lobanova (Shutterstock): 118; Torsten Lorenz (Shutterstock): 222; Dwight Lyman (Shutterstock): 272; Eva Madrazo (Shutterstock): 172, 268; Karl L. Martin (Shutterstock): 237; J. McPhail (Shutterstock): 212; Suponev Vladimir Mihajlovich (Shutterstock): 17, 52, 77, 202, 265; Michelle D. Milliman (Shutterstock): 296; Antonio Jorge Nunes (Shutterstock): 233; Debbie Oetgen (Shutterstock): 259; Jeff Oien (Shutterstock): 87, 161; Ludmila Pankova (Shutterstock): 291; Alvaro Pantoja (Shutterstock): 65, 72; Robert Pearcy (Shutterstock): 157, 214, 287; Mark William Penny (Shutterstock): 285; Steven Pepple (Shutterstock): 198; Perrush (Shutterstock): 73, 128, 146; Sergey Petrov (Shutterstock): 168; Michael Pettigrew (Shutterstock): 159; Pieter (Shutterstock): 10-11; Alyssa Plano (Shutterstock): 22; Cora Reed (Shutterstock): 164-165; Tina Rencelj (Shutterstock): 6, 208; Sara Robinson (Shutterstock): 261; Robynrg (Shutterstock): 109, 127, 136, 141, 181, 297; Ronen (Shutterstock): 62; Lincoln Rogers (Shutterstock): 48, 84; Pavel Sazonov (Shutterstock): 245; Gleb Semenjuk (Shutterstock): 111; Vaide Seskauskiene (Shutterstock): 192; Shutterstock: 4-5, 189, 200, 258; Siberia (Shutterstock): 57; Igor Smichkov (Shutterstock): 31, 223; Victor Soares (Shutterstock): 274-275; Spauln (Shutterstock): 92, 96; Spring (Shutterstock): 247; Lara Stern: 257; Stockphotos (Shutterstock): 238; Dale A. Stork (Shutterstock): 19; Ferenc Szelepcsenyi (Shutterstock): 3, 19, 54, 60-61, 76, 106, 169, 209, 210, 262, 279, 307; Denis Tabler (Shutterstock): 263; TFH Archives: 8, 39, 119, 139, 157, 162, 219, 221, 232, 281; Jeff Thrower (Shutterstock): 102; Ho Ying Tian (Shutterstock): 300; Graham Tomlin (Shutterstock): 105; H. Tuller (Shutterstock): 156, 163; April Turner (Shutterstock): 220; Troy (Shutterstock): 113; April Turner (Shutterstock): 135; John Tyson: 182, 279; Simone van den Berg (Shutterstock): 34, 253; Kim Worrell (Shutterstock): 142; Stavchansky Yakov (Shutterstock): 32; Olga Yermolaeva (Shutterstock): 170; Linda Z. (Shutterstock): 270; Miranda Zeegers (Shutterstock): 190; Terrie L. Zeller (Shutterstock): 58; Dusan Zidar (Shutterstock): 50; 9744444159 (Shutterstock): 290

Front cover: Troy (Shutterstock)
Back cover: Tina Gill (Shutterstock), Mohd Faizal Ahmad (Shutterstock), Trout55 (Shutterstock)